EK LOAN

Voluntary Organizations and Innovation in Public Services

The innovative capacity of voluntary organizations has become a touchstone for their role in providing public services. Across the world there are increasing pressures on voluntary organizations to improve the quality and effectiveness of public services through innovation and change.

This volume uses original research to assess the innovative capacity of voluntary organizations. It provides:

- a conceptual framework for understanding the innovative capacity of voluntary organizations
- empirical evidence detailing the nature and extent of innovation
- an analysis of successful innovators and innovations in personal social services
- the applicability of the for-profit model of innovation to non-profit organizations
- an account of the contingent nature of voluntary organizations' relationship to their external environment and particularly their main funders

The development of a theory of innovation in non-market and non-profit conditions makes this volume an important addition to organizational studies literature.

Stephen P. Osborne is Director of the Voluntary and Non-Profit Research Unit and a member of the Public Services Management Group of Aston Business School, Aston University, UK. His previous publications include *The Public Sector Management Handbook* and *Managing in the Voluntary Sector*.

Routledge Studies in the Management of Voluntary and Non-Profit Organizations
Series Editor: Stephen P. Osborne

Voluntary Organizations and Innovation in Public Services

Stephen P. Osborne

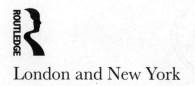

London and New York

First published 1998 by Routledge
11 New Fetter Lane, London EC4P 4EE

Simultaneously published in the USA and Canada
by Routledge
29 West 35th Street, New York, NY 10001

© 1998 Stephen P. Osborne

Typeset in Baskerville by Pure Tech India Ltd, Pondicherry
Printed and bound in Great Britain by
Biddles Ltd, Guildford and Kings Lynn

British Library Cataloguing in Publication Data
A catalogue record for this book is available from the British Library

Library of Congress Cataloging in Publication Data

Osborne, Stephen P., 1953–
    Voluntary organizations and innovation in public services /
Stephen P. Osborne.
        p.   cm.
    Includes bibliographical references and index.
    ISBN 0–415–18256–5 (hc.)
    1. Human services–Great Britain.   2. Social service–Great
Britain.   3. Associations, institutions, etc.–Great Britain.
4. Nonprofit organization–Great Britain.   5. Organizational
change–Great Britain.   I. Title.
HV245.073   1998
361.8′0941–dc21   98–18518
                                                                CIP

For my parents, Frank and Gwendoline Osborne

Contents

Illustrations

ɟ

Figures

Tables

Acknowledgements

To acknowledge everyone who has been of help and assistance in the production of this book would be impossible. They are legion. However, a number of people and events have been especially helpful and these are detailed below.

A number of colleagues at Aston have provided invaluable help in the creative process. In particular I must thank Ray Loveridge and David Johnson, for their encouragement and support, and Paul Golder for his patience both in helping me understand discriminant analysis and in helping me to negotiate the highways and byways of SPSS. Others who have offered invaluable support include Tony Bovaird, Mike Luck, Jill Schofield, Mike Tricker and David Wilson.

Colleagues from outside of Aston have also been invaluable in their suggestions. These include Nicholas Deakin, Norman Flynn, Margaret Harris, Martin Knapp and Diana Leat in Britain, and Helmut Anheier, Aniko Kaposvari, Mark Lyons, Vic Murray and Felice Perlmutter from beyond these shores.

A special acknowledgement is due to the Joseph Rowntree Foundation, which funded the research upon which this book is based, and especially to Pat Kneen from the Foundation for her suggestions and understanding.

Stuart Hay, from Routledge, has been sterling in his support and advice.

Preliminary and emerging findings from the research upon which this book is based have been presented at a number of academic conferences over the past four years, and the comments of the participants at these conferences were invaluable. These have included the annual conferences of the British Academy of Management and of ARNOVA (the Association for Research on Nonprofit Organizations and Voluntary Action), the 1994 European Symposium on the Third Sector, the 1994 ISTR (International Society for Third Sector Research) conference and the 1995 INDEPENDENT SECTOR conference.

Parts of Chapter 2 are based upon material by myself published in Aston Business School Public Sector Management Research Centre (PSMRC) Working Papers, numbers 23 and 24. It has also been adapted as Chapter 1 of *Managing in the Voluntary Sector*, edited by myself and published in 1996 by International Thomson Business Press. Chapter 3 is drawn material by myself published in Aston Business School PSMRC Working Paper number 25 and Research Institute Paper number 9710 and in an article in *Social Services Research* (1995, no. 1; pp. 1–13).

Similarly, Chapter 4 draws upon material published in Aston Business School PSMRC Working Paper number 34. Parts of Chapters 5 to 7 have appeared in adapted forms in Aston Business School Research Institute Papers number 9710 and 9713, *Social Services Research* (1995, no. 4; pp. 57–67), *Local Government Policy Making* (23, 3; pp. 54–62). Further papers drawing upon this material are 'in press' in the *British Journal of Management*, *Local Government Studies*, *Human Relations* and *Public Money and Management* (with Norman Flynn).

The typing (and handwriting translation) services of Jean Elkington and Jane Winder at Aston have ensured that the ideas in my head have made it onto paper.

A special 'thank you' is due for the long-standing support of my family, Marian, Martha and Madeline, who have suffered the creative process along with me and without whom this book would certainly never have been finished.

Last, but by no means least, I must thank all the people who participated in this research, either in the survey or the case-study interviews. They must remain anonymous, but are no less essential for all that.

As always, responsibility for the content of this book lies with me and me alone.

Abbreviations

CAF	Charities Aid Foundation
CVSs	Councils for Voluntary Service
GNP	Gross National Product
ICNPO	International Classification of Non-Profit Organizations
IRS	Internal Revenue Service
NCVO	National Council for Voluntary Organisations
NHSCC Act	National Health Service and Community Care Act
PSMRC	Public Services Management Research Centre
PSS	Personal Social Services
PSSRU	Personal Social Services Research Unit
RCCs	Rural Community Councils
SSDs	Social Services Departments
VNPO	Voluntary and non-profit organization
VBx	Volunteer Bureaux

1 Voluntary and non-profit organizations and innovation in public services

This book concerns the capacity of voluntary and non-profit organizations (VNPOs) for innovation in public services. Its specific focus is the personal social services (PSS) in the UK. Broadly this includes support services to children and their families, the care of adults with special needs (such as elderly people or people with learning disabilities), and services which span both these groups (such as those for people with a need which is not age-specific, such as cerebral palsy).

This is an important topic. As will be seen from the review of the existing literature below, such innovative capacity has often been asserted, both as a core characteristic of VNPOs and as an important contribution by them to the provision of public services.

However, as this review will also demonstrate, there has been a significant lack of research, either to give an empirical grounding to such assertions, or to develop a conceptual model of this innovative capacity which might provide some causal explanation of it. Whilst VNPOs were a minor player in the provision of public services, this assertion had comparatively little social policy import. However, in recent years, they have become significant providers of these services. In part this has been a product of the changing public-policy framework for the delivery of public services toward that of the *enabling state* (Rao 1991); and in part it has been a product of the very perception of VNPOs as possessing a significant potential for innovative activity (as compared to the inflexibility and bureaucracy of local and central government departments). This has had an especial resonance in the PSS, where innovation itself became a key policy goal of the 1980s (King's Fund Institute 1987).

This changing framework is especially apparent in the two key founding documents of the 'mixed economy of care' (Wistow *et al.* 1994) for the PSS in the UK, the Griffiths Report (Griffiths 1988) and the subsequent White Paper on community care services for adults, *Caring for People* (Department of Health 1989). Griffiths promoted the concept of using VNPOs (and other private providers) as the main providers of community care services in order 'to widen consumer choice, *stimulate innovation* and encourage efficiency' [my emphasis] (Griffiths 1988, para. 1.3.4). Similarly the community care White Paper argued that:

Stimulating the development of non-statutory service providers will result in a range of benefits for the consumer, in particular: a wider range of choice of services; *services which meet individual needs in a more flexible and innovative way* . . . and a more cost-effective service. [my emphasis]

(Department of Health 1989, para. 3.4.3)

Although less explicitly, such expectations have also been part of the developing framework for social services for children and their families.

Despite their policy and service import, though, many of these assumptions about the characteristics of VNPOs have remained largely untested (Wistow *et al.* 1994, 1996). This is particularly true of the assertion about their innovative capacity:

[A] comprehensive, not to say imaginative compendium of attributes [of voluntary organisations] has developed. Most such statements of these attributes are based upon conjecture. It is rarely the case that one can detect either an empirical or a conceptual basis for the listings of the desirable features of voluntary organisations *vis-à-vis* other agencies and sectors . . .

The pioneering characteristic of voluntary organisations has been cited so frequently as to become legendary. But like all the best legends the truth has sometimes been colourfully embellished to make a better story.

(Knapp *et al.* 1990, p. 199)

Because of these policy and service developments, it has now become important to put the assertions about the innovative capacity of VNPOs to the test. This book is dedicated to this task. It will provide both an empirical analysis of the extent of innovative activity by VNPOs, and an exploration of possible causal explanations of this activity by which to build an analytic model of the innovative capacity of VNPOs.

In undertaking this task, this book will bring to bear the insights of organization theory upon the study of VNPOs. As will be demonstrated below, there has been a failure to apply these insights to VNPOs previously, and their study has suffered because of this (Knokke and Prensky 1984; Paton 1993). Of late there has been important work done to right this imbalance, and this is discussed in Chapter 2. This book is intended as a further, modest, contribution to this growing literature.

The book is in two parts. The first part details the existing literature. It will commence by exploring the nature of voluntary activity and of VNPOs. It will then undertake a major review of the key literature about innovation. This will require integrating material from two major fields of study. First, it will review the literature about innovations and innovators from the organization studies field as well as some other key conceptual developments in this field which can also contribute to an understanding of this innovative capacity. Second, it will review the literature from the social administration/social policy field about both the innovative capacity of VNPOs and the extent of innovative activity in the field of social welfare. It will argue that these latter literatures are deficient in their analyses of innovative

activity, because of their failure both to define innovation and to develop conceptual tools for its analysis. The review will conclude by drawing upon the insights of
the earlier organization studies literature about innovation in order to develop just
such a definition and analytic tools.

The second part of the book describes and discusses a major empirical study of
the role of VNPOs in innovation in the PSS in the UK. This was carried out over
the period 1990–1994. It begins by outlining the research methodology. It will
discuss the key challenges confronted in designing this methodology and how the
issues of reliability and validity were resolved. It will emphasize that, because of the
exploratory nature of this study in an area where there has been little previous
research, a wholly deductive approach on the basis of a pre-formed hypothesis
would have been counterproductive. It would be akin to the proverbial search for a
needle in a haystack. Rather, the study combined both inductive and deductive
components. The former allowed the nature of the innovative capacity of VNPOs
to be explored and mapped. The latter allowed the testing of theoretical hypotheses
about this innovative capacity. These had been drawn out of the previous literature
and refined in the inductive stage of this study. They were that the innovative
capacity of VNPOs was a product of their formal organizational characteristics,
of their internal *culture*, of their external environment, or of their institutional
context.

The next chapter will present the findings of this research. It will start by
describing the three localities in which it was undertaken. This will be followed
by a mapping of the nature and extent of innovation by VNPOs, and by an
exploration of the basic organizational characteristics which describe the innovators. This section will be based upon a postal survey of a census of all VNPOs
involved in the PSS in each locality. These findings will be analysed using both
simple distributional statistics and chi-squared tests, and also through the use of
Discriminant Analysis.

Having completed this initial mapping, to describe the nature of innovation and
of the innovative organizations, the book will then explore the four possible
causal hypotheses of the innovative capacity of VNPOs outlined above. These
will be explored using three cross-sectional case studies, of innovative, developmental, and traditional organizations (these terms will be defined in detail at a later
stage).

It will be argued that little evidence was found to support the first two hypotheses
but that significant support was found for the last two. This evidence will be built
upon further by exploring the process(es) of innovation found in the case studies, in
order to explore how these causal factors are operationalized.

The final chapter of the book will draw the findings of this research together, to
produce an initial model of the innovative capacity of VNPOs in public services. It
will conclude both by highlighting the ways forward for future research about this
capacity and by drawing out its key lessons for the management of VNPOs and for
central and local government policy making and management.

The contributions of this book to our knowledge about VNPOs are threefold.
First, it will provide the first empirical mapping of their innovative capacity.

Second, it will explore the utility and significance of organization studies theory for understanding and analysing VNPOs. In particular it will explore the extensive sub-literature of organization studies theory concerned with both innovation and innovative organizations. This will not be a one-way process. Much of this sub-literature has been developed from the study of for-profit organizations operating in a competitive environment. The book will also consider the potential contribution *to* organization theory from the study of VNPOs.

Finally, it will offer a conceptual model developed from an integration of the above two contributions, and through this to understand the causal factors and processes involved in realizing the innovative potential of VNPOs in the management and provision of public services. This has import both for future research about VNPOs and for their management. Deutsch (1985) for one has argued that this field of research has great significance to offer to the development of our understanding of contemporary society:

> Innovations and innovation theory have now emerged as major potential modifiers of social and political theory... Innovation is not just a special marginal subject for a few specialists. It is becoming of critical importance in our thought about the social, political, economic and cultural development of modern industrial society, and of the information society that may now be emerging.
>
> (p. 19)

This book is intended as a contribution to this debate and development.

2 Conceptualizing voluntary activity

Introduction

> The good life is an activity not a receptivity; a doing of things spontaneously for the good of the community and the satisfaction of the social instincts in man . . . Destroy, even check unnecessarily, instincts for self-expression and self-realisation which freedom of speech and freedom of association . . . have made possible and we sap the very life stream of the community. It is a spiritual issue which is at stake. It is in a freedom of the spirit that the real energy source lies, in energy, which can transform the material world as a means to the end of the good community . . .
>
> *Voluntary action is experimental, flexible, progressive.* It can adjust more easily than the statutory authority, its machinery and methods to deal with changing conditions and with diversity of cases. This capacity for experiment, for trial and error, is one of the most valuable qualities in community life. [my emphasis]
>
> ('Forward' by Dr Adams, written in 1948, to National Council of Social Service 1970)

This chapter will examine the role of voluntary activity in Western society. It will develop a conceptual framework within which to understand such activity and clarify some definitional issues. It will then focus more specifically upon organized voluntary activity and will summarize briefly the nature and extent of such organized activity in the UK.

At the outset, two points should be emphasized. First, the focus here is upon voluntary activity in *contemporary Western society*. It does not attempt to examine the differing roles or principles of such effort in more diverse societal settings, such as in the developing nations, or in post-communist Central and Eastern Europe. Second, in this initial section, the term 'VNPO' will be used as shorthand for 'organized voluntary effort', without prejudice. The second section of this chapter will need to justify this use, however.

The quotation prefacing this chapter encapsulates many of the popularly held beliefs – and prejudices – about voluntary action. It draws no distinction between individual and organized voluntary action, and assumes an altruism and innovativeness which is contrasted to the vested interests and bureaucracy of the statutory services. This mixture is then posited as 'one of the most valuable qualities in community life'.

This chapter unpackages some of the concepts and principles involved in this heady brew, and offers a typology which will aid in understanding their relationship to one another. Specifically it intends to clarify the relationship of the voluntary ethic, *per se*, to individual and organized voluntary effort.

Developing a typology of voluntary activity

To return to our initial quotation once more, it is possible to discern the mixture of three different conceptual strands within it. The first is that of a free society, where individuals act together in common cause and where state action is seen as, at best, a necessary evil to be held in check, and at worst an unnecessary and unnatural block on individual action. The second strand is that of individual voluntary effort to meet identified needs. The final strand is that of organized voluntary effort. This third strand does incorporate ideas from the first two (in that it is seen as qualitatively better than state action and as based upon individual effort), but it also has its own distinctive features. These features will be discussed in more detail below.

Whilst all three of these strands are clearly intertwined and are best understood as a triad of concepts, each is distinctive, with its own parameters and background ideas. Their relationship is what Van Til (1988) has called the '*volunt . . . question*', and it is his work that must be the starting point for understanding these concepts.

The analysis by Van Til of voluntary activity contained within *Mapping the Third Sector* is one of the major recent contributions to the understanding of this activity, though the particular concern here is his attempt to separate out the above three strands for analysis. He commences with a statement of the core principle of each of these strands, before offering both an empirical basis and normative conceptualization of it. The full typology is reproduced in Table 2.1.

This approach to the conceptualization of the voluntary ethic is a useful one. It helps separate out the differing strands of the concept and makes explicit their empirical and normative implications. However, the approach is not taken through as far as it might be. The starting point of the typology is 'individual action', and its first two components seek to differentiate two types of such action, before moving on to its organized form. This approach is deficient in that it excludes the concept of *voluntary action*, as a societal principle, from its analysis. Yet this is a conceptualization of the voluntary ethic at its most fundamental and one which is found to run through both of the other strands, of individual and organized voluntary action.

Table 2.1 Typology of voluntary concepts I (adapted from Van Til 1988)

Core principle	Empirical form	Normative concept
'Individual action not coerced . . .	Voluntary action	Freedom
. . . and deemed beneficial . . .	Volunteering	Volunteerism
. . . and organized.'	Voluntary associations and non-profit corporations	Volunteerism

Table 2.2 Typology of voluntary concepts II (adapted from Osborne 1996)

Concept	Focus of concern	Normative statement	Background theory
Voluntaryism	Relationship of individual and society	Free or 'active' society	De Tocqueville, Etzioni
Volunteerism	Individual action in society	Voluntary society	Titmuss, Horton-Smith
Voluntarism	Organized action in society	Plural society	Berger and Neuhaus, Gladstone

In order to include this fundamental concept, it is therefore necessary to develop this typology further. This is done in Table 2.2. In addition to clarifying more clearly the concepts involved, the distinctions within the typology have also been refined to better delineate the three strands. This typological development thus allows the specification of the focus of concern of each conceptual strand, its normative goal (or 'ideal state'), and the background theory informing its conceptual construction.

It will be useful here to explore the concepts in Table 2.2 in more depth. With regard to the normative concepts, the first, voluntaryism, refers to the societal principle of voluntary action as a building block for society. The second, volunteerism, combines both of the first two core principles of Van Til, of 'individualism not coerced' and 'deemed beneficial'. The focus here is upon the *individual* action involved. The final concept of this triad is that of voluntarism, and this corresponds to the 'organized voluntary action' of Van Til. This typological development thus allows one to specify the focus of concern of each of these conceptual strands, their normative goals (or 'ideal states'), and the background theory informing the strands.

It is argued here that this typology is an improvement on that of Van Til for two reasons. First it includes a framework to analyse the fundamental principle of voluntary action – voluntaryism – which is missing from the earlier typology. Secondly it breaks down the components of these concepts into comparable units which highlight the distinctions between them most clearly, whilst also making explicit the relationships between them. These concepts, and the implications of this typology, will now be discussed in more detail below.

Voluntaryism

The *Oxford English Dictionary* lists two definitions for voluntaryism. The first, stressing its ecclesiastical origins, concerns the independence of the Church, as an institution, from the state. This is a significant point. In Western society, Christian religious inspiration often formed the basis for early voluntary activity. Some, such as Collins and Hickman (1991), have argued that this is the basis of the distinctive contribution of voluntary activity to society. This point will be returned to below, when considering definitions of organized voluntary effort.

The second definition, more pertinent to this section, defines voluntaryism as 'any system which rests upon voluntary action or principles'. Here it is used to denote that theory of society which emphasizes the primacy of voluntary action, and voluntary relationships, as the core of societal organization. Thus it is a way of conceptualizing the relationship of the individual to society which values individual voluntary effort or activity, as counter-posed to coerced or state-organized action. It is, in essence, the voluntary principle in society.

Such a principle has as its ideal state a society where all action is freely chosen, and can be characterized as the *free*, or *active*, society (the term *voluntary* society has also been used by some authors in this context, but this is to be reserved here for specific usage, in connection with voluntarism). The actuality of such a free society has been well articulated by Schultz (1972):

> [A] society which achieves a high level of social integration but does this with minimum reliance on force and money as organizing principles ... Voluntarism [sic] is one of the goals of such a society as it is also a means which is employed to establish and accomplish societal priorities, and to define and solve societal problems.
>
> (pp. 25–26)

The origins of voluntaryism as a societal principle can be found in the liberalism of the eighteenth and nineteenth centuries, with its emphasis on individual action and its antipathy to state action. The clearest statements of these roots are found in the writings of de Tocqueville (1835, reprinted 1971) on his experiences in America. He identified the principle of voluntary association as an essential component of a civilized society and held up the experience of Americans as the summation of this principle:

> Americans of all ages, all conditions, and all dispositions, constantly form associations. They have not only commercial and manufacturing companies in which all take part, but associations of a thousand other kinds ... whenever at the head of some new undertaking, you see the Government in France, or a man of rank in England, in the United States you will be sure to find associations.
>
> (pp. 376–377)

Whilst de Tocqueville emphasized the importance of voluntary *association* in society, the most eloquent statement on the role of voluntary *action* is probably found in the work of Etzioni (1961, 1968). In *The Active Society* (1968) in particular he develops a theory of society based on voluntaryism, which he contrasts to atomistic (fragmented) and collectivistic (monolithic) societies. This model takes voluntaryism to its extreme. It recognizes few limitations upon the actions of an individual, and views such limitations as being abnormal. He suggests that the individual should be able to 'remould his world at will'.

In conclusion, voluntaryism represents the voluntary ethic as the organizing principle of society, based upon a voluntary relationship between the individual and that society. It is antipathetic to the role of the state. This is the logic of voluntary action taken to its conclusion.

Volunteerism

If voluntaryism represents the fundamental principle of voluntary action as an organizing principle of society, volunteerism encompasses the reality of individual action in society. At its broadest it is a conceptualization of freely chosen individual action. In ideal terms it is the principle of voluntaryism applied to everyday affairs. Thus it can encompass the establishment of a business and the committing of adultery, the joining of a club and the decision about what to have for dinner.

Van Til summarizes Gamwell (1984), who sees an important link between volunteerism and voluntaryism, with such individual voluntary action as the cornerstone of a free society, contributing to both individual and societal health:

> Volunteerism is a quality of participation, which at any time and in any institution empowers the individual and enriches the organizational setting in which the individual is sited . . . [S]uch voluntary action is a critical aspect of the person who is genuinely alive. It may be seen as the hallmark of both the authentic person and the active society, as no mere appendage to the business of life but rather as its very core.
>
> (Van Til 1988, p. 84)

Below this broad level of conceptualization of individual action is a more specific formulation of volunteerism, however, which is concerned with personal voluntary action aimed at the benefit of others. This is commonly called *volunteering*.

The Aves Committee (1969) in the UK, in its study of volunteering in the social services, thought that this was so straightforward a concept as to require no definition. Later analysts have been more concerned to tease out its fundamentals. Darvill and Mundy (1984) provide what could be called the archetypal definition of a volunteer: as a person

> who voluntarily provides an unpaid direct service for one or more other persons to whom the volunteer is not related. The volunteer normally provides his or her services through some kind of formal scheme rather than through an informal neighbouring arrangement.
>
> (p. 3)

Contained within this definition are the three core components of volunteering, which have been confirmed by recent research in Britain into the nature of volunteering (Thomas and Finch 1990; Hedley 1992). The first is an economic one, concerned with the allocation of resources. Voluntary action, like volunteering, is unpaid and seen as a surplus beyond normal economic activity. In this respect it is quite different from the perspective of Van Til, which sees volunteer action as the core of human activity. Here it is denoted as an add-on to such activity.

Second, volunteering is counter-posed to paid, and often professional, caring. At times this may be in a pejorative sense, comparing the idealistic volunteer to the selfish professional (for example, Schultz 1972). At other times, it is used in a more descriptive sense, to contrast the differing roles of volunteer and professional. Guzzeta (1984) has used this distinction to chart the changing role of volunteering in the personal social services in America over the last century, as a result of the professionalization of this function. More recently Brudney (1990) has examined the renewal of interest in partnership between volunteers and professionals, as a result of the worsening social and economic climate.

Finally, volunteering is differentiated from informal helping, either in the form of the family or of neighbours. This is an important distinction because all three are often thrown together as part of a homogeneous *informal sector*. However, Abrams *et al.* (1989) have well drawn the distinction between organized volunteering and neighbourhood helping.

This analysis is further developed by Chanan (1991, 1996) who contrasts the well-meaning but standardized activities of volunteers with the struggles of local people in disadvantaged communities to cope with the 'daily problems of survival caring and disadvantage'. He concludes that volunteering, far from being the freely chosen self-actualization that such individual voluntary action is conceptualized as within voluntaryism, is actually 'a mirror of paid work, especially low grade paid work: hierarchical, externally directed and essentially serving the policies and practices of the organizations rather than the needs and choices of the participants' (Chanan 1991, p. 10). This view of volunteerism strikes at the very heart of its most normative formulation, of the voluntary society, and opens up an important dichotomy within the concept. On the one hand are those writers who emphasize the issue of free choice as a key component of individual voluntary action, and its links to altruism (and voluntaryism). On the other hand are those who emphasize the social determinants of individual action; as will be seen, for this latter group, volunteerism is almost a fraudulent concept.

With regard to the positive analyses of volunteerism, these draw clear links between freely chosen and altruistic individual action. The classic statement of this position is contained within the study by Titmuss (1970) of blood donors in Britain and America. Its conclusions encapsulate well the identified connections between altruism, individual voluntary action, and the good of society:

> In not asking for or expecting any payment of money [British] donors signified their belief in the willingness of other men [sic] to act altruistically in the future, and to combine together to make a gift freely available should they have need for it. By expressing confidence in the behaviour of future unknown strangers they were thus denying the Hobbesian thesis that men are devoid of any distinctively moral sense . . .
>
> [These donors] were free not to give. They could have behaved differently; that is to say, they need not have acted as they did. Their decisions were not determined by structure or by functions or controlled by ineluctable historical forces . . . To coerce a man is to deprive him of freedom . . . [and] by doing so escalate other coercive forces in the social system which lead to the denial of other freedoms and maybe life itself to other men who are biologically in no

position to choose – the young and the old, the sick, the excluded and the inept as well as the sellers of blood.

(p. 239)

This assumption of altruism and freely chosen actions within volunteerism has been attacked by social scientists who take a more socially constrained view of it, and who, in doing so, break its links to voluntaryism. Palisi (1972) has argued for the actual replacement of the concept of individual voluntary action by that of 'differentiated social force', contending that all individual action is the product of social pressures. Payne *et al.* (1972) take this argument further by actually specifying the personal factors which they claim to have empirically identified as the parameters of volunteering. Finally, Zeldin (1983) sees the constraints in the form of larger societal forces, such as unemployment. This is a particularly apposite observation, given the attempts of the recent governments in the UK to use volunteer programmes as a way to combat unemployment amongst young people:

The logic was fairly obvious: since the devil finds work for idle hands, why not keep the unemployed constructively (if not gainfully) occupied with voluntary work? Allied to this was the proposition that there were all these people sitting around on the dole doing nothing, and there were all these tasks needing to be done in the community which society cannot afford to pay for, so why not put the two together? Thus the unemployed would be able to brush up on their work skills, and the community would get some useful work done.

(Sheard 1992, p. 21)

The most sophisticated of the sociological studies of volunteerism are those of Horton Smith. In a seminal paper (1981) he redefines altruism as

an aspect of human motivation that is present to the degree that the individual derives intrinsic satisfaction or psychic rewards from attempting to optimize the intrinsic satisfaction of one or more other persons without the conscious expectation of participating in an exchange relationship whereby these 'others' would be obligated to make similar related satisfaction optimizations in return.

(p. 23)

In these, relational, terms volunteering is not so much concerned with freely chosen altruistic (in the traditional sense) action, but rather with different types of personal reward. Nor did Horton Smith accept the automatic assumption of volunteering as necessarily a force wholly for good within society:

Volunteers are not angelic humanitarians in any sense...Some do very positive things for the general welfare; others are harmful, and selfish in the extreme. Altruism is a variable both among volunteers and among voluntary organizations. Failure to admit this constitutes a failure to face known social and individual reality.

(p. 33)

In conclusion, the concept of volunteerism has been seen to be a more complex and paradoxical one than that of voluntaryism. At its most general level it does carry the voluntary principle epitomized by voluntaryism into the study of individual action, and can be presented as a normative concept epitomizing the positive benefits for the individual and for society of such action. This is the *voluntary society*.

However, below this normative level, the concept is more specifically applied to individual voluntary action for the benefit of others, or volunteering. Here, analyses of the concept vary. One analysis, linked to the normative conceptualization above, emphasizes the role of altruism in such action. Another analysis questions the normative assumptions of freedom and altruism in volunteering, preferring to see it as determined by other social focuses and pressures.

Whichever one is preferred, the locus of analysis is individual action. It is now time to move on and examine the last of our triad of voluntary concepts, voluntarism, which is concerned with organized voluntary action.

Voluntarism

In moving on to the concept of voluntarism, we are moving to the central concerns of this chapter. With voluntarism, the focus shifts to the organizational and institutional level of analysis. It is necessary at the outset to draw a vital distinction between this and individual voluntary action. Whilst it is true that VNPOs may well contain volunteers, it is a mistake to see this as their defining feature. It is also a mistake which is commonly made; for example, the recent study of the funding of voluntary organizations in Britain by central government, carried out by the Home Office (1990), made great play of the cost benefits of volunteer labour and maintained an assumption that VNPOs are also organizations deriving a significant amount of their strength from volunteers.

In fact, volunteers can play a full or a minimal role in VNPOs but this is not the key determinant of voluntarism. This concept does not focus on individual action, but upon the voluntary *organizational* characteristics of the bodies concerned. It is these characteristics which define the *voluntariness* of an organization or structure. They were well summarized half a century ago by Bourdillon (1945a). The essential characteristics of such an organization were not the products of its labour, she contended,

> but of their mode of birth and method of government. A voluntary organisation properly speaking is an organisation which, whether its workers are paid or unpaid, is initiated and governed by its own members without external control. Such a body may well undertake work on behalf of a statutory authority, but if it is to qualify as a voluntary organisation it is essential that it should select or cooperate in selecting what that work shall be and how it shall be done.
>
> (p. 3)

Thus it is the method of its inception and its mode of governance that define an organization as voluntary and which form the key components of voluntarism.

Voluntarism, as a normative concept, views VNPOs as the essential elements of a free society, and harks back to the emphasis of de Tocqueville on the importance of association as the cornerstone of civilization. This conceptualization sees society as a 'rich stew', which the diversity of VNPOs reflects (Cornuelle 1983).

With regard to the method of inception of voluntary organizations, this is posed as the way in which they are able both to reflect the heterogeneity of society and to allow a voice for minority and disadvantaged sectors of society which might otherwise lose out if the state were the sole arbiter of need. In this view, the state is characterized as monolithic and as disenfranchising minorities because of its emphasis on majority rule (the 'tyranny of the majority') in an electoral system. Thus by having the ability freely to form 'voluntary' organizations these diverse sectors of society are able to gain a voice.

With regard to their method of governance, this is similarly argued to add diversity to society, in the manner of the outputs of VNPOs. Because they can choose what they wish to do they are not restrained in their actions either by universalist principles or by legal statute. Hence they add diversity in service delivery in a way that the state is unable to (Gladstone 1979).

Within Western society, such voluntarism is often espoused as an essential component of democracy by allowing sectoral and minority interests to have a voice, by keeping a check on the state, and by adding to diversity in service delivery (see, for example, the report of the Finer Committee – US Department of the Treasury 1977). In its ideal state it posits a wholly plural society, where each sector has a voice and where there are multiple sources of public services. This ideal version of voluntarism once again makes explicit the underlying concept of voluntaryism in organized voluntary activity.

Different advocates have given different weightings to these components of voluntarism. Berger and Neuhaus (1977) emphasize the alienating nature of contemporary society with its 'mega institutions'. They present pluralism as an antidote to this alienation, through the means of 'mediating' institutions (such as VNPOs) which would empower citizens to control their own destinies. Gladstone (1979), by contrast, starts from a similar analysis, and has argued that the post-war centralized, and professionally dominated, state has disempowered individuals and communities and also failed in its goal of a more equal society. However, whilst Berger and Neuhaus concentrate on the role of voluntary organizations in representing and giving voice to the citizenry, Gladstone concentrates more upon their service outputs. It is these services which he sees as promoting choice in society, and in the process as releasing the 'latent ability of "ordinary people" to help themselves and to help each other' (p. 123).

Brenton (1985) has summarized well the breadth of this positive view of voluntarism:

> The voluntary organisation is seen to add diversity and choice to society. It can act as an independent competitor, its independence giving it a moral superiority and a neutrality not possessed by the public sector, which is inherently political. It is seen as innovative, pioneering and experimental,

ready to take risks and adopt new ideas and practices because its members do not generally have the material investments of employees nor the constraints of trade union rules, [and] because the organisation is non-bureaucratised and flexible . . . It is thought to be more cost effective than the statutory sector and it embraces popular participation in a way the statutory services do not. The voluntary agency is assumed to be beneficent, enlightened and public spirited.

(pp. 145–146)

This ideal version of voluntarism, with its belief in a plural society, and antipathy to the role of the state in society, has its critics. Van Til (1988) has noted the tendency to ignore the 'dark side' of voluntarism, and to make an assumption of altruism and social benefit in it, whereas it is as equally likely to be driven by self-interest or hate. Thus he counter-poses the extension to democracy for White racists offered by the Ku Klux Klan chapter, with the restriction to democracy for Black people oppressed by that organization. The contribution of voluntarism to democracy is therefore more ambiguous than its proponents would maintain.

This point is reinforced further by Brenton (1985) who argued that the plural view lacks a structural analysis of the distribution of power within society. In its ideal form, pluralism requires an equal distribution of power within society. As such it is at odds with the existing reality of economic and political power differentials in society. Finally Salamon (1987) has pointed to some of the drawbacks of a plural society in service delivery, and in particular that services will be duplicated, that organizations will be managed in an amateurish way, that need will be met arbitrarily and with poor coverage, and that services become the private domain of organizational leaders to be dispensed at their patronage. For Salamon it is the state which is essential to counter the problems of such organizations, rather than *vice versa*.

Summary

This section has been concerned to develop a typology of concepts of voluntary action, to further its understanding. In doing so, it has taken the work of Van Til as its starting point. It has developed his typology, first to include the concept of voluntary action as the fundamental building block of society. This has been denoted as 'voluntaryism'. It has then subsequently analysed both volunteerism, as individual action, and voluntarism, as organizationed action. It has made explicit the contribution of voluntaryism to these concepts, but also established areas where these differing conceptual strands are at odds with each other.

With regard to voluntarism, this concept has been used to describe the organizational manifestation of voluntary action in society. Whilst it may incorporate some key issues from voluntaryism and overlap with volunteerism, it is a distinct concept in its own right. It offers as an ideal, a plural society based upon self-organization and a multiplicity of service choices, which is opposed to the centralized and monolithic state.

In spite of the critiques of this approach discussed above, it has been a powerful concept in the late twentieth century in the Western world, as the modern states have been perceived to have failed in their tasks of achieving social justice (it is also gathering an increasing impetus in the developing world and in post-communist Eastern and Central Europe, as a core component of the *civil society*; see, for example, Shaw 1990, Fisher 1993, Les 1994, and Osborne and Kaposvari 1997). Voluntarism, it seems, may well be an idea whose time has come. This makes the understanding of the parameters of its key organs, VNPOs, even more essential. It is to this task that the remainder of this chapter is devoted.

Defining organized voluntary activity

This chapter began by agreeing to use the term *VNPO* to denote organized voluntary effort but made the point that this term would need to be explored further at a later stage. That stage has now come. There are a number of ways of describing organized voluntary effort in contemporary Western society, both in terms of individual organizations and of the sector as a whole. These include as *charities and philanthropic organizations* (Butler and Wilson 1990; Gurin and Van Til 1990), as *non-profit organizations* (James 1990; Salamon and Anheier 1994), as *non-governmental organizations* and *para-governmental organizations* (Cousins 1982; Hood 1984) and as *'quangos'* (Pifer 1967, 1975; Barker 1982a).

Each of these terms has its strengths and limitations, and each has been discussed further in Osborne (1993a). However, for this study, it is argued that the term *voluntary and non-profit organization* is the most useful. It is the one which will allow the focus of this book to be upon the contribution of organization studies to the understanding of these organizations, by focusing the analysis on their organizational and institutional characteristics, whilst nonetheless still maintaining a focus upon the voluntary motivation within such organizations.

In doing this, the contribution of the recent work by Salamon and Anheier (1994; see also Anheier 1995) and their colleagues in the Johns Hopkins Comparative Non-profit Sector Project has to be acknowledged as of great import. Although preferring the term *non-profit* for their international comparative study, their focus was also upon the organizational characteristics of such organizations. These characteristics were that they

- were formally constituted organizations;
- were private organizations, and separate from government (though they could receive governmental support for their work);
- were not profit-distributing to their owners or directors;
- were self-governing and 'equipped to control their own activities'; and
- had some meaningful voluntary content, such as voluntary income, volunteer labour or voluntary management.

This is an important approach and one which goes beyond the basic *non-profit* definition to embrace and broaden the organizational dimensions of voluntarism outlined previously by Bourdillon (1945a).

The approach taken here, therefore, will be to use the term VNPO to denote organized voluntary activity, and to draw upon the insights of the Johns Hopkins project in doing so. By applying these insights it is possible to subdivide the two organizational characteristics of voluntary organizations described earlier by Bourdillon into five, to give a more explicit understanding of this phenomenon. Moreover, it is suggested that by placing this definition within the context of this wider definitional debate, it provides it with a robust degree of construct validity.

First, VNPOs must be *formally structured*. The extent and nature of this formalization can vary (from having an agreed constitution to having paid staff, for example). Nonetheless it is apparent enough to separate them out from informal gatherings and meetings.

Second, they should be *founded* independent of state control. They exist because a certain group of people want them to, not because there is some legislative requirement for them. The state (at either local or central level) may have a role in encouraging such organizations to come together but it must not be a prime mover, either by legislating to form such organizations or by being a majority force in their founding membership.

Third, VNPOs should be *governed* by a management committee which is able to decide its own composition, either at the behest of its membership or by its own decisions, and have independent decision-making capacity. Again, they might share this capacity with government but cannot abnegate it entirely.

Fourth, they have a distinctive pattern of *financial management*. VNPOs cannot distribute any surplus accrued by their mission-critical activities, but must reinvest it in services. They are also differentiated from statutory organizations by having voluntary income which is not raised through taxation.

Finally, the *motivation* of a VNPO should not be based upon financial gain, but rather should hold some normative *voluntary* value. In this there is a clear echo of the 'public benefit' clause of the legal definition of a charity. However, it is wider than this, in that it includes activity which has an element of self-benefit (such as self-help groups), but which is excluded under charity law. It is important to emphasize that the nature of this voluntary content can vary. It may mean the participation of volunteers in the fund-raising, management or service-delivery activities of an organization, for example, or the presence of voluntary funds for the organization.

Such a definition is broad enough to include the wide range of truly *voluntary* organizations, whilst excluding those organizations which, although non-profit-making or non-governmental, do not derive their mainspring from voluntarism. Private hospitals are a good example of the non-profit-making and many Housing Associations of the non-governmental organizations. Moreover it does not draw impermeable boundaries between voluntary and other types of organizations, which boundaries have become increasingly blurred. Leat (1995), for example, is presently exploring the similarities between voluntary and for-profit organizations, whilst other authors have questioned their independence from the state, as governmental funding becomes an essential part of their core funding (for example, Pifer 1975). The definition proposed here has the advantage that it allows exploration of some of the inter-sectoral issues raised by the terms 'non-profit' and 'non-governmental organizations', by reference to the four imperatives outlined above. As Anheier (1995) has noted, such an ability to differentiate is needed increasingly, if we are to make sense of contemporary Western society, and the role of organized voluntary activity within it.

As an example of the way that the above overall definition can be used to highlight key commonalities and differences between different types of voluntary organizations, it is instructive to compare what Kramer *et al.* (1993; see also Billis 1991) call *voluntary associations* and *voluntary agencies*. The former are a more informal type of organization, usually relying upon their members for their activity. A voluntary agency, by contrast, is

> more formalized, bureaucratic, and employs paid staff to provide a continuing service to a community . . . While these two organizational forms share many values, norms, and interests . . . when voluntary agencies enter into the world of social service provision, they become more subject to the influence of governmental policy, financing, and regulation.
>
> (p. 173)

Both these organizational types exist within the overall field of VNPOs. However, each has, for example, different characteristics, as outlined above, and different issues to confront. These issues and challenges are exposed by use of the definition and its component dimensions outlined above.

The scope of VNPOs

Having decided upon the appropriate terminology, it is now necessary to look at the scope of the activity which we have thus defined. O'Neill (1989) is in no doubt about this in America. He estimated that his 'Third America' actually employs 7 per cent of the American workforce, and accounts for 6 per cent of the GNP (in 1986), whilst its total assets amount to over $506 thousand million (in 1987).

The size of the voluntary sector in the UK is smaller, but no less impressive. A major recent study of the income and expenditure of the voluntary sector in the UK has provided a similar estimate for this country. The study estimated the sector's income to have been £9,094.3 million and its expenditure to have been £8,498.5 million in 1991, or 1.6 per cent of GDP (Osborne and Hems 1995, 1996).

The range of VNPO activity is equally diverse. In America, the National Center for Charitable Statistics (1986) lists 26 types of tax-exempt activity (based upon the categories of the American IRS), each one of which is itself split down into numerous subdivisions. Even the more limited classification of the British Charity Commission (concerning charitable work alone) lists 10 categories of activities (Bennett 1983). Finally the International Classification of Non-profit Organizations (ICNPO), of the Johns Hopkins Project, differentiates between 145 types of activity, across 27 major categories of activity (Salamon and Anheier 1994).

This organizational diversity has led some to question whether it is possible to speak of a cohesive societal sector comprised of VNPOs (the 'voluntary sector'). A range of studies have come down against such a sector, on the grounds that it obscures and masks the diversity of the organizations within it, as much as it illuminates any common characteristics (see, for example, Hatch 1980; Brenton 1985; Kramer 1990). Most recently, Leat (1995) has argued also that it fails to recognize the similarities between VNPOs and other forms of organization.

Others have suggested that if sectoral analysis is to be employed then it is best approached through the concept of a *third* or *independent* sector counter-posed to government and business (for example, Seibel and Anheier 1990). However, this approach is problematic in that, on the one hand, it emphasizes the independence of VNPOs from the other sectors rather than their increasing interdependence. On the other hand, it coalesces VNPOs together with neighbourhood and informal groups in a way which belies their differentiation. In doing so it risks losing the distinctive characteristics of both VNPOs and community and neighbourhood groups in a way unhelpful to the understanding of both (Abrams *et al.* 1989; Chanan 1991).

Because of these difficulties some analysts have proposed to differentiate further the sectoral analysis, suggesting a five- or even seven-sector model (see Horton Smith 1991, for the former; and Caiden 1982, and Schuppert 1991, for the latter). Such multi-sectoral approaches, however, dis-aggregate the components of analysis to such an extent as to question whether the effort is really worth it. Thus it returns one to the concept of the separate sector for VNPOs.

It is argued here that the concept of a voluntary sector does have its use, though within strictly defined criteria. It is essentially a descriptive rather than analytic term which draws attention to those organizations which possess the distinctive features of VNPOs described above. Such a descriptive term is a useful aggregation in that it describes their joint features, is able to accommodate their interdependence with other types of organizations (which is the reality for contemporary voluntary organizations), and does not mask the heterogeneity of their objectives and activities. To pursue more detailed analysis, however, it may well be necessary to differentiate sub-sectors of organizations from this broad category.

This latter approach will be the one adopted in this book. It is actually very hard to say a great deal at the general level of the voluntary sector. It is necessary to be more industry-specific in approaching fields of organizations which share common boundaries and issues. This is the approach to be adopted here, with a specific focus upon VNPOs in the field of the PSS. Further research would be necessary to explore its validity for other fields of activity. The issues involved in such a task have been well summarized by Kramer *et al.* (1993):

> Fields of service differ in their size, core technology, external environment (such as the extent of competition), roles, and relationship to government, all of which influence the structure and performance of [voluntary organizations] ... Indeed, differences among VNPOs in various fields may be greater than those between different forms of 'organizational ownership', which are

increasingly blurred ... For example Knapp *et al.* (1990) found that there were greater differences in costs among VNPOs than between them and their statutory counterparts.

(p. 171)

Conclusions

This chapter began by developing a typology of *voluntary* concepts, moving from the conceptualization of voluntary action as an organizing principle in society (voluntaryism) to its application to individuals (volunteerism) and organizations (voluntarism). This typology also drew attention to the 'ideal state' toward which each of these conceptual principles would contribute. In the case of voluntarism, it was toward a plural society, where VNPOs would reflect the heterogeneity of society and represent the diversity of opinions and aspirations within it as well as offering choice in service delivery. This was contrasted with the monolithic and centralist tendencies of the state, which would reduce this diversity to its lowest common denominator and provide an undifferentiated range of services.

From this clear conceptual understanding of organized voluntary effort, this chapter has gone on to argue for the continued general use of the term *VNPOs* rather than some of the other alternative terms proposed. It has argued that although the analyses behind the other terms do contribute to our wider understanding of organized voluntary effort (for example, by enabling us to understand their role in the allocation of resources), the continued use of the *voluntary* concept maintains the link between such organizations and their underlying conceptual principle of voluntarism. The key features of such organizations are their formal existence, independent foundation and governance, non-profit distribution, and a meaningful element of voluntary motivation.

It has also been argued that such VNPOs can usefully be described as making up a voluntary sector, but subject to three clearly comprised parameters. First, it is only a descriptive term with regard to the features defined above. It does not reflect any homogeneity in objectives or activities; in fact these are extremely diverse. Second, the sectoral model does not imply a complete independence from other sectors of society, such as business or governmental organizations. The reality is one of interdependence. Third, it is not possible to ascribe organizational characteristics to the sector as a whole. Rather these need to be used in a targeted way upon specific sub-sectoral fields, and on the basis of empirical evidence.

This chapter has dwelt upon these definitional concerns at length. This has not been because of their own intrinsic interest − if, indeed, they have any. Rather it has been to create a clear conceptual framework within which to situate and discuss the more specific concerns of this book, within a field of study often flawed by its lack of conceptual clarity and rigour. It is to these more specific concerns that we must now turn.

3 Innovations, innovators and innovating

This chapter is intended to review the key literature about innovation. Its starting point will be a review of the organization studies literature upon the nature of innovation. This will be followed by a discussion of some other key conceptual developments in this field, which will be of use in the subsequent analysis. It will continue with an exploration of the social administration and social policy literatures about the role of VNPOs in innovation and about innovation in the PSS. A final section will bring these literatures together to highlight the key research questions to be addressed in the remainder of this book.

This latter task of integration is an essential one. Over a decade ago, Knokke and Prensky (1984) noted the lack of attention that organization theory had given, and continued to give, to VNPOs. More recently, in an excellent review of the field, Paton (1993) has lamented the dearth of material in the UK in particular which applies organization theory to the study of such organizations:

> [A]lthough the amount of [such] work has increased noticeably in recent years, this is not a substantial body of work, and the amount of 'proper research' in particular is very limited. To some extent, this simply reflects the absence in the UK of an indigenous management research tradition, and a long-standing preference on the part of funders to support policy studies... But another reason for the limited amount of work is the fact that few mature researchers have given much attention to this field...
>
> Another weakness is the fragmentation of the work that has been undertaken. Too often, the studies that have been produced amount to statements, rather than contributions to a discussion... The most obvious division is between those who approach voluntary and non-profit organizations from the direction of social welfare administration, and those that approach [them] from the direction of organizational theory and management... This diversity could be a source of strength – if there was also a recognised focus and meeting ground for work on the organization and management of voluntary and non-profit organizations.
>
> (Paton 1993, pp. 21–22)

This is not to say that such work is not being done. In the UK, for example, both Wilson (Butler and Wilson 1990; Wilson 1992) and Huxham (1993; Huxham and

Vangen 1996) have produced important work upon VNPOs from the perspective of organization theory. Moreover, in the US such important scholars as DiMaggio and Powell (1988) and Singh *et al.* (1991) are also now making significant contributions.

This present study is thus very much part both of the growing recognition of the relevance of organization theory to the study of VNPOs, and of the contribution that the study of these organizations can make to organization theory. It also exists at that very cusp of organization theory and social-welfare administration which Paton identified above and which offers such rich potential for cross-fertilization of ideas and mutual learning.

Where this study is rather more unique is in its application of the 'innovation studies' sub-literature to the study of VNPOs. As will be demonstrated below, this has been (almost) wholly neglected in the discussion of their innovative capacity, which has been conducted largely within the parameters of the social administration literature. Yet not only has this literature an important contribution to make to this discussion but this discussion also has the potential to contribute back to the further development of organization theory. The starting point for this process will be the organization theory literature about the nature of innovation.

The nature of innovation

Introduction

> The general topic of innovation has inspired vast amounts of research, theorizing, speculation, and wishful thinking. The extensiveness of the research and theorizing has been well documented ... the extensiveness of the speculation and wishful thinking is less easily documented, but nonetheless real.
> Innovation is advocated ... by sundry philosophers, journalists, politicians, industrialists, and social reformers.
>
> (Kimberly 1981, p. 84)

The study of innovation has formed an important part of the social sciences since their inception. The early studies were economic ones concentrating on the role of innovation in macro-economic change, and were developed by the founding fathers of both market and Marxist economics – Adam Smith (1910), Marshall (1966) and Marx (1974).

In the twentieth century this macro-economic conception was developed further in the work of Schumpeter and Kondratiev. Schumpeter (1939) drew links between the development of the market and innovation, and emphasized the role of the entrepreneur. Kondratiev (1978) linked innovation into the cyclical pattern of macro-economic growth and development, with each cycle linked to a key invention and its subsequent innovation. Scholars in this tradition maintain that the Western economies are now in the fifth Kondratiev cycle, based upon the new information technology (for example, Barras 1989).

Whereas the studies of the nineteenth century and early part of the twentieth century concentrated upon this macro-economic concept of innovation, the last fifty years have seen a greater emphasis upon its micro-economic implications, together with a widening of its study to include sociological, political and psychological perspectives. A particular concern has been to explore the impact of this macro-economic framework upon the micro-level behaviour of individual firms and organizations. Key studies here have been those concerning the links between the competitive environment and the urge for firms to innovate in order to gain a competitive advantage (Porter 1985; Gomulka 1990), and those concentrating upon the role of innovation in the organizational life cycle (Bessant and Grunt 1985).

This approach has been an important component of the organization and management studies literature which has developed over the twentieth century. Indeed innovation is seen as such a fundamental issue in this literature that it has focused the attention of the four great management 'gurus' of the present day: Kanter (1985), Drucker (1985), Peters (1988), and Adair (1990).

This section will begin by reviewing this substantial literature about innovation from the organization studies and management fields. It will commence by reviewing attempts to define innovation and to differentiate it from invention. It will then go on to examine the nature of innovation. In particular it will discuss the need for a conceptual typology of innovation and link this to the perceived attributes both of innovation and of innovative organizations. It will also highlight the three most significant hypotheses about the causal factors which produce innovative capacity (that it is a function of their structural characteristics, their internal culture or their external environment). These will be linked to a fourth hypothesis (that it is a function of their institutional framework), which is developed in the subsequent section that provides a review of some of the wider issues in organization studies. The present section will end by looking at attempts to develop models of the process of innovation and its management.

Defining innovation

One of the difficulties in reaching a consensus upon a definition is the sheer heterogeneity of studies of innovation. Within the purely academic sphere the extent of discussion of innovation is enormous. The present author encountered twenty-three different definitions of innovation in preparing this chapter.

One example of this heterogeneity will suffice to make the point. Within the confines of the business management literature, innovation has a range of definitions which portray it quite specifically as the key tool used by entrepreneurs to change the profit-yield of resources and to produce an advantage over their competitors:

> Entrepreneurs innovate. Innovation is the specific instrument of entrepreneurship. It is the art that endows resources with a new capacity to create wealth. Innovation indeed creates a resource.
>
> (Drucker 1985, p. 27; see also Heap 1989)

Contrast this with the more wide-ranging definition developed by Rogers and Shoemaker (1971), and which echoes the earlier seminal work of Barnett (1953):

> An innovation is an idea, practice, or object perceived as new by an individual. It matters little ... whether or not an idea is 'objectively' new as measured by the lapse of time since its first use or discovery ... If an idea seems new to the individual, it is an innovation.
>
> (p. 19)

Despite this diversity it is nonetheless possible to suggest four features which form the core of a definition of innovation. The first of these is that an innovation represents *newness*. Beck and Whistler (1967) argue for an absolute definition of such newness, as literally 'first use' of a piece of new knowledge. However, most studies have preferred to use a relative definition of it, as relating to something new to a specific person, organization, society, or situation, irrespective of whether it represents a genuine 'first use' (Knight 1967; Mohr 1969; Pettigrew 1973; and Zaltman *et al.* 1973).

Ultimately it is wrong to see these views as alternatives. Rather they represent different forms of innovation. Kimberly (1981) brings them together by suggesting the twin concepts of *objective* and *subjective* innovation. The former is something which is significantly different from what has gone before; it is, quite literally, a 'first use'. The latter is something which is seen as new to those involved in its adoption, but is not necessarily its first use; it represents the diffusion of an idea/process developed elsewhere to a new situation (and may also involve its modification/ adaptation in this process). A similar differentiation has also been made by Downs and Mohr (1976), between *intrinsic* and *extrinsic* innovation.

The second feature of innovation is its *relationship to invention*. Whilst there is a consensus that invention is the actual generation of new ideas, there is none as to whether this is an intrinsic part of innovation. Urabe (1988) asserts that innovation

> consists of *the generation of a new idea* and its implementation into a new product, process, or service ... Innovation is never a one-time phenomenon, but a long and cumulative process of a great number of organizational decision making processes, ranging from *the phase of generation of a new idea* to its implementation phase. [my emphases]
>
> (p. 3)

Although this view is supported by a number of authors (Thompson 1965 and Adair 1990, for example), it is not a unanimously held one. Other studies differentiate innovation from invention. These see innovation as being the *process of adoption or implementation of a new idea,* whereby new ideas are converted into an actual product or service (Knight 1967; Aiken and Hage 1971; and Twiss 1987). Linked to the previous point this might be either the first use of such new knowledge, or its diffusion to a new situation.

Again it seems foolish to create an unnecessary counter-position here. What is clear is that innovation always involves the adoption and implementation of new ideas, and may sometimes also involve their actual invention or discovery.

The third facet of innovation is that *it is both a process and an outcome*. Whilst many studies concentrate upon its processual nature, as a process of transformation (Thompson 1965; Pettigrew 1973; Urabe 1988), it is also possible to talk of an innovation as the actual product of this process (Kimberly 1981). However, the foci of these two approaches are different, and it is important to be clear which is being addressed in any particular study.

The final feature is that innovation must involve *change or discontinuity*, both in terms of the transformation of an idea into actual reality, and also in terms of its impact upon its host organization (Wilson 1966; Nystrom 1979; and Robert and Weiss 1988). The key here is to differentiate *development* from *innovation*. Both are forms of organizational change and both, over time, can lead to significant changes in the configuration of an organization and/or its market. However, organizational development occurs within the existing product-service-market paradigm. Neither aspect of the paradigm is changed, but one or both of them may be modified and developed over time. With innovation, by contrast, there is change in this paradigm. Innovation leads to change occurring in the configuration of the product-market paradigm and leads to the creation of a new one. This 'paradigmatic shift' changes the nature of the product/service and/or the market for it in a way that is discontinuous from what has gone before.

This issue of discontinuity is an essential distinction to make (Tushman and Anderson 1985). Whilst, in the long term, incremental change can lead to significant changes in the production process or in the nature of a good or service, these changes occur within the existing paradigm (the improvement in the efficiency of canals as a transport system in the late eighteenth century, for example). Innovation, however, changes the prevailing paradigm (as with the replacement of canals by railways in the nineteenth century).

Pulling the threads of our four features together, it is possible to propose a general definition of innovation as the introduction of newness into a system usually, but not always, in relative terms and by the application (and occasionally invention) of a new idea. This produces a process of transformation which brings about a discontinuity in terms of the subject itself (such as a product or service) and/or its environment (such as an organization or society).

Classifying innovation

As with definitions of innovation, the organization studies literature is not short of typologies for classifying innovation. The focus here will be upon the five most common classifications. Whilst this might not be entirely exhaustive, it does cover the most important approaches.

The simplest typology classifies innovation according to its original impetus. Thus innovation is classified as resulting from either *research push* (that is, from the development of an innovation on the basis of research) or *market pull* (that is, from the development of an innovation on the basis of marketing analysis). Although useful in explicating the origins of innovation, this typology is limited in its usefulness. As Freeman (1982) has noted, push and pull factors are often both involved in the origin of an innovation. Consequently, it is important to understand the relationship between them, as the work by Burgelman and Sayles (1986) has begun to do. Moreover, it has an implicit assumption in it that invention is an integral part of the innovation process. As we have seen above, this is not always the case.

A second typology also focuses on the origins of innovation, though this time at an organizational level. This approach derives from the work of Cyert and March (1963). They argue that innovation can be classified as either *distress innovation* (arising because an unsuccessful organization needs to change to avoid extinction) or *slack innovation* (arising because an organization is successful, and so has sufficient surplus resources to carry the risks of innovation).

This approach is useful because it does focus attention upon the resource issues involved in innovation and relates them to their organizational context. However, its environmental analysis lacks sophistication; for example, it takes no account of other environmental factors which might stimulate innovation, such as a shift in the prevailing public-policy paradigm (Rothwell and Zegveld 1981). At the organizational level it also, once again, presents a dichotomous typology. It fails to allow for the analysis of innovation by organizations that are not in either of the stated extreme situations.

The third approach to a typology is based upon the perceptions of the beneficiaries or users of an innovation. In one of the smaller number of studies of innovation in public organizations, Daft and Becker (1978) make the important point that innovations are not a homogeneous group of entities but can have a range of different attributes. Which of these will be emphasized will depend upon the perceptions of the most significant stakeholders. Different groups will emphasize different of these attributes. Thus, in analysing the development of a new teaching programme, they show how its innovative content could differ dependent upon which group (students, teachers, administrators) was most influential in its development.

This approach is developed further by Von Hippel (1978, 1982). He adopts a *cui bono* ('who benefits') approach, similar to that of Blau and Scott (1963) in their analysis of formal organizations. In particular he looks at the differing level of benefit to be achieved by the user and the manufacturer of an innovation, and argues that ultimately it is the perceptions of the beneficiaries which are most telling in defining the nature of an innovation. Atuahene-Gima (1996) has also used this perspective to differentiate between the success factors for innovation in the manufacturing and the service sectors.

It is perhaps unfair to describe this approach as a true typology. It has not been developed so formally. Nevertheless it is an important contribution to understanding the different types and perceptions of innovation, by concentrating attention upon the producer–user/beneficiary relationship.

The fourth approach is probably the one adopted most commonly. This classifies innovation by its outcome(s). The usual framework is to look at whether the innovation is one which is a genuinely new *product or service* for the end-user, or if it is a new *process* for producing existing products and services (Bessant and Grunt 1985). Some studies have specified a wider range of outcomes. Knight (1967) adds organizational structure and personnel innovation to product and process; Starkey and McKinlay (1988) add work organization and management innovation to them; and Zaltman *et al.* (1973) are most ambitious, creating five types of innovation: product, process, organizational, personnel and policy. At its simplest, this product–process way of classifying innovation has the benefit of simplicity, and additionally draws attention to one of the core characteristics of innovation identified in the previous section (that is, whether it is a process or an outcome).

A more ambitious development of this kind of typology is where classification upon the basis of product and process innovation is employed as the starting point for a larger model of the process of innovation as a whole. In this model, product innovation is seen as *radical* innovation, which represents true discontinuity with the past and which redefines the organizational environment. Abernathy and Clark (1988) call this 'creative destruction', because it allows a qualitative jump forward in product definition which can render all existing organizational competencies obsolete. Process innovation, by contrast, is seen as *incremental*, providing continuity with the past by refining existing organizational competencies for more efficient production. In this sense, this classification is a way of differentiating between true innovation and organizational change.

A further version of this model links these two processes together with the life cycle of organizational development. Radical product innovation is thus linked to new industries and firms, where technological jumps are being made. By contrast, incremental process innovation is linked to established industries and firms, where efficiency and profitability can be developed by refining existing product processes (Holloman 1980; Urabe 1988). This approach to classification is found in its most developed form in Bessant and Grunt (1985).

As with the typologies discussed previously, this approach has its strengths. It draws the links between innovation, its organizational environment, and its impact upon that environment. However, whilst the process–product dichotomy can be useful, when used in isolation, it does have drawbacks. It forces one to focus on one or the other, when in fact both might be of interest. As noted above, an inherent characteristic of innovation is that it has both a processual and an outcome content. This typology obscures this important point by making them alternatives. Moreover, even advocates of this approach in the manufacturing sector (Bhoovaraghaven *et al.* 1996) acknowledge that it has its limitations in the service sector, where production and consumption occur contemporaneously (Normann 1991).

The life-cycle model is also often too static and linear in its presentation. At one level it confuses the discontinuity of innovation with the incremental development of organizational change. As Herbig (1991) has noted, no matter how incremental an innovation might be across an industry or sector as a whole, for the individual firm its impact is to produce discontinuity, marking a break from its practices of the past. Abernathy *et al.* (1983) have also made the important point that this life cycle is not a one-way process: it is possible for industries and firms to *de-mature* and to revert to an earlier stage of the life cycle.

Abernathy and Utterbach (1988) make the point that a particular innovation can be a product innovation for one company (which perhaps produces a new machine) but a process innovation for another (which uses this machine to change its production process). This does not mean that the distinction is unimportant. On the contrary, it can be extremely important to explore the differing impacts of an innovation upon its producers and end-users. However, as a means of classifying innovations in a mutually exclusive way, it has clear limitations.

The final approach to classification of innovation is in many ways the most satisfying. This derives from the work of Abernathy. Initially, Abernathy (1978) also adopted a linear life-cycle model, though he took this a stage further by integrating concepts, from Burns and Stalker (1961), of organic and mechanistic organizations (which concepts will be discussed further below), the former being linked to radical innovation and the latter to incremental innovation.

However, in Abernathy *et al.* (1983), he moves away from this linear and positivist view of industrial development, and argues that it is possible for organizations to *de-mature*, to move away from the standardized mass production of a mature company, with an emphasis upon process innovation, and once more embrace diversity of product production, with a reasserted emphasis upon radical innovation. This de-maturity, he argues, could frequently be brought about by a major change in the environment of an organization.

Developing from this more dynamic, and satisfying, analysis of the organizational life cycle, Abernathy *et al.* go on to develop a two-dimensional typology of innovation, based upon its impact both upon the production processes of an organization and upon the existing markets and users of a product or service (Figure 3.1). Thus, architectural innovation changes both the markets for a product or service and its production (the classical radical innovation). Regular innovation, by contrast, refines existing production processes and markets (incremental

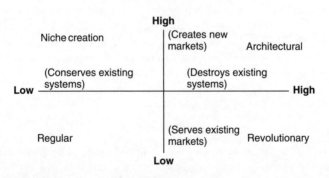

x-axis – impact of innovation on the production system
y-axis – impact of innovation on the market

Figure 3.1 Typology of innovation in Abernathy *et al.* (1983)

innovation). Niche-creation innovation is one which preserves existing production competencies, but creates new markets and users for a product or service, usually by re-packaging or re-marketing it. Finally, revolutionary innovation applies new technology to the production process for existing products and markets, creating an efficiency gain.

This approach is important because it does not treat product and process innovation as separate entities but rather explores the relationship between the two, as it does between the producers and end-users of a service or product. It dis-aggregates the concepts of *product* and of *process innovation* to explore their relationships with the user group of an innovation, as well as with each other. Nor does it necessarily link one type of innovation to a specific point in the life cycle of an organization. Instead it allows for this cycle to, quite literally, be cyclical, and encounter the same conditions again, if in a different plane. Further, it allows the issue of discontinuity and continuity to be explored, in terms of the impact of a new process or product/service, thus allowing true innovation to be differentiated from organizational development. For these reasons, this classification is a qualitative move forward, away from the traditional linear ones described previously.

In summary, then, this section has reviewed a number of approaches to classifying innovations, based upon their source (in processual and organizational terms), their users and beneficiaries, and their outcomes. These all illuminate important aspects of innovation but, it is argued, none by itself supplies a satisfactory classification of innovation. For this it is important to examine some of the relational issues, rather than relying solely upon one-dimensional typologies. In this context, the typology developed by Abernathy *et al.* is felt to be the most satisfying. This highlights the different relationships possible between the impact of an innovation upon the production of goods or services of an organization, and upon its impact upon its actual and potential users and beneficiaries.

The characteristics of innovation

> The reason why innovation theory does not easily tell us what we want to know . . . is that there is a failure to pin-point precisely what our questions are. It turns out that one cannot simply wonder about innovation and have all of one's curiosity resolved by a compact, unified, parsimonious collection of theoretical statements. Social scientists have tried to develop many of these statements, but they tend to answer different questions, if any at all, and do not easily connect with one another.
>
> (Mohr 1987, p. 13)

Zaltman *et al.* (1973) make an important distinction in differentiating the attributes of *innovations* from those of *innovators*. This subsection therefore will review the literature with regard to the characteristics of innovations, followed by the process of innovation and its management. The following subsection will then move on to examine the key issues in relation to the innovators.

The attributes of innovations

These are explored in most detail in the studies of Rogers and Shoemaker (1971) and Zaltman *et al.* (1973). The former study details five optimal attributes which it argues that users of an innovation require, in order for it to be successfully adopted (relative advantage over what preceded it, compatibility with existing technologies/skills, ease of comprehension by end-users, trialability, and the observability of its results and achievements). The Zaltman study lists nineteen dimensions along which the success of an innovation can be evaluated.

Other, more limited studies have been undertaken since. Cooper and Kleinschmidt (1993), for example, argue for product differentiation as being the major factor in identifying successful innovations. Such one-dimensional approaches do not convince, however, when compared to the earlier studies. Altman *et al.*, for example, take a contingent approach to these dimensions and stress that it is important in any given situation to differentiate between which of these are the necessary attributes of a successful innovation and which are of secondary importance. Finally, Daft and Becker (1978) combine this latter approach with a typology of innovation outcomes, to develop a matrix for the analysis of successful innovation.

Like many of the approaches to classifying innovation discussed in the previous section, these approaches to the attributes of successful innovation have been criticised for their over-rationality. Clark (1987) argues that existing studies have been dominated by economics and have also concentrated upon isolating variables rather than upon highlighting their relationships to each other. Clark and Stanton (1989) further argue that the process of the transformation of knowledge has been neglected by concentrating upon the intrinsic attributes of innovations. They also contend that such an attributional approach to innovations assumes that they are a homogeneous group of entities. In fact they argue that they are heterogeneous 'bundles of elements', which need a dynamic and relational rather than a static and discrete analysis.

Another criticism of the study of the attributes of innovations is the inherent assumption that innovations must be good. Indeed, the role attributed to innovation in market economies is almost that of a normative good. As will be seen below, innovation is assumed to be a key linkage between a competitive environment and the behaviour of individual firms (Drucker 1985; Porter 1985). This is especially true of the influential work of the 1980s of Tom Peters (Peters and Waterman 1982; Peters and Austin 1985; Peters 1988). However, other critics have taken issue with this assumption. Knight (1967), Rosner (1967) and Kimberly (1981) had all previously argued that it is possible for innovations to have negative effects both upon their adopters and upon society in general. For firms, innovations can be expensive to develop and they risk being prey to imitators who copy (and improve) their innovations, whilst not risking the development costs. Similarly, for society an innovation can have immense social costs (in terms of pollution, for example), despite any economic benefits. This latter point has led Mole and Elliot (1987) to argue for the importance of public control of innovations, to limit their social costs.

Atuahene-Gima (1996) has also pointed to the need to distinguish between the characteristics of successful innovations in the manufacturing and the service sectors.

Finally, Van de Ven (1988) has also argued against the positivism implicit in many studies of the attributes of innovations, which assumes an implied link between goodness and usefulness: 'Innovation is often viewed as a good thing because the new idea must be useful – profitable, constructive, or solve a problem. New ideas that are not perceived as useful are not normally called innovations: they are usually called mistakes' (p. 105).

To conclude, the studies of the attributes of innovations do have some insights to offer. They do, for example, draw attention to the dimensions involved in their successful adoption. However, it is not possible to use these dimensions in a mechanistic predictive way – Zaltman *et al.* (1973) are right to point out the contingent nature of these attributes. Moreover, there is an assumption of an inherent benefit in innovation which belies its potential costs. These include lost opportunities to develop in other directions and the costs to firms of the actual process of innovation, as well as their possible social costs. These more negative aspects of innovation also need to be taken into account in developing a more rounded view of it.

The process of innovation

The study of the process of innovation is one with a great lineage, stretching back to the political philosophy of Machiavelli. Traditionally, innovation has been viewed as a linear process. This view is well characterized by Mole and Elliot (1987): 'The innovation process typically involves a series of stages ranging from the idea of invention, through the product design, development, production, and adoption or use' (p. 14). Other studies have challenged this linear model. As early as 1966, Wilson argued that the process was not linear but cyclical, with key feedback points within it. More recently Pelz (1985) and Clark (1987) have also argued against a linear model as being too static and one-dimensional. Rather they argue that it is multi-dimensional and multi-directional.

However one models the entire process, though, it is agreed generally that three dimensions are involved in it: an optional one of invention, and two essential ones of implementation, and diffusion.

INVENTION

The invention stage is, as the earlier discussion suggested, an optional stage. Innovation can often mean solely the application of new knowledge rather than its 'invention' or discovery. This is an important activity in its own right, nonetheless.

As discussed earlier, one of the key arguments in the literature is whether the generation of new ideas is pulled by 'pure' research (Burns and Stalker 1961), or 'pushed' by market and consumer demand (Von Hippel 1978, 1982). Inevitably, perhaps, recent studies have synthesised both the above perspectives, arguing that both have a role. In particular, Abernathy *et al.* (1983) have argued for an understanding of the source and impact of inventions in relation to both new knowledge and the market.

IMPLEMENTATION

This is often seen as the core of innovation, involving the introduction and adaptation of a new idea within a new environment. Four interlinked factors are identified in the literature as important to an understanding of this stage. The first is the organization itself. Research has suggested that different organizational characteristics are appropriate to different stages of the innovation process: whilst an open decentralized organization is required for the generation of ideas, a hierarchical and centralized one is more effective for their implementation. This analysis has been supported by Normann (1971), Aiken and Hage (1971), and Rowe and Boise (1974). The issue here is the relationship between the open communication required in the invention stage (Tidd 1995) and the management direction needed in the implementation stage, which often involves negotiating opposition to change. A separate but linked analysis concerns the relationship between efficiency and innovation within organizations and the extent to which it is possible to achieve both these organizational states simultaneously (Heap 1989).

The second factor is the importance of an organizational environment committed to innovative change. The key factor here is the development of organizational values and an organizational environment which encourages and stimulates innovation (Starkey and McKinlay 1988).

This links into the third identified characteristic, which is the role of individuals in the process of implementation. Again, as previously noted, individuals can operate at different levels. Schon (1963) and Knight (1987) both point to the role of the product champion in managing the implementation of a new product or service. By contrast Hage and Aiken (1967), Hage and Dewar (1973) and Hage (1980) all emphasize the role of senior management as providing leadership and innovative values for the innovative organization. These issues will be discussed further below, in the section on the characteristics of innovating organizations.

The final factor in the implementation stage is that of its micro-process within the organization. Here the debate centres on whether this is predominantly a rational or a political (i.e. inter-personal) process. Carson (1989) and Adair (1990) make a case for a wholly rational approach, in which the implementation of innovation is rigorously planned. However, this is strongly challenged by a number of empirical and theoretical studies (notably Kimberly 1987, Golden 1990, and Frost and Egri 1991). The case is most strongly made, though, in the seminal work of Pettigrew (1973):

> Political behaviour is likely to be a special feature of large-scale innovative decisions. These decisions are likely to threaten existing patterns of resource sharing. New responses may be created and appear to fall within the jurisdiction

of a department or individual who has not previously been a claimant in a particular area. This department, or its principal representative, may see this as an opportunity to increase its, or his, status and rewards in the organization. Those who see their interests threatened by the change may invoke resistance in the joint decision making process. In all these ways new political action is released and ultimately the existing distribution of power is endangered.

(pp. 20–21)

In the late 1980s, efforts were made to bring these schools together in a 'contingency' model of managing change (Beer and Walton 1987; Nadler 1988). These emphasize the importance of bringing rational and political processes together, dependent upon the specific environmental configuration of an organizational innovation.

Whichever approach is preferred, and the preference here is towards the contingency model with its emphasis upon environmental analysis, all analysts are clear upon the need for a positive management role. This is discussed further below, in the section on the innovators.

DIFFUSION

The final stage of the innovation process is diffusion. This is the means by which a specific innovation is transmitted from one user on to others, be they individuals or organizations. The key work in the study of diffusion is undoubtedly that of Rogers and Shoemaker (1971). They specify a process by which awareness of new knowledge is followed by persuasion by its proponents and its subsequent testing, to decision making. Basing their work on an extensive review of diffusion studies and communication theory, they argue that the pattern of diffusion of an innovation will follow a *normal curve*, moving from the 'innovators' through to the 'laggards'. If this distribution is viewed cumulatively, rather than discretely, it forms the 'S' curve which is the basis of much analysis of individual innovation diffusion.

This detailed study has formed the basis of much analysis of the diffusion process, though it has been criticized for its over-emphasis upon the role of the individual, rather than of the organization. However, some important modifications have been suggested. Three are especially important.

First, Mohr (1987) has argued that the traditional model of diffusion has excluded the importance of evaluation in the process, which makes it a cyclical process, rather than the traditional linear one. Second, Mort (1991) has argued against the use of *diffusion* as a metaphor for the process and instead favours *percolation*. This is because it concentrates attention upon the environment in which innovation takes place, rather than seeing it as a self-contained process.

Finally, Herbig (1991) has argued also against the 'S' curve as helping in understanding the impact of innovation upon an organization. He contends that this model implies an incremental continuity to the process which might well describe the diffusion process for an industry or market as a whole. However, as was noted earlier, the impact upon individual organizations within this environment is to produce discontinuity. In these circumstances he argues that catastrophe theory is more appropriate for aiding understanding of the process of innovation.

A theory of innovation?

[I]nnovation is not a homogeneous category. All innovations share the characteristic of newness, but beyond newness the array of innovations adopted by any organization may be a mixture of types each having different attributes ... some types of innovation ideas percolate up the organization, some are imposed from above, and other types of ideas move in both directions. The consequence of this heterogeneity is that the adoption of ideas from different innovation sub-categories will be related to different organizational and environmental factors and will follow different processes. Studying one innovation category will produce markedly different findings from the study of another category.

(Daft and Becker 1978, pp. 120–121)

This section has taken in a 'grand tour' (or perhaps 'package trip'?) of innovation, from the perspective of the organization studies literature. It began by defining innovation and by developing a typology of it. It then moved on to look at the characteristics of innovations before concluding by discussing the actual process of innovation.

Such a broad review is unlikely to produce closely linked conclusions. Nonetheless, a number of important points do rise to the surface. First, innovation is about the introduction and adoption of new ideas which produce a change in the existing relationships between an organization and its internal and external environments. Second, any typology of innovation needs to take account of its impact on both these environments. An example of just such a typology is that of Abernathy *et al.* (1983). Third, the process of innovation involves an optional stage (invention) and two compulsory ones (implementation and diffusion/evaluation). Fourth, it is essential to emphasize the issue of *discontinuity* in discussing innovation, and in differentiating it from other, more incremental, forms of organizational change. Finally, the management of the changes inherent in innovation involves both rational and political components. The precise balance between these needs to be analysed for any particular innovation.

The key question in concluding this review is to ask whether this literature offers a single unifying theory of innovation. The answer to this is a resounding 'no'. As will have become clear in this review, the act of innovation is a nexus of a number of heterogeneous elements. To try to bring all of these within the realms of one theory stretches the credibility of our bounded rationality. Such a conclusion is not original, and has been well argued before (Downs and Mohr 1976; Daft and Becker 1978; Clark 1987; Mohr 1987).

However, if it is not possible to construct a single theory of innovation, it is possible to develop some guidelines for its understanding. First, there is a need for more focused research within clearly defined fields of innovation. These fields should be homogeneous enough to be able to produce generalizable results (within that field) and be developed with a view to comparison with data from other fields. Again, this is no new insight. A similar call was made by the SAPPHO team in the early 1970s (Achilladelis *et al.* 1972; Rothwell 1975). The importance of defining the field of analysis to organizations with a shared environment, or niche, has also been demonstrated by the 'organizational ecology' studies of recent years (Hannan and Freeman 1989).

Second, any theory needs to be developed within a model of contingency, which acknowledges the situational specifics of innovation. Thus the emphasis should not be upon defining static configurations of characteristics which might define innovative organizations. Rather it should be upon developing an understanding of the relationships involved in the event and process of innovation. This is a complex task. At the very least it requires two-dimensional analyses, such as those of Nystrom (1979) and Daft and Becker (1978). It could also make use of three dimensional models, such as catastrophe theory (Herbig 1991), rather than the more one-dimensional models, such as diffusion theory (Rogers and Shoemaker 1971).

Finally, the development of a contingency model of innovation theory requires a greater understanding of, and weighting given to, the effects both of the characteristics of innovative organizations and of the external environment upon innovation. This is discussed in greater detail in the next section.

In sum, this section has argued against the development of overblown and over-ambitious innovation theory. In its place it calls for a series of smaller-scale innovation models, within specific contexts. These need to be based upon the contingency paradigm and in particular need to acknowledge the influence of the external environment as a key variable in the process of innovation.

The attributes of innovators

In reviewing the literature, three distinct foci can be drawn out, to explain the innovative capacity of an organization. These are its formal structure, its internal environment, and its external environment and its relationship to this. Each of these will be examined in turn.

Organizational structure

The starting point for any discussion of this factor has to be a clear conception of what formally constitutes an organization. Zaltman *et al.* (1973) give a clear definition of the formal aspects of an organization: '[It is] a social system created for attaining some specific goals through the collective efforts of its members. Its most salient characteristic is its structure that specifies its operation' (p. 106).

Early work on the relationship between organizational structure and innovation emphasized the importance of the overall configuration of an organization. This is best epitomized by Burns and Stalker (1961) and Thompson (1965). The former, highly influential, study counter-posed the mechanistic organization to the organic one. The former relied upon highly specified and distinct organizational special-isms among its staff, with a strong vertical line management. The latter, by contrast, had a high degree of task complexity and sharing, and a more horizontal organiza-tional structure with a greater degree of lateral connection. Burns and Stalker hypothesized that the mechanistic organization was most suited to stable conditions whilst the organic one was more adaptable in unstable conditions, and by implica-tion, more innovative. This model was supported by Thompson, who contrasted the bureaucratic organization (as centralized and formalized) with the innovative organization, which possessed more participative management and freedom of communication: 'The bureaucratic orientation is conservative. Novel solutions, using resources in a new way, are likely to appear threatening. Those having a bureaucratic orientation are more concerned with the internal distribution of power and status than with the organizational goal accomplishment' (1965, p. 5).

Following on from these studies, later ones were concerned to break down these 'ideal' types into their constituent parts, in order to examine their impact. In particular, the issues of centralization of power, formalization of roles, and organi-zational complexity were explored. Some of these studies confirmed the model of Burns and Stalker. Thus, for example, Hage and Aiken (1967) contended that centralized decision making did indeed inhibit the ability of an organization to innovate, whilst organizational complexity encouraged openness and the exchange of ideas.

Other studies took a more paradoxical view in their analyses, however. Wilson (1966) argued that there was a contradiction between the types of organizational structures required for the generation (or invention) of innovative ideas and for their implementation. The former process did indeed require open non-hierarchical structures. The latter, however, benefited from a centralized structure which could be forceful in implementation. This position was similarly argued by Sapolsky (1967) and Zaltman *et al.* (1973). Even Aiken and Hage (1974) subsequently mod-ified their earlier position to suggest that the ability of organizations to be innovative could vary over time, dependent upon their needs and their environment.

The earlier static model of Burns and Stalker thus has subsequently been replaced by a more contingent one. This acknowledges that organizational struc-ture is a significant predictor of innovative capacity, but that innovation may well require different organizational structures at different stages of the process, or that a specific organization will need to be able to cycle between different modes of structure, dependent upon its needs in relation to innovation.

The internal organizational culture

The second group of studies which have attempted to explain the innovative capacity of the innovators are those concerned with their internal culture. These studies have tended to concentrate upon three issues – the size of an organization, the nature of organizational leadership, and the nature of organizational life (such as the communication channels and processes within an organization and the complexity of organizational tasks).

With regard to organizational size, a whole range of early studies found a clear relationship between the greater size of an organization and its ability to innovate (Mansfield 1963; Becker and Stafford 1967; Mohr 1969; and Langrish *et al.* 1972). However, later studies have taken a different view, starting with the seminal SAPPHO study at the University of Sussex, which associated small organizational size with innovativeness (Freeman 1973; Stroetman 1979; Ahlbrandt and Blair 1986). This debate has continued, with Pavitt (1991) and Haveman (1993) advocating the significance of small size and Azzone and Maccarrone (1993) that of large size.

Da Rocha *et al.* (1990), summarizing the arguments, suggest that the proponents of size as a predictor of innovation are actually using this as a proxy for resource availability (in terms of capital, personnel and expertise), whilst those supporting smallness are similarly using it as a proxy for a less bureaucratic organizational structure and for greater freedom for individual action. Damanpour (1996) has also argued for a contingent model which relates the significance of organizational size to environmental uncertainty.

Overall, the decision on the relationship of size to innovation is one still to be proven. Certainly there is no one clear conclusion relating it to innovation as a whole. It remains to be seen whether more specific studies can locate size in a more contingent way, in terms of different stages, or types, of innovation.

Moving on to organizational leadership, there is little dispute in the literature that senior management commitment to innovation is a key factor in innovative organizations. However, three distinct roles can be delineated in this unanimity.

The first is the role of the general manager to direct their organization, and to enable/make things happen (Kamm 1987; Baden-Fuller 1995). As was noted earlier, the implementation of innovation can require a 'hands-on' and directive managerial approach at a senior level, if innovative ideas are to be turned into reality. Boeker (1997) has argued that the positive performance of 'top teams' is a key determinant of successful organizational transformation.

A more normative version of this argument is the emphasis upon entrepreneurship as a key trait in senior management for innovative organizations, where the emphasis is upon resource acquisition and its transformation into products or services. Drucker (1985), quoted previously, is a good example of this approach, as are Robert and Weiss (1988):

> Innovation is the tool of entrepreneurs . . . This simply requires a willingness to see change as opportunity instead of as threat and to employ some process for the orderly examination of change. Innovation is the entrepreneur's method of moving extra resources and assets from low yield and profitability to areas of high yield and productivity.
>
> (p. 8)

A further modification of this approach, though, is that of the 'intra-preneur' (Pinchot 1985; Knight 1987), who is 'a corporate employee who introduces and manages an innovative project within the corporate environment, as if he or she were an independent entrepreneur' (Knight 1987, p. 285).

A second role envisaged for management in innovation is the creation and management of an organizational culture. This was first suggested by Burns and Stalker (1961) and has been given considerable prominence in the work of Hage (Hage and Aiken 1967; Hage and Dewar 1973; Hage 1980). Here the role is not so much the proactive development of innovation as the creation and support of a climate which supports innovation throughout the organization. Innovation and change hence become basic values of the organization. More recently this view has been expressed succinctly by Jelinek and Schoonhoven (1990): 'A strategy for innovation is contained not in "plans", but in the pattern of commitments, decisions, approaches, and persistent behaviours that facilitate doing new things . . . [Managers] behave, make decisions, and commit in ways that persistently foster innovation' (p. 203). It is important to realize that this requires a distinct managerial approach to be taken. Nystrom (1979) and Heap (1989) have pointed out that there is an irreconcilable tension between the needs of an organization to be efficient and to be innovative. They maintain that a choice needs to be made between the mass production of standardized products/services, with limited risks but often small profit margins, and innovation of new products/services, with greater risks but also potentially greater profits. The two choices require different leadership styles. Despres (1991) has argued that the failure to understand this dichotomy, and the limitations of the rational model of management has been one of the major brakes on the innovative capacity of organizations. Further, Colville and Packman (1996) have argued that, even where the nature and significance of cultural management is understood, it can be notoriously difficult to achieve.

The final leadership role is somewhat different from the above two. It is not necessarily located at a senior management level, and indeed may often be represented by a lower-level figure in the organization. This is the role of the *product champion* or *hero innovator* who supports an innovation at its early stage of development, even when it does not seem to accord with the strategic direction of the organization. Both Schon (1963) and Fischer *et al.* (1986) argue that this role is required because of the inability of formal organizations to respond to change. Thus a mediator is needed to balance the present needs of the organization for stability against its future need for change.

Moving on to the final aspect of the internal environment of an organization, its organizational life, three factors have been emphasized here. These are the nature of the staff group of an organization, the complexity of the tasks that they undertake, and the nature of organizational communication.

All three of these factors were integrated in the early model of Burns and Stalker (1961), of the organic organization. Subsequent studies have sought to separate out these factors rather more. Both Aiken and Hage (1971) and Iwamura and Jog (1991) have argued for the educational and professional level of the staff group of an organization as being a key factor in promoting innovation by that organization. Doudeyns and Hayman (1993) have also argued for it as a key statistical indicator of the innovative potential of organizations. In contrast, Zaltman *et al.* (1973) and Abernathy and Utterbach (1988) have emphasized the importance of task complexity as promoting innovative activity within organizations.

Most recently, attention has been turned to the role of communication channels and patterns within organizations as a key factor in their innovative potential. Poole (1981, 1983a, 1983b; Poole and Roth 1989) has been a most influential scholar in developing this perspective and Van de Ven *et al.* (1989) subsequently integrated this factor into their holistic model of innovative organizations. Albrecht and Hall (1991) have also maintained that internal communication is *the* key factor in organizational capacity to innovate.

Given the complexity of organizational life, Rickards (1985), probably sensibly, recommends a *contingent* approach (Lawrence and Lorsch 1967) which examines the interplay of these, and other, internal factors. Importantly this approach also places these internal environmental factors in the context of their interrelationship with the external environment of an organization. The wider role of this external environment as a potential factor in the innovative capacity of organizations must now be examined.

The external organizational environment

The central problem of some of the organization studies literature is that it tends to treat organizations as if they exist in a vacuum. Whilst a number of studies, from as far back as 1969, have recognized the importance of the external environment in innovation, they have had little to say about the nature and extent of its influence (for example: Mohr 1969, 1987; Abernathy and Utterbach 1988). This has led some to dismiss the utility of the innovation studies literature, as being unable to predict innovative capacity and trends, precisely because of its neglect of environmental issues (Mensch 1985). However, this is an area whose contribution is growing. As will be seen below, though, this contribution has its own problems.

Those studies which have addressed the external environment have usually stemmed from one of three sources. The first source is those studies which have their roots in the economics literature and which have been concerned almost wholly with the activities of for-profit organizations in the market place.

The focus there is the issue and impact of the competitive environment. A core component of this approach is the link between this competitive environment, innovation, and a competitive advantage for one firm over other firms within this market. Thus, the spur of inter-firm competition defines the direction and nature of any innovation. This in turn gives the successful innovator a competitive advantage through which to gain a price and/or market-share advantage over its competitors (see Kamien and Schwartz 1982; Nelson and Winter 1982; Gomulka 1990; Nelson 1993a; and Morris and Westbrook 1996).

In the words of one of the major advocates of this view, innovation

> is one of the principal drives of competition. It plays a major role in industry structural change, as well as in creating new industries . . . of all the things that

can change the rules of competition, [innovation] is among the most prominent.

(Porter 1985, p. 164)

The argument is most concisely summarized by Nelson (1993b):

> For-profit business firms in rivalrous competition with each other are the featured actors [in innovation]. Firms innovate in order to gain competitive advantage over their rivals or to catch up with them. A firm that successfully innovates can profit handsomely. On the other hand, in an industry where competitors innovate, a firm is virtually forced to do so, or fall further behind.
>
> (p. 364)

> In most industries a company gains profit from its innovation by getting it out into the market ahead of its competitors, moving rapidly down the learning curve, and supporting the product and improvements to it through sales and service efforts.
>
> (p. 367)

A second rather different perspective upon the inter-organizational environment is provided by the network perspective (Powell *et al.* 1996; Robertson *et al.* 1996). Camagni (1991a) focuses upon the *innovation milieu*, which is defined as 'the set ... of mainly informal social relationships [within] a limited geographic area' (p. 3). From this perspective, innovation is seen to arise not out of the competition between organizations, but from their interaction. Alter and Hage (1993) argue that there is now a move away from competitive relationships with other organizations within a particular market and toward collaboration.

> Until recently, US corporations adopted organizational structures that were large and centralized ... Corporate strategy was to eliminate competitors to gain control over their buyers or suppliers, and the methods were merger, price war, and large advertising budgets ... Profit making organizations' primary objective, of course, was to gain maximum leverage over needed resources by besting rivals by whatever means were at hand.
>
> Today, however, many companies are developing structures that are smaller, decentralized, and based on strategies of cooperation and horizontal relationships ... [This] has led to a variety of obligational networks, bound together by sub-contracts and comparative contracts among small firms, and strategic alliances and joint ventures among large and small firms.
>
> (p. 2; see also Tidd 1995)

This is happening because of the increasing complexity and open-endedness of many organizational goals, and because of the desire to share risks in an uncertain market. Nohria (1992) agrees, arguing that organizational networks are now an essential component of *the new competition*, where expertise and knowledge are so widely dispersed that collaboration with some organizations in your market sector is essential to gaining a competitive advantage over other organizations (see also Burt 1982, 1992; and Best 1990). In this model, innovation can only occur through collaboration, which brings together the knowledge, capital and personnel necessary for its achievement (Kreiner and Schultz 1993). An important issue here is that networks are seen, not as an alternative to competition, but as a different and currently more effective way through which to achieve a competitive advantage.

The second source is those studies which have adopted an explicitly contingent approach to the study of organizations, emphasizing the interrelationship between the structure and internal environment of an organization with its external environment as being the key trigger to innovative activity (Astley and Van de Ven 1983; Rickards 1985). From this literature it is possible to discern two interrelated views about the impact of this interrelationship. These are concerned with the relationship of an organization to its end-users, and its overall strategic orientation to the market (Berry 1994).

The role of the end-users in shaping the innovative capacity of organizations has been a consistent theme in much of the organization studies literature (Von Hippel 1978, 1982; Freeman 1982; Twiss 1987; Robert and Weiss 1988), as discussed above, and views marketing as one of the prime motivators of innovation. Probably one of the most forceful proponents of this view, though, was Tom Peters: 'The excellent companies are better listeners. They get a benefit from ... closeness that for us was truly unexpected. Most of the real innovation comes from the market' (Peters and Waterman 1982, p. 193).

The second view places this relationship to end-users within the overall strategic orientation of an organization. At one level this concerns the direct commitment to innovation as a goal (or *the* goal) of an organization, highlighted in relation to organizational leadership previously (Nystrom 1979; Heap 1989). More fundamentally, however, it concerns also its wider strategic orientation to its environment.

The seminal work here is certainly that of Miles and Snow (1978) and Pfeffer and Salancik (1978), though more recent formulations of this approach can be found in Astley and Van de Ven (1983) and in Cho *et al.* (1996), while in Beekum and Ginn (1993) is a rare application to the public sector. Zahria and Pearce (1990) also provide an excellent critique of this model. The core argument here is that organizations have a choice in the way in which they relate to their external environment. This environment is a complex multifaceted reality, and managers can choose what they focus on within it, and how they choose to interpret what they see there.

Miles and Snow developed four managerial *gestalts*, or mind-sets, through which to analyse these strategic approaches. These are:

- *the defender*, who seeks stability and offers a limited product line, with an emphasis upon efficiency;
- *the prospector*, who seeks a dynamic environment and offers a broad or changing product line to respond to this;

- *the analyser*, who seeks a balance between stable and dynamic markets, and who offers a mix of efficient and flexible products; and
- *the reactor*, who reacts on the spur of the moment, with no consistent strategy.

In these gestalts, it is the prospector and the analyser who are likely to unlock the innovative potential of an organization, through their dynamic approach to the environment.

The environmental approach to innovative capacity thus includes two compatible views as to its causality. The first concerns the impact of that environment itself. This has invariably been posed in terms of the market environment, and the argument has been developed in terms of whether the search for increased profits in this market has promoted innovation through either competition or collaboration. The second approach has concerned the strategic response of organizations to their environment and the extent to which this has seen innovation or stability as the best means through which to achieve organizational survival and growth.

Yet if these approaches identify different routes for the release of the innovative capacity of organizations, they converge nonetheless upon the acceptance of the prevailing environmental paradigm as being one of the market. They are alternatives only in that they identify different perspectives upon this paradigm.

Conclusions

This section has explored the contribution of organization studies to the understanding of innovation. It has discussed the definition and classification of innovation, and outlined three hypotheses about the causality of the innovative capacity of organizations. However, this does not end the potential contribution of this literature to the concerns of this book. There are other areas which have a potential contribution to make. These are outlined in the next part of this chapter.

Some wider issues in organization theory

The previous part of this chapter examined in detail the sub-literature of the organization studies field concerned with the innovative capacity of organizations. Before moving on to the second substantive literature that this book draws upon (the social administration/social policy literature), it is important also to consider several other aspects of organization theory which may contribute to its theoretical perspectives. Clearly, there is not space here to cover the entire remit of this literature. However, it is important to cover four main aspects. These are contingency theory, exchange theory, systems theory and institutional theory.

Contingency theory

This has already been mentioned in passing in this chapter. It was developed first by Lawrence and Lorsch (1967) and further by Galbraith (1973). The central premises of this approach are that there is no one best way to organize, that not all ways of organizing are equally effective, and that the best way to organize for any particular organization depends upon its relationship to its environment. This approach was a real challenge to those previous models, such as that of March and Simon (1958), which viewed organizational form as relating to a hierarchy of organizational goals.

In this hierarchy of goals, each level is

> considered as an end relative to the levels below it and as a means relative to the levels above it. Through the hierarchical structure of ends, behavior attains integration and consistency, for each member a set of behavior alternatives is then weighted in terms of a comprehensive scale of values – the 'ultimate' ends.
>
> (March and Simon 1958, p. 63)

By contrast, Lawrence and Lorsch saw successful organizational structure as guided not by internal rationality but by external adaptiveness. Different environments placed different demands upon organizations, and required different organizational structures with which to meet these demands – though as Scott (1990) has noted, how the 'demands of the environment' or the 'best adaptation' are defined is not always clear.

A further development of this contingency approach is found in those who take a more strategic approach. They criticize the conventional contingency theorists for failing to consider the issues of power and of the decision-making process inside organizations:

> They draw attention to possible constraints upon the choice of effective structures, but fail to consider the process of choice itself in which economic and administrative exigencies are weighed by the actors concerned against the opportunities to operate a structure of their own and/or other organization members' preferences.
>
> (Child 1972, p. 16; see also Hickson *et al.* 1971; Pfeffer 1978, 1981)

Thus, rather than seeing organizational structure as being contingent upon environmental adaptiveness, these theorists emphasize rather the political decision-making process and the distribution of power within an organization as the key contingencies of organizational structure.

Contingency arguments play an important part in many key studies of innovation (Rickards 1985; Wolfe 1994) and have an important part to play in understanding the innovative capacity of voluntary and non-profit organizations.

Exchange and network theories

These theories have their pedigree within the sphere of political economy. The focus of exchange theory is upon the relative power of different parties to a relationship, dependent upon such factors as their financial resources, access to information, independent decision-making capacity, and degree of legitimacy. The expectation is that organizations will seek to minimize the uncertainty of their environment by combining with others to act. To some extent it can be seen as the behavioural counterpart of the contingency theory of organizational structure, discussed above.

According to Benson (1975), organizational relationships will depend upon the degree of consensus over the respective roles of the parties, their agreed tasks and approaches, their relative evaluation of the importance of the others to their own goals, and the pre-existing patterns of activity between them. He makes an important point in identifying the networks of organizations which arise from these resource dependencies as being *emergent* rather than *planned* phenomena. Aldrich (1976) argues further that such resource-dependent relationships are an inherent part of the competitive environment, because resources are in short supply.

More recently, the concept of the *organizational network* has received extensive consideration in the literature (Nohria and Eccles 1992). Network analysis (Knokke and Kuklinski 1982) has long been a descriptive tool used to explore organizational relationships, though its ability to build analytic and predictive theory has sometimes been doubted (Pfeffer 1982).

However, contemporary proponents of a network approach argue that this potential is now being fulfilled. Nohria (1992) has outlined five basic premises of a network approach to organizations:

1 All organizations are in important respects social networks and need to be addressed and analyzed as such . . .
2 An organization's environment is properly seen as a network of other organizations . . .
3 The actions (attitudes and behaviors) of actors in organizations can be best explained in terms of their position in networks of relationships . . .
4 Networks constrain actions, and in turn are shaped by them . . .
5 The comparative analysis of organizations must take into account their network characteristics.

(pp. 4–7)

Elsewhere, Burt (1992) has applied this approach to explain the workings of the competitive market:

Opportunities spring up everywhere; new institutions and projects that need leadership, new funding initiatives looking for proposals, new jobs for which you know of a good candidate . . . The information benefits of a network define who knows about these opportunities, when they know, and who gets to participate in them. Players with a network optimally structured to provide these benefits enjoy higher rates of return to their investments because such players know about and have a hand in, more rewarding opportunities.

(p. 62)

These approaches are clearly important to the consideration of the relationship between organizations and their environment. In particular they offer opportunities to understand the mechanisms through which the contingent adaptation of organizations takes place, whether in relation to the environment or to the prevailing patterns of power and interests.

Again, significant contributions to understanding innovation have come from this network perspective (Tidd 1995; Powell *et al.* 1996; and Robertson *et al.* 1996). These will need to be considered further below.

Systems theory

This approach is one which has developed out of the field of organizational sociology. Scott (1990) has developed an important typology of three types of organizational systems. Two of these are essentially inward-looking. The first of these is *rational systems*, where 'Organizations are collectivities orientated to the pursuit of relatively specific goals and exhibiting highly formalized social structures' (p. 23). The second is *natural systems*, which are 'collectivities whose participants share a common interest in the survival of the system and who engage in collective activities, informally structured, to secure this end' (p. 25). Scott contrasts these with *open systems*, where 'organizations are systems of interdependent activities linking shifting coalitions of participants; the systems are embedded in – dependent on continuing exchanges with and constituted by – the environment in which they operate' (p.25).

Thus organizations as open systems are dependent upon their environment for the achievement of their organizational goals.

> From an open systems point of view, there is a close connection between the conditions of the environment and the characteristics of the system within it: a complex system could not maintain its complexity in a simple environment. Open systems are subject to what is termed the *law of limited variety* – 'a system will exhibit no more variety than the variety to which it has been exposed in its environment'.
>
> (p. 85)

> The organization as an arrangement of roles and relationships is not the same today as it was yesterday or will be tomorrow: to survive is to adapt, and to adapt is to change.
>
> (p. 93)

In many respects there is a great deal of synergy between this and the two previous approaches discussed. Scott himself highlights the extent to which Lawrence and Lorsch (1967) saw contingency theory as a meta-theory within which to integrate the three models of rational, natural and open systems:

> [They] argue that if an open system perspective is taken – so that any given organization is viewed not in isolation but in relation to its specific environ-ment – then the rational and natural systems perspectives may be seen to

identify different organizational types which vary because they have adapted to different types of environments . . . The two extremes depicted by the rational and natural systems models are not viewed as different aspects of the same organizations . . . but rather as different forms of organizations. And, as emphasized by the open systems perspective, the nature of the form is determined by the type of environment to which the organization must relate . . . Thus we arrive at the contingency argument: there is no one best organizational form but several, and their suitability is determined by the extent of the match between the form of the organization and the demands of the environment . . .

The open systems perspective is viewed by Lawrence and Lorsch as the more comprehensive framework within which the rational and natural systems perspectives may be housed, since each of the latter constitutes only a partial view depicting particular organizational adaptations to differing environmental conditions.

(Scott 1990: 97–98)

Without wishing to square the circle unnecessarily, there are also clear links between such an open systems approach and the focus of the network theorists upon the inter-organizational network as the key locus of analysis.

Other key literature exists also. The organizational ecology literature (such as Hannan and Freeman 1989; Hannan and Carroll 1992; Baum 1996), for example, has something to say about this topic, but from the macro-view of whole sectors and industries, rather than the micro-focus here of individual organizations. However, there is one further sub-literature of great significance to this thesis. That is the field of institutional theory and analysis.

Institutional theory

This concerns the impact of institutional forces, the hidden 'rules of the game' that can affect both the commission and the interpretation of action (Lane 1993). Of all the fields of organization theory, this is probably the one which has had most to say directly about voluntary and non-profit organizations. DiMaggio and Powell (1988), in a seminal paper, echoed the foci of the open systems approach, and argued for institutional forces as a key feature of 'organizational isomorphism' for voluntary organizations: as they become part of organizational fields dominated by the more powerful (and resource-rich) governmental organizations, so their work and direction become inevitably constructed by these powerful organizations. Euske and Euske (1991), Singh *et al.* (1991) and Tucker *et al.* (1992) have developed this argument in relation to VNPOs, and contend that they are especially vulnerable to such institutional forces, for two reasons.

First, because VNPOs

have somewhat indeterminate technologies, they are limited in their ability to demonstrate their effectiveness in terms of conventional output, efficiency, or process criteria. Under these conditions social criteria, like the satisfaction and approval of external constituencies, are more likely to be used to judge effectiveness. This suggests that [voluntary organizations] are specifically more vulnerable to conditions and constructs that have their origins in the institutional environment, and that factors such as the acquisition of external institutional support significantly affect their survival chances.

(Singh *et al.* 1991, p. 392)

Second, and as a further development of this argument, Tucker *et al.* (1992) suggest that organizational survival for voluntary organizations is in particular dependent upon their gaining legitimacy in the eyes of the 'higher-order collectivities' – that is, their prime funders. They are therefore 'specifically vulnerable to conditions that have their origins in the institutional environment and...their interconnectedness with the external institutional environment significantly affects their survival chances' (p. 50).

The issue of legitimacy is a particularly important one. Indeed, Singh and Lumsden (1990), writing from the perspective of organizational ecology, highlighted this as one of the key issues in institutional theory:

[The concept of] legitimacy...is, of course, central to institutional theory... because the isomorphism of an organization with the institutional environment enhances legitimacy and so provides greater access to resources, which reduces mortality rates...Acquisition of external legitimacy and institutional support significantly reduces the death in a population of voluntary organizations.

(p. 184)

This issue of legitimacy has been a core focus of many recent research initiatives by institutional theorists (such as Sutton *et al.* 1994 and Dacin 1997).

Institutional theory is thus one of the few branches of organization theory to address the organizational issues of VNPOs in detail, and to provide some useful insights about the way that their actions are both enabled and constrained (for example, Euske and Euske 1991). Admittedly, it has not addressed the issue of their innovative capacity directly. But, because of its potential for explanatory power about the behaviour of such organizations, it will form the basis of our fourth causal hypothesis about the innovative capacity of VNPOs – that it is a function of their institutional framework. Because of this, this section will conclude with an explication of the key dimensions of institutional theory.

The institutional paradigm is a very 'broad church' indeed. Loveridge (1993) has criticized this broadness and the wide diversity of approaches and levels of analysis included within this paradigm, in contrast to 'the simplicity of rational choice theory underlying most economic analysis' (p. 1033). In reply, institutional theorists themselves would argue for this as a strength of their approach. Sen (1977) argued against the idea of the 'rational fool', on the grounds that it assumed not just a rationality belied by human interaction, but also a 'steady-state' personality at odds with contemporary psychological theory. Freidland and Alford (1991) similarly argued that neo-classical economic models were incapable of truly explaining societal interaction, because they concentrated upon prices rather than values. These authors are not lone voices.

Granovetter (1985; see also Baum and Oliver 1992 and Oliver 1996) developed a core concept of institutional analysis, by arguing both against such under-socialized (economic) explanations of human behaviour as above, and against over-socialized ones, which saw individuals as slaves to a societally derived script. Rather, he argued, one had to understand how individual action and agency were embedded in their social context:

> Actors do not behave or decide as atoms outside a social context, nor do they adhere slavishly to a script written for them by the particular intersection of social categories that they happen to occupy. Their attempts at purposive actions are instead embedded in concrete, ongoing systems of social relations.
>
> (p. 487)

Finally, and perhaps most radically, Etzioni (1993) has contributed further by developing a conceptual framework within which to understand value-based choices. He argued that:

> Most choices are made on the basis of emotions ... or values; they are not products of deliberation. And when deliberation does occur, it is often far from extensive, let alone complete. The individual's limited intellectual capability cannot be overcome by training; in fact science itself is far from a fully rational endeavour.
>
> (p. 1068)

This analytical concentration upon individual and societal interaction has meant that, over time, institutional theorists have worked upon a number of different levels of analysis. Selznick (1949), for example, focused upon the process of structural adaptation, whilst Meyer and Rowan (1977) highlighted the processual and ritualistic nature of organizational behaviour. More recently, DiMaggio and Powell (1988; see also Dacin 1997) have illuminated the construction and impact of institutional fields upon organizational behaviour. The diversity of the most recent institutional writing (whether viewed as a strength or a weakness) is also well illustrated by the excellent volume edited by Powell and DiMaggio themselves (1991).

Here there is not space for an extensive discussion of institutional theory as a whole. Rather the intention is to provide a focus for an exploration of the specific institutional focus upon the innovative capacity of organizations.

Powell and DiMaggio (1991) define the new institutionalism (as opposed to the 'old institutionalism' of Selznick) as emphasizing

> the ways in which action is structured and order made possible by shared systems of rules that both constrain the inclination and capacity of actors to

optimize as well as to privilege some groups whose interests are secured by prevailing rewards and sanctions.

(p. 11)

Lane (1993) goes on to define institutions as

> the humanly created constructs in the interaction between individuals. They are the rules and norms resulting in formal and informal rights and obligations which facilitate exchange by allowing people to form stable and fairly reliable expectations about the actions of others.
>
> (p. 166)

Five issues are highlighted by this institutional approach. The first is that of the environmental embeddedness of organizations, highlighted earlier in the work of Granovetter. Again, it is important to emphasize that this does not presuppose a one-way moulding of action by the social environment. Rather, it is an interactive process of moulding and being moulded. Actors and environment are both significant.

The second issue is the importance of organizational processes, not as rational entities derived by information gathering and decision making, but rather as organizational myths and rituals which endow legitimacy onto these organizations within their organizational field. Meyer and Rowan (1977) best presented this argument, maintaining that organizations created myths of organizational structure which both shaped them and provided them with a source of external legitimacy, by providing conformity to the prevailing societal norms and customs. They argue that this is an inherently rational, not irrational, process, for to fail to do so would threaten the resource flow and the ultimate survival of the organization.

The third issue is the consequent role and meaning of 'organizations' in such institutional environments. North (1990) has argued that, if institutions provide the 'rules of the game' that societal actors must play, then organizational forms, structures and processes are strategies for survival within these rules. Greenwood and Hinings (1988) were more specific about the factors involved:

> Organizational structures, should be seen as embodiments of ideas, beliefs, and values which constitute an over-arching and prevailing ... 'interpretative scheme' ... [An organizational] design archetype is thus a set of ideas, beliefs, and values that shape prevailing concepts of what an organization should be delivering, of how it should be doing it, and how it should be judged *combined with* structures and processes that serve to implement and reinforce those ideas.
>
> (p. 295)

The fourth key issue of institutional analysis concerns the types of networks through which organizations interact with their environment(s). Scott and Meyer (1991) were important here in developing the concept of the 'societal sector', which they defined as (1) a collection of organizations operating in the same domain, as identified by the similarity of their services, products or functions, (2) together with those organizations that critically influence the performance of the focal organizations ... The adjective *societal* emphasizes that organizational sectors in modern societies are likely to stretch from local to national or even international sectors. The boundaries of societal sectors are defined in functional, not geographic terms: sectors are comprised of units that are functionally interrelated even though they may be geographically remote.

(pp. 117–118)

The final issue is that of the isomorphic pressures that the institutional forces within such sectors exert upon their population of organizations. This argument was most developed in the seminal paper of DiMaggio and Powell (1988) as noted above. They argued that the increased interdependence of organizations within such societal sectors is leading to the homogenization of these organizations, because of 'coercive', 'mimetic' and 'normative' pressures. Barley and Tolbert (1997) have also examined the processes through which institutionalization occurs for organizations, drawing links with the concept of 'structuration' (Giddens 1984).

In summary, institutional analysis focuses attention upon the relationship between organizations and their societal environment. It emphasizes the interdependency both of this relationship and of organizations within a societal sector. The central question of such analyses is upon the adoptive processes through which organizations survive, and the pressures which produce these processes.

Clearly, as noted above, such an approach has the potential to offer significant insights into the understanding of innovative capacity of VNPOs, as being an activity embedded in their institutional relationships with their key stakeholders. Perhaps suprisingly, it is the avenue which has been least explored in the innovation studies literature, as a factor in the release of innovative potential. However, some work has been done, though on the margins of the organization studies field: Feller (1981), for example, has developed the concept of *conspicuous production* to explain innovative activity in the public sector. In many respects, however, the full contribution of institutional theory to our understanding of innovation is yet to be made.

In order to successfully develop an institutional argument about the nature of this institutional contribution, a useful general approach to institutional analysis has been outlined by Lane (1993). He has maintained that one must specify three factors in order to build an institutional argument: the key institutional forces involved, how they affect decision making, and how to provide an explanation for their force. This will be attempted here below, in exploring the potential of institutional theory to contribute to an understanding of the innovative capacity of VNPOs.

The innovative capacity of VNPOs: the challenge for organization theory

The chapter has so far reviewed both some of the wider aspects of the organization studies literature and the innovation studies sub-literature. In bringing to bear the insights of this literature upon the innovative capacity of VNPOs, this book will have two key tasks. The first will be to test out these insights and to question what they can contribute to the understanding of the innovative capacity of VNPOs. In doing this, four causal hypotheses about this innovative capacity will be evaluated: that it is a function of their organizational structure, of their internal environment, of their external environment, and/or of their institutional framework.

The second task will be to reverse the telescope, and ask what contribution the study of VNPOs can make to the further refinement of organization theory, particularly in relation to the behaviour of organizations in the absence of the profit motive. Some important work has already been carried out along these lines. This includes North (1990) upon the non-financial transaction costs of political decisions, Huxham (1993; Huxham and Vangen 1996) upon the stimuli to collaborate in the absence of competition, and Loveridge (1992) upon the management of technological change within the public sector. Before addressing this task, this chapter must now move on to explore the second major literature that it draws upon, that of social policy.

VNPOs and innovation in the personal social services

This section is intended to cover three issues. First, it will discuss the literature, such as it is, on the innovative capacity of VNPOs in the personal social services (PSS). Second, it will review the wider literature on innovation in the PSS. It will end by bringing these two literatures together and discussing their strengths and limitations for our understanding of the innovative capacity of VNPOs in the PSS. In doing this, it will draw on the organization studies literature detailed previously, in order both to facilitate this process and to consider its potential contribution to our understanding of this capacity.

VNPOs and innovation: the growth of a legend

The innovative capacity of VNPOs, like many of their other ascribed characteristics, such as flexibility and a non-bureaucratic structure, has achieved something of the status of a legend. The basis of this, in Britain at least, is certainly within historical fact, for VNPOs were the pioneers of many social services in the nineteenth century (Prochaska 1988). The expression of this innovative capacity was formalized early in the twentieth century in the work of the Webbs (1911):

> [L]ooking back on the social history of the last hundred and fifty years, we must recognise that nearly all our successful developments in the way of collective provision for any class, have been preceded and rendered practicable by private experiments . . . It is the first, the highest, and in many ways the most useful duty of the voluntary agencies to perform this indispensable service of invention and initiative and purposeful experimenting.

(pp. 240–241)

This expression subsequently became the official perception of VNPOs and was embedded in the foundation of the welfare state by Beveridge (1948):

> The capacity of voluntary action inspired by philanthropy to do new things is beyond question. Voluntary action is needed to do things which the state should not do . . . It is needed to do things which the state is most unlikely to do. It is needed to pioneer ahead of the state and make experiments.
>
> (pp. 301–302)

This view, in various forms, has been repeated often since then. The Ministry of Health in 1959 asserted that innovation was likely to be 'the most valuable contribution of voluntary organizations to social welfare' (Ministry of Health 1959), whilst the Younghusband Report on services for people with a handicap claimed that innovation was an essential contribution of VNPOs to society (Young-husband *et al.* 1970). This view was also reiterated in the report of the Wolfenden Committee (1978) about the future societal role of such organizations.

More recently, this innovation legend has found a place in the reports of both the Barclay Committee, on the future of social work (Barclay 1982), and the Wagner Committee, on residential care (Wagner 1988). Most recently, it was a key assertion of the efficiency scrutiny of VNPOs carried out by the Home Office (1990) and has also received endorsement by leaders of both the Conservative and Labour Parties (NCVO 1991; Labour Party 1990).

In none of these statements, however, is any evidence produced to corroborate this claim. What was, at one time, an empirical statement of fact, has been transformed, through the uncritical and sometimes inappropriate reiteration (and reification?) of the work of the Webbs and of Beveridge, into a normative statement of the importance of voluntary action. As will be seen below, however, despite figuring in a number of studies in Britain and America, the evidence in support of this innovative role is by no means clear-cut.

The arguments in support of the innovative role

Even within the academic literature, wholly normative statements upon the in-novative role of VNPOs are not unknown. Rose (1974) and Peyton (1989) have both asserted that innovation and social change are a principal purpose (and contribution to society) of VNPOs. No evidence has been produced to support these assertions, though, nor analyses made to suggest why this might be so.

Other studies have eschewed such normative statements to develop analyses of why VNPOs might take on an innovative role in society. Broadly, four reasons have been presented to account for it. The first is what can be called the *categorical constraint* argument. This is that, because government is constrained in its ability to experiment by the requirement to provide universal and/or statutory services, then VNPOs (which are not constrained by such an imperative) must perforce take on this role. This view was reflected in the early work of the Webbs:

> The public authority is bound down by Statute and by authoritative Orders of
> the Central Executive Department, as well as limited by the disinclination of
> the local Ratepayers to expend money in unfamiliar ways. 'We must not
> experiment with the Ratepayers' money' is perpetually an effective plea . . . In
> a Voluntary Agency, a person with new ideas, or a group of enthusiasts for new
> methods of treatment . . . can put new devices to the test of experiment.
>
> (pp. 240–241)

It has been put forward more recently also by Douglas (1983) and Knapp *et al.*
(1990b).

A second line of argument has been offered by Poulton (1988), who saw the
innovative nature of VNPOs as deriving from *their links to their local communities* and
their consequent ability to respond quickly to developing local needs. A third
argument was presented by those who saw their innovative capacity as a result of
the organizational features of VNPOs. This view was given a classic statement by
Mellor (1985):

> Because of its independence, and often because of its relative smallness of size,
> the voluntary body is able to experiment, by doing old things in new ways, or
> trying out quite new services, and in doing so take the risks which might be
> more difficult for a large and essentially more bureaucratic state concern.
>
> (p. 11)

The final approach, drawing upon the institutional model outlined in the previous section, argues that their innovative capacity is not so much an inherent part
of VNPOs, but is rather imposed upon them by *the institutional framework* within
which they operate (see Singh *et al.* 1991, quoted above). In this model, innovation
is not a product of the normative superiority of VNPOs, but of their dependence
upon 'higher-order collectivities' (Tucker *et al.* 1992) for their survival. Innovation is
thus a tactic to gain legitimacy with these organizations, rather than, necessarily, an
end in itself.

Yet if all these studies offer legitimate reasons why VNPOs might be innovative,
they do not provide evidence to support their arguments. Increasingly, therefore,
these assertions have come under attack from critics.

The arguments for a modified innovative role

The first group of critics are those who continue to support the innovative capacity
of voluntary organizations, but in a modified or circumscribed form. There are
three strands within this group.

The first strand of studies maintain that the changing nature of the statutory–
voluntary relationship, and in particular the increasing dependency of the latter
upon the former for funding, has inhibited the ability of VNPOs to act independently, and consequently to be innovative (Gronbjerg 1982; Lipsky and Smith 1989;
Ware 1989). The proponents of this argument do see VNPOs as having an

innovative capacity but, in contrast to the institutionalists, have argued that this potential is being smothered by the changing organizational environment.

A second argument has been presented by Kramer (1981) in his major study of VNPOs in the welfare state. This is that, although VNPOs may indeed develop new services or programmes, they are invariably only minor modifications of existing services, rather than genuine innovations:

> Authentic social innovations, true innovations that are original or the first of their kind, are the exception. More common are 'new programs' or changes that extend, expand or improve an existing voluntary service...
> ... almost without exception, the service programs inaugurated are smaller-scale, non-controversial, and incremental, if not marginal, extensions or improvements of conventional social services to a clientele previously under-served.
>
> (p. 178)

In Britain, empirical support was given for this view by two studies of the role of VNPOs in Scotland in developing schemes for unemployed people which also served the community (Connor 1987; Connor and Wilkinson 1988). The intention of these had been to be innovative projects also. However, the researchers concluded that, although the projects themselves were important ones, their innovative content was limited to marginal improvements upon existing services.

A final view was presented by those studies which accepted that there was indeed a genuine innovative capacity within VNPOs, but that this was limited to certain types of such organizations. Young (1976) argued that the innovative capacity of VNPOs was dependent upon their staff adhering to an innovative value system; Johnson (1987) has linked the innovative thrust specifically to small VNPOs; and Saxon-Harrold (1990) has argued that innovation was a function of only those VNPOs which adopted an overtly innovative management strategy – that is, that it was a variable rather than a constant.

The arguments against the innovative role

The second group of critics are those who have argued against the innovative capacity of VNPOs, and have done so in two different ways. The first approach is to take issue with the use of the term *innovation* without any attempt to define it. It thus becomes a 'totem' to be used by VNPOs in establishing their primacy over state provision. This view was well presented by Carter (1974) in a survey of over three hundred social welfare agencies in Canada. He concluded that innovation had become a 'term without meaning', and was often used as a tactic by which to assert the hegemony of voluntary organizations over the statutory ones.

The second approach is to argue that the innovative role of VNPOs is a real but historical one. Kamerman and Kahn (1976) have maintained simply that VNPOs no longer perform the innovative role. Others (Schorr 1970; Moore and Green 1985) have argued that not only are VNPOs no longer innovative themselves, but that this role has been taken over by the statutory agencies. Kingsley (1981) and Osborn (1985) have taken this further by suggesting that, by continuing to expect VNPOs to be innovative (and by funding them upon this basis), the state has actually limited the contribution that they could make to other areas of service and in other ways.

Conclusions

This section has reviewed the arguments for and against the innovative capacity ascribed to VNPOs in public and social policy. It has found many assertions, and normative statements, but little evidence. This makes it hard, if not impossible, to choose between these models – and certainly does not justify a blanket claim of an innovative capacity for VNPOs in the PSS.

A further difficulty is the lack of common ground about what innovation actually means. Only Kramer (1981) of the above studies made any attempt to define it in a rigorous fashion. Given this lack of a guiding definition or an operational model of innovation, it is suprising that less attention has been paid to organization theory to provide just such essential tools.

In fact, only two studies of significance could be identified which drew upon this organization literature. The first is that of Perri 6 (1993), in the field of vocational training. This was a legitimate attempt to develop a workable matrix classification of innovation by VNPOs, by explicitly drawing upon this organization studies literature. However, the attempt was a flawed one, for two reasons. First, the reference to the organization studies material was partial and drew upon the older and more mechanistic literature (such as Burns and Stalker 1961, and Rogers and Shoemaker 1971). In particular it missed out on some of the recent, and more sophisticated and dynamic, discussions of innovation (such as Abernathy *et al.* 1983; Van de Ven *et al.* 1989). This led it to try to create unnecessarily strong dichotomies between, for example, product and process innovation, where the distinction was by no means so clear-cut.

Second, the dimensions of the classificatory matrix which the paper develops are problematic. One dimension involves precisely the above attempt to differentiate product and process innovation, when both might be bound up in the same innovation, depending upon which views of the innovation one took. The other dimension draws similarly arbitrary distinctions between the stages of invention, innovation and diffusion, which hark back to the older one-directional and linear models of the process (such as Rogers and Shoemaker 1971), rather than the more contemporary cyclical models (again such as that of Van de Ven *et al.* 1989; and also Herbig 1991). Finally, and most crucially, attempts to use the matrix have proved difficult, and have foundered upon the operational difficulties that these above points have given rise to (Randon 1993). Important as the attempt has been, therefore, it has been flawed both conceptually and as an empirical tool.

The second study (Nelson 1993b) has a much stronger base in the literature and is more persuasive for that. Indeed, Nelson himself is one of the foremost theorists in developing the economic approaches to innovation. Frustratingly, though the focus of the paper is narrow and contributes little to this present discussion, its context is technological innovation in an American industrial setting, and the focus is upon the capacity of private universities to stimulate research and development, compared to their public counterparts.

Beyond these two studies, the field is barren. The full contribution of organization studies to our understanding of the innovative capacity of voluntary organizations is yet to be made.

Innovation in the PSS in Britain

The emphasis in the management of the PSS in Britain has changed over the last thirty years. In the 1960s, with the rationing of the war and post-war years not long gone, the emphasis was upon establishing a minimum basic entitlement for everyone, within the context of an expanding welfare state. The 1970s and early 1980s, however, saw a period of retrenchment of mainstream services, as the resource base of the welfare state contracted, compared to the expanding population and its changing demography and to developing perceptions of need.

The period since the mid-1980s has seen a third phase develop, with 'innovation' as its watchword. This has encompassed both innovation for reasons of efficiency, because of the growing population of adults and children recognized as having special needs, but with no commensurate increase in the resource base, and innovation for reasons of effectiveness, because of the pressure on services to meet increasingly individual definitions of social need. Certainly, since the early 1980s, the social administration and social policy literature about the PSS has produced a large number of studies of innovation within its stated field. It will be argued here, however, that the majority of these have been descriptive, or evangelical. Moreover, frequently they have been written within the framework of the professional social-work paradigm. There is nothing wrong with this in itself; indeed it is an important contribution to the development of efficient and effective social-work services. However, these studies have failed to address the equally important organizational and managerial issues which innovation raises, and have frequently been written (once again) in isolation from the organization studies literature, which could have contributed much to an understanding of these issues.

Accordingly, this section will commence by reviewing the existing studies of innovation in the PSS and draw some conclusions from these. Whilst it cannot pretend to review every such study, it is argued here that those discussed are typical of the field. In particular, it will pay attention to those studies which have attempted to develop a model of innovation in social welfare. It will move on to argue that, as was the case with the literature upon the innovative capacity of VNPOs, there is a lack both of good empirical evidence about innovation in the PSS and of a framework by which to analyse it. A final section will draw these two literatures together with that of organization studies, and explore what potential contribution the latter can make to the former.

As indicated previously, there have been numerous studies of innovation in the PSS, particularly in the 1980s. This section will concentrate upon reviewing the key papers in four areas: the prevailing social policy paradigm, the management and organization of the PSS, child-care services, and community care services for adults.

Innovation and social policy

One of the key developments of the late 1980s and early 1990s was the promotion of innovation to the status of a social policy goal in its own right. On the one hand, this sprang from the overriding concern of the then Conservative government with introducing a more business-oriented and competitive paradigm into the provision of public services. The intention here, combining a mixture of Schumpeterian and neo-classical models of economics, was both to introduce the winds of 'creative destruction' into these services through competition and to encourage cost efficiencies through the expansion of the market model into the provision of public services. These intentions have been the subject of critical analysis by, among others, Le Grand (1991).

On the other hand, there was also pressure from public-sector and professional advocates to raise innovation to the status of a policy goal. The King's Fund Institute (1987) certainly argued for the centrality of innovation in the community-care reforms, though without ever really defining what this meant. In a more polemical vein, Smale and Tuson (1990) at the National Institute of Social Work argued for innovation to be elevated to the status of a method of social-work intervention. The Department of Health has also explored the model of *outcome funding* as a way of allocating scarce governmental funding for the PSS, with an emphasis upon innovation as an indicator of success (Williams and Webb 1992).

Yet if innovation has become a rather indeterminate policy goal, there have been few studies of the rationale for, or impact of, it. Those that have addressed this issue have primarily been American, rather than British. Feller (1981), for example, has suggested that this concentration upon innovation was an example of 'conspicuous production' – that is, that it was a way of managers proving their effectiveness in an arena where few, if any, objective measures of success existed. A similar argument has also been advanced from the standpoint of the institutional analysis of organizations by Singh *et al.* (1991).

Innovation in the management and organization of the PSS

The decade of the 1980s is well framed by two major attempts at innovation in the organization of the PSS. It began with the *patch-work* movement, which attempted to shift social services departments (SSDs) away from a traditional bureaucratic model of organization, with an emphasis upon professional skills, to a community-based orientation, with an emphasis upon community organization and networking (Hadley and McGrath 1980; Hadley 1981).

Although it has never quite produced the revolution that its proponents hoped for, it has had nonetheless an impact in arguing for a more community-based orientation to the provision of social services. It received official backing of a sort, in the report of the Barclay Committee (Barclay 1982), though perhaps this report is less well remembered than patch-work itself.

The 1980s concluded with another innovation intended to make the PSS more community-based, this time in the specific field of community care services for adults. There is little doubt that it was the work of the Personal Social Services Research Unit (PSSRU) at the University of Kent which spearheaded this attempt. It represented an attempt both to design care services which more clearly addressed the individual needs of those at risk, and to do so in a more cost-efficient way as demographic pressures threatened to produce a financial time-bomb for the government. These intentions ultimately culminated in the passing of the National Health Service and Community Care Act (NHSCC Act) in 1991.

The literature on this organizational innovation is extensive, with a great deal originating from the PSSRU itself (see, for example, Davies and Challis 1986; Davies *et al.* 1990; Knapp *et al.* 1990a). It is undoubtedly more rigorous in its evaluation of this initiative than are the studies of patch-work. Much of this derives from the lucid theoretical framework provided by the *production of welfare* model of the PSS and pioneered again by the PSSRU (Knapp 1984). However, both developments are lacking in any analysis of the nature and process of innovation itself.

This is also true of the other studies of management innovation in social work. Goldberg and Warburton (1979) reviewed the management of workloads in SSDs and developed an alternative *case review* model; Healy (1989) produced a major review of management innovation practices in SSDs; Hardy *et al.* (1989) reviewed innovative management arrangements for joint working in the PSS; and Sommer-lad and Hills (1990) reported on a Department of Health pilot scheme to try and develop innovative ways of stimulating local voluntary action. All these studies provided good descriptions of the work undertaken and provide many valuable lessons for future practice. The best (particularly Goldberg and Warburton, and Hardy *et al.*) also produced some evaluation of the implementation of innovation. However, overall, there is a lack of any attempt to analyse innovation as a process itself, or to borrow from the organization studies literature for an understanding of the nature of the phenomenon. Whilst some important work has developed in the US (notably Berry 1994 on strategic approaches to innovation and public manage-ment), this work has been piece-meal and discrete, rather than inclusive.

Innovation in child-care services

The 1980s and 1990s have also seen a number of major innovations in child-care services in Britain (for an overall summary, see Kahan 1989). Some relate to discrete therapeutic interventions, such as cognitive behavioural work with chil-dren (Ronen 1994) or child-centred casework (Hughes 1995). Two will be con-centrated upon here: the moves to de-institutionalize the juvenile justice system and local authority care for children, and the introduction of the Children Act 1989.

The moves against the institutional, and particularly custodial, treatment of juvenile offenders built up a head of steam in the late 1970s. Studies at that time emphasized the intrusive nature of social welfare services; the ineffectiveness of attempts to treat juvenile offending within a social pathology model, and also of custodial sentences; and the role of social workers in sentencing juveniles to these intrusive and ineffective measures (see, for example, Cornish and Clarke 1975; Morris and McIsaac 1978; Osborne 1984). These issues were brought together in the work of Thorpe *et al.* (1980) and the subsequent development of a *systems management* approach to juvenile justice (Morris and Giller 1987; Schall 1997).

Within the civil child-care system, pressure also developed to move away from a residentially-based service to one which supported children in the community (for a summary of the research in this area see Utting 1991). Research also centred upon specific initiatives in community-based child-care services, such as family centres (Gibbons 1990), and schemes to support children as they left care (Stone 1990).

Finally, the Children Act 1989 has spawned a whole range of innovations, both in the forms of child-care services and in the processes by which they are delivered. Although it is still early in the implementation of this Act, some preliminary studies have been produced, often themselves piloting new forms or processes of service delivery (for example, Parker *et al.* 1991; Connelly 1994). Like the material on organizational innovation, though, all these studies on child-care fail to address the innovation process itself.

Innovation in community care

For an approach to social welfare services conceived in the 1960s the gestation period of community care has been a long one. There are signs, however, that this may finally come to fruition, following the passing of the NHSCC Act. There are still difficulties to be overcome, not least the resourcing of the service. However, the 1980s saw a series of innovations in the delivery of community care services. At the most general level, the work of the PSSRU in piloting and evaluating community care innovations has already been noted. Some more recent studies have also examined specific aspects of this initiative, such as the work of Barritt (1990) on innovations in community care in non-metropolitan areas, and Barnes and Wistow (1992) on the problems of sustaining initiatives beyond the pilot stage.

There have also been studies of innovations within particular client-based services. Thus Marks and Scott (1990) and Ramon and Giannichedda (1991) have both reviewed innovative approaches to the delivery of mental health services, whilst Grant and McGrath (1987) examined a community-based approach in Wales to services for people with learning difficulties (the All Wales Strategy), and Connelly (1990) and Ross (1995) have looked at services for people with disabilities.

Undoubtedly the largest group of studies, though, concern services for elderly people. Ferlie and his colleagues have produced almost a library of such studies on their own (for example, Davies and Ferlie 1982; Ferlie 1983; Davies and Ferlie 1984; Ferlie *et al.* 1984a, 1984b, 1989). The emphasis in all Ferlie's studies is upon the efforts of the statutory authorities to produce more efficient ways of meeting the needs of elderly people within their own communities.

More generally, Marshall and Sommerville (1983) and Isaacs and Evers (1984) have evaluated innovative community-based services for elderly people, in Liverpool and Birmingham respectively, and Fisher (1994) has looked at the specific issue of the role of male carers. Butler (1985), Kraan *et al.* (1991) and Myrtle and Willer (1994) have also provided overviews of a range of developments of community care services for elderly people. Once again, though, the innovation process itself is ignored.

Understanding innovation in the PSS

All of the studies reviewed above provide both valuable insights into the new types of services developed in this field, and an invaluable source literature for those wanting to design new services. The best have also evaluated the impact of these innovations in the field. However, as should now be apparent, there have been few attempts to address the issue of understanding the nature of the process of innovation in social welfare services. An earlier study had found this to be the case in the 1970s (Delbecq 1978), and little seems to have changed since then.

Perhaps this is to do the literature an injustice; no doubt many of its authors would argue, quite rightly, that this was not their purpose. If not their purpose, however, it is still nevertheless a task essential to the greater understanding of the provision of social welfare services. This section will therefore review that limited number of attempts to develop such an understanding.

Four approaches to understanding innovation in social welfare can be identified from the literature. Hasenfeld and Schmid (1989) have pinpointed the life cycle of social services organizations as the key parameter of the development of innovative services. In doing so they were drawing upon a sizeable theme in organization studies (for example, Bessant and Grunt 1985). However, their approach was a discursive one, with little evidence produced to support their position and with no attempt to develop the implications of their framework for the actual management of innovation in the PSS.

A second approach to understanding innovation was taken by those studies which concentrated upon the role of strategic management and planning. Work in the 1970s by Rothman (1974) and Rothman *et al.* (1976) proposed a planning-based model of innovation in the PSS which emphasized the importance of such strategic planning in developing innovative services. The 1976 study took the form of a manual for service managers to use in developing innovation in the organization. This work was later brought together in the *social marketing* model of Rothman (1980; see also Berry 1994), which provided a rationalist model of planning to produce innovation.

This rationalist approach has been explicitly challenged by later studies, influenced by the work of the management 'guru' Tom Peters (for example, Peters and Waterman 1982). In particular, Golden (1990) has argued that her empirical studies have indicated that, far from requiring careful planning, successful innovation in human services is the result of 'groping along'.

Both these approaches draw attention to the managerial and strategic role in innovation in the PSS, and the Golden study was also based upon empirical evidence. Yet both approaches were too narrow in their focus to provide a holistic understanding of innovation. In particular, they ignored the impact of the social environment upon human service organizations in the development of innovative services, and the Peters and Waterman study also, by its commitment to the rationalist model, ignored the often irrational (or at least, arational) and apparently paradoxical nature of change within organizations.

The third approach was one taken by a number of studies and was to relate innovation specifically to the need to counter the bureaucratic nature of public services. Young (1976) has argued that this bureaucratic nature of public services inhibited their ability to innovate, which required entrepreneurial exercise. Gershuny (1983), in polemical vein, has also argued that innovation in public-sector welfare services was required to make them more efficient so that they could meet the growing needs of service recipients rather than provide job security for public-sector employees. However, once again, no evidence was produced to support these implications. Moreover, the argument was structured in the form of exhortations to practising managers, rather than within a conceptual or analytic framework.

The fourth approach, of Ferlie *et al.* (1989), did produce such a framework, embedded within the production-of-welfare model discussed above. It also produced evidence to support its analysis – of the relationship between innovation and the need for efficiency. The major drawback with this analysis is that it was limited to examining a subset of innovations within the PSS: that is, those concerned with the need to innovate in established mature services where environmental factors (in this case, demography and funding) had produced pressure for change. Thus, it ignored a whole range of innovative developments which spring not from the need for efficiency but rather from other imperatives, such as the need to address a newly defined need (a good recent example of this being services for people with AIDS).

These points were well drawn together by Baldock (1991) and Baldock and Evers (1991). These studies pointed to two possible pressures to innovate. The first was for 'bottom-up innovation', where a social or demographic change led to pressure for a new form of service in one locality, and which produced ad-hoc innovation. This was often on a small scale, and was hard to replicate elsewhere or to integrate into the existing statutory services. It was based explicitly, however, upon meeting the expressed needs of the local community and frequently used existing resources in a new way. It thus expanded choice, but often at the cost of efficiency to the welfare system as a whole.

This was contrasted with 'top-down innovation', which sprang directly from the growing resource constraints of the statutory welfare services. This was directed at meeting an already recognized need more efficiently, by targeting existing services more accurately, by sharpening the boundaries between different services so as to utilize the cheapest, or by developing new cost-efficient forms of service.

The approach of Baldock is undoubtedly a helpful one in understanding innovation in the PSS, in that it takes account both of organizational and of environmental factors in the development of innovation. He does not take the approach sufficiently far, though. In presenting a simple dichotomy between needs-led and efficiency-led innovation, he ignores the intermediary cases, where the parameters of innovation could derive from both imperatives. A good example of this is the development of community-based living arrangements for adults with learning difficulties. Here there is both a needs-led pressure, because of the recognition that this is a far more appropriate way in which to provide homes for such adults, and an efficiency-led pressure, derived from the increasing number of adults requiring such community living options to be organized by SSDs, as a result of the closure of hospital-based accommodation.

In conclusion, it is suggested that the above attempts at understanding innovation within the PSS suffered from three faults. First, as has been a common refrain in this review, many of the studies lacked an empirical base and were often framed in a polemical or discursive manner. Second, they frequently adopted a simple linear and/or rationalist model of innovation, which belied its dynamism and complexity. Even the work of Baldock, which is probably the most complex attempt, was based on a simple dichotomy.

Third, several of the studies were so narrow in their approach as to ignore the breadth of innovative activity in the PSS. Finally, the majority of studies were constructed in almost total isolation from the organization studies literature. Ferlie *et al.* (1989) did discuss the implications of the work of Burns and Stalker (1961), whilst Rothman also referred to the work of Rogers and Shoemaker (1971). However, as with the work of Perri 6 previously discussed, this is to but touch upon the range of material available and not necessarily upon the most sophisticated.

If a proper understanding of innovation both in the PSS and by VNPOs is to be developed it is suggested here that it is necessary to take greater cognizance of the organization studies literature. This is essential in order both to construct a meaningful conceptual framework for the understanding of innovation and to develop effective tools for its analysis, in constructing a framework. This task is approached in the final section of this chapter.

Combining the literatures – the present state of knowledge and research questions for this study

So far, this review has kept the organization studies literature on innovation and the VNPO/PSS literature separate. It is now time to integrate them. In doing so, two arguments will be made. The first is that the study of VNPO and of the PSS will benefit from far greater attention being paid to conceptual developments found in the organization studies literature. Second, this latter literature will also benefit from insights developed from the study of VNPOs; specifically it will allow the discussion of innovation in an environment where competition is not the norm.

The organization studies perspective on VNPOs and the PSS

Contributions from the organization studies literature

Three general issues from the organization studies literature about innovation are particularly relevant to understanding innovation both within the PSS and by VNPOs. First, with regard to the nature of innovation, it is important to be clear about the significance of *discontinuity* as a core element of innovation. One issue to be teased out in the research discussed below is the differing roles and impacts of service *developments* (that is, the gradual improvement of existing services to the existing users of an organization) compared to actual *innovation*. This distinction is never really drawn out in the VNPO and the social administration and social policy literatures. However, its import is clear from the organization studies literature, in terms of its impact both upon its host organizations and upon their relationship with their end users.

Second, with regard to the nature of the innovators, it is important that the insights of the contingency approach be appreciated. This interrelationship between the host organization of an innovation and its environment is one which often seems to be lacking in the existing social policy literatures. It is true that some studies discussed above do talk about the role of end-users in influencing innovation, as in the *bottom-up* innovation of Baldock and Evers (1991). However, this is but one element of the overall environment. The organization studies literature has provided some useful guidance over the full range of factors to be considered in this context.

Finally, the organization studies literature has provided a crucial conceptual framework for considering the causal factors involved in the innovative capacity of VNPOs. Where these issues have been considered previously in the VNPO literature, they have been raised on a purely empirical, or even normative, basis. The organization studies literature gives a conceptual clarity to these issues which has been missing from the discussion till now. Drawing upon the insights of this organization studies literature, it is possible to develop four hypotheses about the innovative capacity of VNPOs. The first three stem directly from the innovation studies sub-literature. These are that this potential is a function of the organizational characteristics of VNPOs, of their internal culture, and of their external environment and their relationship to it. To these can be added a fourth hypothesis developed in the one area of organization studies to have considered VNPOs in any depth. This is the field of institutional analysis. The fourth hypothesis is therefore that the innovative capacity of VNPOs is a function of their institutional framework, and their relationship to it. Interestingly, whilst the first three hypotheses have an empirical basis, but little testing out in relation to VNPOs, this last hypothesis has a direct relevance to VNPOs, but no empirical basis. The theoretical bases of these four hypotheses are detailed in Table 3.1.

In order to enable the evaluation of these hypotheses to take place, the organization studies literature has a final contribution to make to the study of the innovative

Table 3.1 Theoretical bases of the four hypotheses

	Basis	
Hypotheses	Voluntary sector literature	Organizational studies literature
Organizational	Mellor 1985	Thompson 1965
Cultural	Johnson 1987	Hage 1980
Environmental	Poulton 1988	Rickards 1985
Institutional	Singh et al. 1991	Not explored in detail

capacity of VNPOs. This is to provide a conceptual typology of innovation in social policy initiatives.

Developing a classification of change and innovation in social policy

As discussed above, the issue of discontinuity is a core element of any definition of innovation. This is important in differentiating gradual organizational development, which may nonetheless produce major changes in service delivery over a period of time, from the actual process of innovation. This conceptual clarity will be important for this study, in differentiating *genuine* innovation from *ascribed* innovation. As Carter (1974) made clear, the term 'innovation' is often used in a pejorative and normative sense by the staff and supporters of voluntary activity and organizations, whilst the social administration/policy literature has frequently used a lax definition of it. It is argued here that, by reference to the organization studies literature, one can develop more rigour in the understanding and codification of the innovative capacity of VNPOs in the field of the PSS, and indeed of innovation within the wider field of social policy implementation, which delineates it both from such developmental and traditional organizational activity.

To summarize the existing VNPO and social administration literature briefly, the work of Perri 6 (1993) and Nelson (1993b) have been the only notable attempts to use the organization studies literature to understand the innovative capacity of VNPOs. Their strengths and limitations have been discussed above.

Within the literature upon innovation in the PSS there have been, similarly, limited attempts to conceptualize organizational change and innovation. Even those which were conceptually developed, such as that of Baldock and Evers (1991), were more descriptive than analytic.

It is argued here that a useful approach to classifying and understanding organizational change and innovation in social policy can be evolved by modifying the approach of Abernathy et al. (1983), discussed above. There is a developing managerial literature which is concerned both with understanding public services in terms of the markets that they serve (Crompton and Lamb 1988) and with viewing their management within a general management context rather than a service or professional one, such as social work (Nutley and Osborne 1994). This literature suggested that it could be possible to develop a classification of change and innovation within the social policy and social services terrain, by adapting the model of Abernathy *et al.* In terms of such social services, therefore, the *method of production* is not (usually) a technological process which is transformed by the application of new scientific knowledge. Rather it is frequently an interpersonal (or sometimes inter-organizational) process, but one which can nevertheless be changed by the introduction of new knowledge – whether it be about, for example, the needs of service users, or the efficiency and effectiveness of methods of care.

Similarly the actual users, or clients, of social services are very much the *market* for these services, as much of the new literature upon such services is suggesting – such as the growing literature on the application of marketing techniques to service management (Walsh 1989), as well as the more theoretical literature covering such developments as *quasi-markets* and *the mixed economy of care* (Le Grand 1991; Wistow *et al.* 1996).

The typology presented here was developed upon the basis of these assumptions and by the modification of the original model of Abernathy *et al.* to take account of them. This modified typology is displayed in Figure 3.2. This typology situates innovation as part of organizational change in general, allows different modes of innovation to be clarified, and distinguishes it from incremental organizational development. The *x*-axis now becomes concerned with the impact of an organizational change upon the actual services that an agency produces (that is, whether it involves the existing services of an agency, or the creation of new ones). The *y*-axis is concerned with the relationship of an organizational change to the clients of a social services agency (that is, whether it meets the needs of an existing client group of the organization, or a new one). Such a modification thus produces four types of

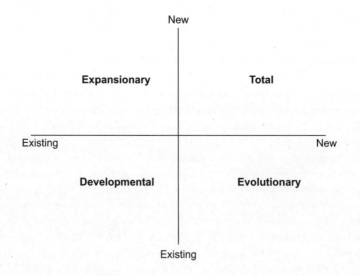

x-axis – services of the agency
y-axis – needs of the client (end-user) group

Figure 3.2 A typology of organizational change in the human services

organizational change – total, expansionary, evolutionary and developmental. These four archetypes allow organizational changes to be understood, therefore, both in terms of their impact upon the actual services that an agency offers and upon the clients that it is serving, as well as the interrelationship between these dimensions. Its ability to capture this interrelatedness goes to the heart of service production, as outlined above by Normann (1991) – that services are produced and consumed contemporaneously and that their consumers are as active in their production as are their host agencies.

Four examples taken from the PSS will make this typology more rooted in the real world. An example of a *total change* taken from the research reported below was a hospital 'Friends Association'. This had traditionally offered practical support (such as small cash payments or transport to or from hospital) to the in-patients of that hospital. However, as the hospital itself was run down, this association changed both its client group, to support chronically ill people living in the community, and its actual services, to begin to offer counselling and domiciliary care services. This is the classic 'radical innovation', thus, with the organization addressing a new client group and providing new services.

An example of *expansionary change* could be the recent moves within the probation service to utilize the non-custodial alternatives developed for work with juvenile offenders (under 16 years old) for work with young offenders (aged 16–21). This is using methods of service already developed by the agency but to meet the needs of a new group of clients. Another example could be the transfer of the 'systems management' approach, developed by many social services departments (SSDs) in their work with juvenile offenders, to work within the civil child-care system.

An *evolutionary change* might be the new forms of service developed over the past five years to provide care in the community for adults with special needs. These meet the needs of an already defined client group, such as elderly people, but with new forms of social services, such as care management.

Finally, a *developmental change* could be the refinement of the role of home-care assistants in supporting elderly people at home, so that their work is targeted more clearly upon those tasks required to ensure that the person can continue to live in the community. This is addressing a client group already defined and utilizing existing methods of service; however, it is doing so in a modified way, in order to meet its objectives more efficiently.

This approach is a potentially useful one for the study of social policy, for two reasons. First, and most importantly, it allows *innovation* to be clearly delineated from incremental *organizational development*. Using the definition of innovation derived above, it is clear that the total, expansionary and evolutionary types of change which this typology clarifies all involve discontinuity for the organization, in terms of its services and/or its client group. Developmental change, however, does not. It modifies existing services to an existing client group. The typology is hence a potentially important tool for differentiating organizational innovation and development in practice.

This is not an academic point but rather an essential distinction to make. Organizational development poses different managerial challenges for an organization, compared to the challenges that the discontinuity of innovation involves. To take one example, persuading and enabling staff to develop their existing skills base is a task of a wholly different order from enabling them to abandon these skills for new ones, as would be the case with total and evolutionary change. Further, managerial issues for the three types of innovation are different also. Whilst the focus for evolutionary change might be upon the aforementioned acquisition of new skills by organizational staff, for expansionary change the balance would be more toward convincing organizational clients that a service developed elsewhere is relevant to their needs. This classification exposes these differences both for analysis by the researcher and for resolution by service managers.

Second, the typology allows the exploration of the relationship between the staff of an agency (the *producers*) and the end-users of a service (its *market*) in the process of innovation. This is important both because of the role of both these groups in defining innovation and because of the contribution of both groups to the process of service production; as discussed above, the end-users of a service are not simply its passive recipients but are active in its production process (*prosumers*, as Normann 1991 calls them). Again, this typology helps clarify this interrelationship and the changes being experienced by each partner to it.

A helpful approach to evaluating the utility of such a typology as this one is provided by Deutsch (1966). This approach has been used recently by, amongst others, Salamon and Anheier (1994). Deutsch argued that, to be useful, a new typology needs to combine an appropriate mix of four factors. These are its *relevance* to the topic under consideration and the empirical evidence which relates to it; its *economism* compared to alternative typologies; its *predictive powers*, in terms of its *rigour* (its potential to offer insights to each step of its analysis), its *combinatorial richness* (the range of alternative scenarios that can be generated from it) and its *organizing power* (its ability to be generalized across different situations and data); and its *originality*, in that it contributes something new to the body of knowledge within which it is located.

Whilst Deutsch emphasized that no typology could meet all these criteria, it is argued here that this present one scores strongly against these criteria. Its relevance can be seen to the extent that it allows an essential distinction between innovation and organizational development to be made, as well as allowing for different types of innovation to be differentiated. This is important both for research about innovations in the PSS, and social policy in general, and for their better management.

Economism is less of an issue here, given the lack of any real alternative typologies at present. However, its predictive power is considerable. In the research reported here, the typology has shown itself able to embrace a range of relationships between the mode of service production and the clients of an organization (combinatorial richness), and to have the ability to incorporate different organizations and localities (organizing power). Further work is required now to test it across different organizational industries and fields. Finally, the originality of the model is strong. It is the first such typology of the innovation in social policy implementation which addresses organizational and managerial issues, and which draws upon the considerable organization studies literature in doing so.

This typology is not the 'last word' in attempting to understand the nature of innovation in social services. It does not specify the origin of any organizational change (that is, to use the classification of Baldock, whether it is a 'bottom-up' or a 'top-down' innovation). Nor does it acknowledge fully the effect of the social environment upon innovation, by concentrating on the market of its end-users alone. However, these are tasks of analysis *within* this classification and it is argued here that they are facilitated by this more relational approach.

This typology is, nevertheless, one which had great utility for the study reported here. Hopefully, it is also a contribution both to furthering our understanding of the complexity of innovation in social policy in general, and in the PSS in particular, opening this issue up for further study and evaluation.

Organizational theory from the perspective of the voluntary organization literature

If organization theory can make an important conceptual contribution to the study of VNPOs and innovation in the PSS, the reverse is also true. As was discussed above, much of organization theory makes assumptions about the nature of innovation. It often equates it, for example, solely with technological change (in the index to Porter 1985, for example, under the entry '*innovation*' it says '*see technological change*'). More crucially, it makes invariably a central assumption about the relationship of innovation to the market economy, viewing it as the key link between a competitive environment and the profitability of individual firms. Much as this assumption highlights key issues for some for-profit organizations it also obscures potential discussion about the equally important non-competitive spurs to and consequences of innovation.

This area has recently been receiving more attention from writers interested in developing models of how organizations operate in the absence of competition. Huxham (1993; Huxham and Vangen 1996), for example, has developed the concepts of 'collaborative capability' and 'collaborative advantage' in this context. She has argued that in much of the discussion of for-profit organizations collabora-tion is assumed to develop where it will lead to a better competitive advantage for an organization, and increased profitability. By contrast in the governmental and non-profit sectors this spur to collaboration is absent. It is therefore necessary to produce a different analysis of collaboration which not only illuminates the world of non-profit organizations but also contributes to organizational theory as a whole.

There is clearly an analogous issue in relation to organization theory about innovation, and its assumption of the centrality of a competitive environment. Given the present state of organization theory about innovation, as detailed above, one of the issues to be addressed in relation to voluntary and governmental organizations is why they should choose to innovate in the absence of competition. This is an area where the study of VNPOs, and this study in particular, has a relevant contribution to make to the organization studies literature.

Conclusions

This chapter has taken an extended tour of three literatures about innovation – those of organization studies, of VNPOs, and of social administration and social policy. It has then thrown these literatures into relief by contrasting and combining them. Although a rather lengthy process, this has been essential in developing the conceptual territory that the research discussed below will inhabit.

Four points arise from this exercise. First, the case for the innovative capacity of VNPOs is not proven. There is a deal of normative assertions and/or pejorative argument about it, but little empirical work.

Second, much of the discussion about innovation in the PSS suffers from a lack of conceptual clarity about the nature of innovation, and from a lack of attention to management issues. A good deal of it is descriptive and/or concerned with professional issues of therapeutic intervention.

Third, attention to the organization studies literature can offer some clarity to the above discussions by providing both a conceptual framework for classifying innovation and a series of propositions about its causality. This task has been begun in this chapter.

Finally, the study of innovation of VNPOs in the PSS has also a contribution to offer to organization theory. This concerns the spur(s) to innovation in the absence of a competitive environment.

Out of these insights arise four research questions which will be the focus of attention for the remainder of this book. The first is the empirical and descriptive question of mapping the nature and extent of *innovations* produced by VNPOs in the field of the PSS. The second is the question of the causality of the innovative capacity of VNPOs (*the innovators*) identified above. The third question is the extent to which the answers to the above questions can be combined, to produce an initial model of the innovative capacity of VNPOs in the PSS. The final question to ask is whether this model can offer also a contribution to the evolution of organization theory, by developing an explanation of innovation in a non-competitive environment.

4 Research methodology

This research study which forms the core of this book could be placed within both the quantitative and qualitative research meta-frameworks (Bryman 1988a). Rather than counter-pose these frameworks unnecessarily, the approach adopted here will be to draw upon the strengths of both. The first part of the research will be within the quantitative framework. Working inductively, it will seek to structure and map the innovative activity of VNPOs. The second part will be within the qualitative framework. This part will work deductively, to explore four possible hypotheses about the processes through which the innovative capacity of VNPOs is realized. The findings from both these sections will then be integrated to form the initial model of the innovative capacity of VNPOs. This inductive–deductive cyclical structure has been recommended for research about innovation by, amongst others, Wolfe (1994).

This chapter will outline the methodological approaches employed in this study. It will commence by providing an operational classification of VNPOs for it, and will then describe its structure and process. It will conclude by describing the research tools employed in the study and by demonstrating their reliability and validity. The larger theoretical arguments behind the choice of methodology and its design are not entered into here. This wider discussion can be found in Osborne (1997).

Developing the research methodology used in this study

Classifying VNPOs in this study

There are numerous approaches to classifying VNPOs. As has been well noted elsewhere (Hatch 1980), none of these is necessarily right or wrong. They are, rather, more or less useful in the context in which they are being applied.

The approach taken here is to use a simple two-dimensional matrix. The one dimension of this concerns the orientation of the organization – that is, whether it is concerned with the needs of its members alone (self-oriented), or with the needs of other people who are not members of the organization (other-oriented). This latter type of organisation is further distinguished between service-delivery organizations, concerned with direct services to individual clients, and intermediary organizations, providing services to other organizations.

Table 4.1 A classification of VNPOs

Client group	Orientation		
	Self-oriented *(self-help groups)*	*Other-oriented* *(service delivery)*	*Intermediary* *(infrastructure support)*
Children and families	Parents group	Family centre	Play Association
Adults	Social club for deaf people	Residential home	
General	Support groups for children and adults with a specific condition (such as muscular dystrophy)	Community transport scheme	Council for Voluntary Service

The second dimension concerns the client focus of the organization. This might be upon children and their families, upon adult community care, or upon generic social needs which could affect children or adults.

This two-dimensional approach is one which has been used elsewhere with success, notably in the Wolfenden Committee (1978) and in Handy (1988). It is illustrated in Table 4.1 with explicatory examples of each type of organization within the matrix.

This approach has three advantages. First, it allows one to explore if either of these dimensions is significant in the innovative capacity of VNPOs. Second, because this approach has been used elsewhere it has a level of construct validity within the field and can also be related to this other work. Finally, it is simple. A more complex classification could almost certainly have been used (such as one based upon the international classification of non-profit organizations developed for the Johns Hopkins international comparative research project). However, this could pose the danger of the classification method coming to dominate the study, rather than being a tool. In this study, therefore, a version of Occam's Razor was applied to the classification of VNPOs – *as simple as it can be, as complex as it has to be.*

The structure and process of the research study

The structure of the research

This research consists of three parts. The first is concerned with exploring and mapping the extent and nature of the innovative activity of VNPOs. It is concerned with the *innovations* produced by voluntary organizations. This will produce, for the first time, an empirical description of such activity.

The second part involves testing the four causal hypotheses which could offer explanations of the capacity of VNPOs to produce the innovations detailed in the first part. It is concerned with voluntary organizations as *innovators*. This part will be analytic rather than purely descriptive.

The final part of the study is concerned with integrating the findings from the previous parts of this study, to build an initial model of the innovative capacity of VNPOs. It is thus primarily concerned with theory building. It also, though, relates the research reported here back to the literature explored earlier, and considers its contribution to this prior literature. This structure not only allowed different aspects of the innovative capacity of VNPOs to be explored, it also allowed for a level of cross-validation between the different stages involved. It should be emphasized that this representation of the research structure is very much an ideal one, to facilitate its understanding. The reality of the research process is often both less linear and less rational (Cameron and Quinn 1988; Pettigrew 1990). This is not to say that such a representation of the structure is a fiction. In fact it represents where the bulk of work in each stage was loaded and also the place of each stage in the research process. It may, perhaps, best be considered a two-dimensional representation of what was in actuality a three-dimensional process.

Finally, such a representation of the structure underplays some of the opportunistic and serendipitous aspects of research (Buchanan *et al.* 1988). A good example of this latter point is the extent to which the three (geographically chosen) localities for the case studies turned out to be utilizing three differing mechanisms for the co-ordination of the provision of the PSS (as discussed below). This was not planned for, but did improve immeasurably the analysis of the study.

The research process

This is illustrated in Figure 4.1. The stages of this process will be discussed briefly below.

THE FEASIBILITY STUDY

The first stage of any study is to define a research area and to map out a distinctive topic for analysis. This is essentially an iterative process of reviewing the key literature and of discussing possibilities with significant peers and key informants in the sector. The topic of the innovative role of VNPOs was suggested by the profile being given to it in social policy developments in the late 1980s and early 1990s. The policy intent was to replace the unitary financing and provision of the PSS by local government with a purchaser–provider split. Local government was to become the planner and purchaser of services, whilst the independent sector (including VNPOs) was to become the provider (Griffiths 1988; Department of Health 1989). The origins of this policy development were complex and beyond the remit of this study. A good summary of them is to be found in Wistow *et al.* (1994, 1996).

A review of the literature and exploratory discussions revealed a remarkable lack of any substantive work upon this topic. Further discussions and reading suggested several key themes which could be explored in this proposed study:

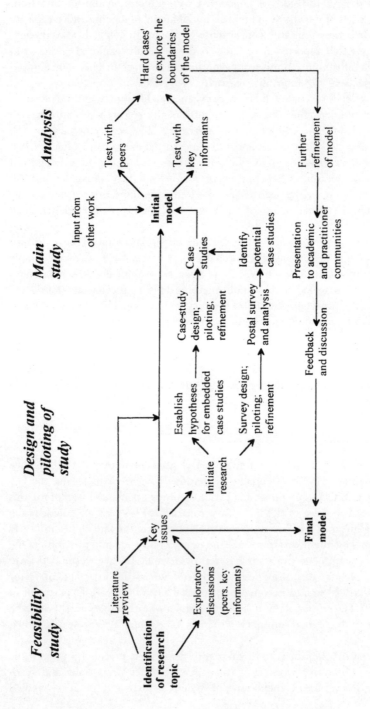

Figure 4.1 The research process

- the ways in which innovation was perceived by the key actors;
- the extent of actual innovation by VNPOs in the PSS;
- the parameters governing the innovative capacity of VNPOs, and the under-lying forces and relationships which shaped this capacity;
- the process of innovation within VNPOs; and
- the extent to which it was possible to use organization theory to develop a model of the innovative capacity of VNPOs.

On the basis of these issues a research proposal was developed to address them.

THE SURVEY AND CROSS-SECTIONAL CASE STUDIES

The survey stage of this study was intended to achieve three goals:

- to establish what the key actors within VNPOs understood by *innovation;*
- to map the extent of innovation, both in terms of the perceptions of the key actors involved and in terms of the theoretically derived understanding of innovation; and
- to test out some basic organizational parameters which might structure the innovative capacity of VNPOs.

The cross-sectional case studies were designed to test out the four hypotheses of the innovative capacity of VNPOs derived from the literature (above).

THE SURVEY

This was intended to provide the initial overview of the innovative activities of VNPOs. Moser and Kalton (1971) and de Vaus (1986) provide good studies of the survey process. The first stage is to decide upon the type of sample to be employed. It was decided to use cluster sampling both because of its exploratory nature, which excluded pre-stratification of the sample, and because of the lack of a robust sampling frame for the diverse voluntary sector (Osborne and Hems 1995).

Moser and Kalton (1971) describe cluster sampling as 'a multi-stage sampling [technique] in which maps, rather than lists or registers serve as the sampling frame' (p. 118). In this case this involved a census of all VNPOs involved in the field of the PSS in a locality to be taken, without any prior decisions about the key variables involved. This had important advantages for this study. First, it allowed one to include the full diversity of VNPOs working in the PSS, from small self-help groups to the large national charities, without prejudging the relevance of any of these. Second, it allowed different spatial environments to be explored.

In this case it was decided to focus upon a rural, an urban, and a suburban environment. This allowed the study to explore whether the dimensions of these different spatial environments were influential or not. It also allowed a more in-depth look at the institutional and network factors at play in each locality and provided the basis for the later cross-sectional case studies. This cluster sampling approach has been used before in research about voluntary organizations, to good effect, and notably in the research which formed the basis of the Wolfenden Report (Wolfenden Committee 1978; Hatch 1980).

The questionnaire to be used in the survey was designed to produce data about the way in which VNPOs perceived innovation, as well as about its extent. Some basic organizational parameters were also obtained to assist in mapping this data in relation to the spread of innovative activity. Because of this it did not give any predetermined definition of innovation. Rather, it asked the respondents to give examples of innovation, where appropriate, by their own organization. This was felt to be more effective than asking them to define innovation, which would have been more of a test of their command of the English language; it also provided good case examples of innovation for the study. These self-perceptions of innovation were subsequently tested out against the typology of innovation in social policy derived above, in order to validate (or otherwise) their perceptions.

The questionnaire was piloted on a small sample of local voluntary organiza-tions, not in one of the sample areas, and refined following this stage. It was then posted to each locality in series, together with a covering letter and a Freepost return envelope.

The information from the survey was subsequently analysed in two ways. First, the typology of innovation was used to map the extent and distribution, and detail the type, of innovative activity engaged in by VNPOs. Second, the basic organiza-tional characteristics were matched against this classification to describe the VNPOs involved in this activity. These characteristics were also analysed in two ways. First, basic distributional statistics were used to explore possible patterns and their significance estimated using chi-squared tests. Second, these basic statistics were used to drive more complex and relational analyses, using the technique of discriminant analysis. These analyses, and their findings, are discussed in greater detail below. In isolation, such a survey would be of limited use. De Vaus (1986) notes that surveys are poor at establishing causation, can often take behaviour out of its context, can supply a spurious rationality to limited data, and simply are unable to consider some aspects of a topic (such as processual ones). In recognition of these limitations this study combined the survey with a series of cross-sectional case studies.

THE CASE STUDIES

Case studies can either be single, unitary, entities, or a cross-section of entities joined by a common focus (Yin 1979). In this study the latter approach was adopted. Three cross-sectional case studies were developed. These were structured across the different localities involved and focused on three different groupings of VNPOs. The first consisted of VNPOs with a demonstrable in-novative capacity; the second consisted of organizations which had developed their services but without the element of discontinuity essential to genuine in-novation – that is, those concerned with *developmental* activity; and the final case consisted of organizations which had not felt the need to develop or innovate in their service delivery, and so were continuing to provide the traditional services which they had previously provided. These case-study groupings were developed utilizing the typology of innovation designed earlier and used to analyse the survey data. The case-study procedures and protocols are discussed further below, in Chapter 6.

The case studies were developed in a series, moving from one research site to the next in an iterative manner. This approach allowed emerging propositions to be tested out, as the study moved from one locality to the next one. For example, it became clear early in the first area that the issue of local networks was a significant environmental factor. This was examined in further detail in the second site, and a tentative hypothesis about this factor was formed. This hypothesis was then tested further in the final research site.

A central part of case-study methodology is the collection and analysis of data. Yin (1979) specifies six sources of this:

- documentation,
- archival material,
- interviews,
- direct observation,
- participant observation, and
- physical artefacts.

The first four of these were utilized here.

Analysing such data can be problematic because of the sheer quantity of it as much as anything. Yin urges that the analysis be linked to the theoretical under-pinning and the research propositions of any study, if it is not to degenerate into plain description and/or incoherent analysis.

Even then, however, it is easy to see one becoming overwhelmed by the sheer weight of data. Because of this, methods of data reduction are an essential part of any case-study research. Miles and Huberman (1984) in their excellent source-book of analytic methods for case studies argue that these methods are not simple mechanical processes prior to analysis:

> Data reduction is not something separate from analysis. It is part of analysis. The researcher's choice of which data chunk to code, which to pull out, which patterns summarize a number of chunks, what the evolving story is, *are all analytic choices*. Data reduction is a form of analysis that sharpens, sorts, focuses, discards and organizes data in such a way that 'final' conclusions can be drawn and verified. [emphasis in original]
>
> (p. 21)

From this perspective, Miles and Huberman offer a series of data reduction tech-niques, based upon matrices and grids, to facilitate the analysis of case-study data. These types of approaches have been employed with effect in this study.

As noted previously, these three case studies were structured to test four hypotheses about the innovative capacity of VNPOs, developed from the literature review above. These four hypotheses and their theoretical bases were specified in Table 3.1 above. They are:

- that the innovative potential of VNPOs is a function of the organizational characteristics of these organizations, such as their structure, formalization and autonomy (*the organizational hypothesis*);
- that the innovative potential of VNPOs is a function of the internal culture of these organizations, such as their size, organizational leadership and channels of communication (*the cultural hypothesis*);
- that the innovative potential of VNPOs is a function of their relationship to their external environment (*the environmental hypothesis*); and
- that the innovative potential of VNPOs is the result of their institutional framework (*the institutional hypothesis*).

Table 4.2 outlines the methodological tools used to explore each of these hypotheses. These tools are described in more detail in the relevant chapters below.

Table 4.2 Methodological tasks and data sources employed in the cross-sectional case-studies

Methodological tools	Data sources
Organizational hypothesis	
Aston Measures, discriminant analysis and analysis of variance	Organizational leaders
Semi-structured interviews	Organizational leaders and other staff
Documentary analysis	Documents (where available) [plus evidence from the survey]
Cultural hypothesis	
Kirton Adaptation Innovation Inventory	Organizational leaders
Aston Measures	Organizational leaders
Structured interviews	Organizational leaders
Semi-structured interviews	Organizational leaders and other staff/ trustees/service users, where available [plus evidence from the survey]
Environmental hypothesis	
Semi-structured interviews	Organizational leaders/staff/trustees/service users/other key informants
Network analysis	Direct observation/information from other semi-structured interviews
Institutional hypothesis	
Semi-structured interviews	Organizational leaders/staff/trustees/service users/other key informants
Documentary analysis	Service contracts/organizational documents, where available

Reliability and validity in this study

Reliability

In the survey component of this study reliability has been approached in two ways. The first was to assess the reliability of the operationalisation of the key concepts to the study and the use of them made by the author. The issue here was the extent to which repeated classifications of responses to the survey would yield consistent findings.

A version of the test–retest procedure was used to do this. A random sample of twenty-seven returned questionnaires (15 per cent of the total returns) was reclassified by the author, three months after the original classification. This was undertaken both for the classification of the organizations (in terms of their orientations and their client groups) and for the classification of the innovation described (in terms of the classification on the innovation described in Chapter 1 above).

With regard to the classification of organizations by their client group, the reclassification was entirely consistent with the original one (i.e. a reliability of 1.00). With regard to the classification of the organizations by orientation, the reclassification agreed with the original one in 88.9 per cent of the sample (a reliability of 0.89). Finally, with regard to the presence of innovation, the reclassification again agreed with the original one in 88.9 per cent of the sample (a reliability of 0.89). This gives an overall index of the reliability of the classification of the author of 92.6 per cent (0.93).

The second method used to test the reliability of the survey related to the reliability of the statistical tests performed upon it. This was undertaken using the *power analysis* tests developed by Cohen (1977). The basis of this work is the relationship between the significance of a test, the size of the sample, and the sample's relationship to the total population:

> [T]he reliability (or precision) of a sample value is the closeness with which it can be expected to approximate to relevant population value. It is necessarily an estimated value in practice, since the population value is generally unknown ... [Reliability] may or may not be directly dependent upon the unit of measurement, the population values and the shape of the population distribution. However, it is *always* dependent upon the size of the sample.
>
> (p. 6)

From this basis, Cohen develops a series of tests to establish the reliability of different statistical procedures carried out upon a population. In particular he specifies the minimum sample sizes required for these procedures to be reliable. Using these tests requires making a number of statistical assumptions and their validity is limited by these. Nonetheless, they were a useful adjunct to analysis. The detailed statistical rationale for identifying power analysis is found in Cohen (1977).

On the basis of this rationale, and with the assumption that one is seeking a 'medium'-sized effect in the statistical tests (from the fact that this is only one part of the overall study) and at a level of statistical significance of 0.05 (the usual statistical convention), then the minimum sample size is required to be at least 87. In fact in this study it is 195, which would suggest that the statistical analyses are reliable, within reasonable parameters.

Moving on to the case-study elements of the research design, a case-study protocol was utilized to enhance reliability. This included:

- an overview summary of the project which was distributed to all respondents, together with an introductory letter, to ensure a basic level of understanding; and
- the use of pro-formas for the semi-structured interviews and full interview schedules for the structured interviews, to ensure consistency in the structuring of interviews and data collection.

This format was felt to offer sufficient consistency between interviews and over the case studies as a whole whilst not providing a strait-jacket to them.

Validity

The search for validity is the most testing of all research goals (Carmines and Zeller 1979; Kirk and Miller 1986). Because of this, five procedures were included to this end. First, the classifications used in the survey stage of this research were themselves operationalized versions of theoretically validated concepts, which offers a level of construct validity to them. Second, in order to test the validity of my making classificatory judgements in the survey, these judgements were tested against those of another academic researcher. This was done by providing a random sample of twenty questionnaires for reclassification by this other researcher. This procedure is recommended by, amongst others, de Vaus (1986). The findings of the validation procedure were as follows.

With regard to the classification of organizations by their client group, the reclassification agreed with my own in 85 per cent of the cases (an index of 0.85). With regard to the classification of organizations by their orientation, the reclassification agreed with my own in 95 per cent of the cases (an index of 0.95). Finally, with regard to the presence of innovation, the reclassification agreed with my own in 80 per cent of the cases (an index of 0.80).

Third, with regard to the case studies, *methodological triangulation* (Denzin 1970) was employed. This approach is particularly recommended by Kirk and Miller (1986):

> [T]he most fertile search for validity comes from a combined series of differ-
> ence [*sic*] measures each with its idiosyncratic weaknesses, each pointed to a
> single hypothesis. When a hypothesis can survive the confrontation of a series
> of complementary methods of testing, it contains a degree of validity unobtain-
> able by one tested within the more constricted framework of a single method.
>
> (p. 30)

Wherever possible, further validation of specific instruments was sought by using ones which had been validated elsewhere previously, rather than developing wholly new ones. Examples of these were the abbreviated version of the Aston Measures employed (Inkson *et al.* 1970) and the Kirton Adaptation Innovation Inventory (Kirton 1976). The range of instruments was summarized in Table 4.2.

It should be noted that *data triangulation* was also employed within the case studies, to improve validation. It was recognized that information from a single source might well be biased. As a consequence, in each case study, information was sought from a minimum of two sources, and often more. This not only provided validation of perceptions, but also highlighted important conflicts and differing perceptions.

Fourth, feedback on the findings of the study and their interpretation was also sought, in order to ensure the validity of the views of the researcher in relation to those in the field. This feedback took two forms:

- in the case of individual organizations, summaries of the findings of the researcher were circulated to respondents, to check both their accuracy and interpretation; amendments were made if necessary; and
- in the case of the overall interpretation of the case studies and the developing model, not only were papers summarizing these circulated to key respondents but (in the case of the cross-sectional case studies) feedback meetings were held in each locality to discuss the findings of the study and their import (again, on the basis of this feedback, amendments were made as appropriate).

This approach to validity is an important one, though Abrams (1984) has warned against taking it to extremes, when it may turn into 'a series of furious arguments, wrangles, and recriminations. The lesson seems to be that overt respondent validation is only possible if the results of the analysis are compatible with the self image of the respondents' (p. 8).

A particular concern also exists with the use of retrospective interviews with senior managers within case studies. This is an established technique which has been used extensively in management research (for example, Mintzberg *et al.* 1976; Kanter 1983; Feeser and Willard 1990; and Huber and Glick 1993). However, recent critics have suggested that such interviews can be prone to poor memory recall and inaccuracy (Golden 1992). However, a recent re-evaluation of this work and its data has suggested that such interviews can have a high degree of validity, provided proper case-study protocols are adopted throughout (Miller *et al.* 1997). That was the approach adopted in this study.

Finally, in the search for validity, different theoretical perspectives were tested out to help make sense of the findings of the study. These were in part operationalized in the four causal hypotheses, but were also considered at the model-building stage of the study. They included the institutional analysis (Powell and DiMaggio 1991) and systems theory (Scott 1992).

Conclusions

This section has addressed the two issues of reliability and validity in this research study. In conclusion, the position of Kirk and Miller (1986) bears reiteration. They emphasize how the search for reliability and validity is not so much a precise science, as a judgemental art:

> The assumptions underlying the search for objectivity are simple. There is a world of empirical reality out there. The way we perceive and understand that world is largely up to us, but the world does not tolerate all understandings of it equally . . . [Therefore] it seems worthwhile to try to figure out collectively how best to talk about the empirical world, by means of incremental, partial improvements in understanding. Often these improvements come about by identifying ambiguity in prior, apparently clear views, or by showing that these are cases in which some alternative view works better.
>
> (pp. 11–12)

Initiating the research process

The loci of the study

As has been noted previously, a central problem in research about VNPOs is the construction of an appropriate sampling or analytic frame. The sector is highly diverse and fragmented. Moreover, there is no one central database of voluntary organizations to which researchers can go in order to construct their sampling or analytic frames. A number of databases do exist (such as those of the Charity Commissioners, the Inland Revenue, the Charities Aid Foundation (CAF) and the National Council for Voluntary Organisations (NCVO) to name but a few). However, each is highly partial: the register of the Charity Commission, for example, contains only registered charities whilst that of the CAF covers only those organizations to which it routes payments (Osborne and Hems 1995).

Indeed the state of the existing databases is so problematic that, for a recent major study of the income and expenditure of charitable organizations upon behalf of the Central Statistical Office, a key task for the research team was the construction of a unified database from which to construct their sampling frame (Osborne and Hems 1996). Yet even this database was partial in relation to the large number of small charitable organizations in existence. Whilst such an approach was legitimate in examining the economic structure of the sector, where the bulk of income and expenditure is weighted toward the largest 5 per cent of such organizations (Clare and Scott 1994), it would distort in the extreme any approach which examined service provision at the local level. Here the full spectrum of organizations needs to be considered.

Because of this, the approach taken was one based upon obtaining in-depth data on three locality, or cluster, samples. Again, as noted above, this approach has been used before to good effect in studies of the voluntary sector, and notably in the research which formed the basis of the Wolfenden Report (Wolfenden Committee

1978; Hatch 1980). It allows the research to capture the richness and diversity of the sector at the local level, and also to explore the impact of important local factors, such as the role of the statutory bodies in relation to voluntary organizations and the local political economy.

In this study, three localities were explored, representing a rural, a suburban, and an urban social environment. A precondition of contact with the voluntary and statutory organizations concerned was their anonymity. The three areas will therefore be given pseudonyms, though their genuine social characteristics are discussed below.

The three areas were respectively, *Southshire* (the rural area), *Bellebury* (the suburban area), and *Midwell* (the urban area). The characteristics of their organizational environments are summarized in Table 4.3, and the key social indicators for each locality are displayed in Table 4.4.

Southshire is a large rural county in the South of England recognized as suffering high levels of rural deprivation and isolation, and a large part of it is classified as a priority area (a *Rural Development Area*) for action by the Rural Development Commission. Traditionally, Southshire had been a Liberal stronghold. In 1993 the County Council was made up of 41 Liberal-Democrat members, 21 Labour, 18 Conservatives and 5 others. The County Council members were circumspect about the development of the *contract culture* for the PSS, but certainly were not opposed to it.

The organizational environment in Southshire is diverse. The County Council itself is a large one. There are three Divisions, with each Division having a high degree of autonomy. The Department is co-ordinated by a hierarchical series of planning committees, which link localities into the Council. Depending upon the view one took, this could be seen as either ensuring the accountability of the Council as a whole to its local areas and responsiveness to their needs, or as a means for senior managers to maintain their ultimate power within the agency,

Table 4.3 The organizational environments of each locality

Environmental feature	Southshire	Bellebury	Midwell
Locality type	Rural	Suburban	Urban
Political make-up	*Hung* (Liberal Democrats as largest party)	*Hung* (Conservatives as largest party)	Labour
Orientation to the *contract culture*	Willing agnostic	Early proponent	Pragmatic opponent
Nature of the local voluntary sector	Very diverse, with sub-networks within the overall locality	Diverse, structured around three urban areas, but within one network	Concentrated, and defined in relation to the local authority
Orientation of the local authority to the voluntary sector	Corporatist, within a hierarchical framework	Keen to develop a *mixed economy of care*, with this sector as a core component	Strong view of which voluntary bodies were *in* and which were *out*

Table 4.4 Social characteristics of the three localities

	England	Area 'A' Midwell	Area 'B' Southshire	Area 'C' Bellebury
Total population	46,382,050	285,090	550,026	127,701
Population density (persons per hectare)	3.6	33.9	1.2	4.0
% of population under 16 years old	20.1	20.6	20.9	18.7
% of population over pensionable age	18.7	19.5	23.3	24.8
% of population with long-term illness	12.8	15.1	13.9	14.1
% of males unemployed	9.7	14.0	8.7	8.5
% of females unemployed	4.7	6.5	4.2	4.1
% with over 1 person per room	2.1	3.2	1.5	1.8
% single-parent households	3.7	3.9	3.2	2.9
% of households with children under 5 years old	12.8	13.8	11.2	10.9
% of households with 3 or more children under 16 years old	4.7	7.0	4.0	4.5
% of population identifying themselves as black	6.2	14.7	0.7	2.3

Source: Adapted from OPCS, 1992

through the hierarchical chain of command. The third possibility is that it could combine both functions.

The field of VNPOs active in social services is also diverse. It is probably best characterised as a series of interlocking networks, based on different geographic loci, rather than one field. Certain key agencies, and individuals, operate on a County basis and provided links between these networks. These are either umbrella bodies such as Rural Community Councils (RCCs), the Councils for Voluntary Service (CVSs) or Volunteer Bureaux (VBx), or else the larger VNPOs which operate at a County level (such as RELATE and the Childrens Society). Around these individuals and agencies the organizational environment has a number of separate loci, which operate with their own organizational networks, and to an extent independently of the other localities.

Six such localities can be identified in Southshire: North Coast, focused on two small towns; Moors, an isolated and sparsely populated area in the north of the County; Central County, comprising a swathe of small market towns across the centre of Southshire; County Town, a far more populated and urban area, centred around the administrative centre of the County; Holiday Bay, a region centred around a fading holiday town, but with a number of isolated villages bordering upon it; and Southwest, an area which in many respects felt itself separate from the rest of the County and which comprised several significant market towns and another isolated moorland area.

The issue of the co-ordination of the local voluntary sector is such an important issue for the local umbrella bodies that they had formed their own 'umbrella body of umbrella bodies'. The purpose of this is both to try to unify and co-ordinate voluntary action across the County, and also to offer a unified voice to the County

Council which is perceived as using the diversity of Southshire as an excuse for not liaising with local VNPOs. The status of this body is contested, however, by some of the larger voluntary agencies. These have their own routes into the Council and object that this co-ordinating body does not have either their resources or their significance. This debate is ongoing.

Bellebury, also in the South of England, is an affluent suburban area though with a high elderly population. It had been a traditional Conservative authority for many years, though recently it had become a *hung* District Council, as was the County Council of which it was a region. In 1993, the District Council comprised 22 Liberal-Democrat members, 19 Conservatives, 7 Labour and 1 other; the County Council comprised 41 Conservative members, 30 Labour and 28 Liberal-Democrats. The local authority had pioneered the *purchaser–provider split* in the PSS and continued to be highly committed to this approach.

Bellebury District comprises three main areas: Bellebury town itself, the largest urban area and comparatively affluent; Dog Bay, a faded seaside town which is economically run-down; and Mayshed, another fading coastal town but with a more affluent middle-class bedrock to it. Despite their proximity, each of these towns operates comparatively independently. Age Concern, for example, has independent branches in each town and each addresses its local area.

The District is densely populated with local VNPOs, the local CVS producing a 94-page directory of such organizations. They tend to operate around one of the suburban towns, and few attempt to be District-wide. One CVS covers the entire District, but each town has its own Volunteer Bureau, which acts as a mini-umbrella body for that part of the District. Despite its relative smallness, compared to Southshire, the voluntary sector in Bellebury also has difficulty in speaking with one voice, though the three networks are rather more closely drawn around the CVS than is possible in Southshire.

Bellebury District is covered by one area office of the Social Service Department, split into *purchaser* and *provider* units. A Regional Planning and Commissioning Team is also based in a nearby large town, and covers three District Councils in the County. The Regional Planning Officer describes services as being developed by a process of contractual tenders which the Department offers out. Many of these are on a negotiated basis: that is, the Department decides which agencies to invite to tender and upon what basis their bids will be evaluated. Some, however, are also offered on an open and competitive basis, with price competition being the key (the developing framework around such a contract culture is explored in more detail in Wistow *et al.* 1994, 1996).

Midwell is an inner-city locality in the West Midlands. It scores highly on a range of indicators of social deprivation and is the subject of a number of government interventions aimed at the inner cities.

Politically, the local authority is a long-standing example of British *municipal socialism* with a ruling Labour group under no threat from the opposition parties. In 1993 the District Council was made up of 42 Labour members, 24 Conservative and 6 Liberal ones. This ruling group was, and continues to be, deeply opposed to the contract culture and the idea of the *purchaser–provider split*. However, it is also a highly pragmatic group, and works invariably through compromise and tactical manoeuvring rather than political confrontation.

As would befit such a densely populated area, Midwell has a similarly dense voluntary sector. Organizations can be both Borough-wide and based upon one or two wards in Midwell. The Social Services Department (SSD) is a major funder of much activity and, for this reason, the voluntary sector in Midwell tends to define itself in relation to that body. To an extent, two different voluntary sectors exist – that which has links to and support funding from the SSD and that which operates independently from it. The local CVS had attempted previously to bridge the two communities but with limited success. Indeed, its own relationship with the SSD was problematic. This had led to the withdrawal of funding by the local authority, part-way through this study, and the collapse of the CVS. The SSD funded another voluntary body to take on the umbrella role. However, it is very much part of the voluntary sector linked to the SSD and consequently has difficulty in pulling together the local voluntary sector as a whole.

Establishing research contacts

In each of the chosen localities, the first step was to contact the major local umbrella body, in order to discuss the proposed study. The utility of it to them was emphasized, in terms of developing their information and knowledge about the local voluntary sector. In each area, enthusiastic support was forthcoming from this body, and this support was vital to the success of the study. They saw some benefit to themselves from the study and so were more likely to participate. Similar contact was also made with senior officers of the SSD in each area.

The local umbrella groups were used in four ways. First, their knowledge of the extent of the local voluntary sector (usually formalized in local directories) was utilized in order to create the initial sampling frames for each locality. Second, their understanding of the dynamics of this sector, and its interaction with the statutory agencies, was used as a starting point for building up an environmental profile of the locality. Third, they were invaluable in encouraging local voluntary groups to participate in the study, both through articles in their local newsletter and by discussing it at meetings. Finally, they were an invaluable first sounding board for the emergent findings of the study.

Conclusions

This chapter has developed and justified the methodological approach of the research study upon which this book is based, outlined its reliability and validity, and detailed the loci in which the research took place. To conclude, three points should be emphasized. First, because of the lack of both theoretical and empirical studies of the innovative capacity of VNPOs it has been necessary to draw upon the quantitative and qualitative traditions in designing this research – the former to structure the field of study and the latter to explore causal and processual issues.

Second, the research proceeds upon both an inductive and a deductive basis. It works inductively in structuring the field, because of the lack of data about it; and it works deductively in exploring causality, by evaluating four hypotheses about the innovative capacity of VNPOs, derived from the organization studies literature.

Finally, it is important to emphasize the need to use both methodological and data triangulation (Denzin 1970), wherever possible, in this study. The phenomenon under investigation is a diffuse and complex one, involving interaction between innovations and innovators, both within their social environment. This calls for multiple sources of evidence to test and prove the emergent findings of this study.

5 Mapping and defining the innovative activity of VNPOs

The purpose of this chapter is to answer two sets of questions. The first set examines the nature and extent of innovative activity carried out by VNPOs. At issue here is first the sort of activity that they *themselves* define as being innovative, and then how this range of activity relates to a more theoretically derived definition of innovation. The second set of questions concerns the basic characteristics of those organizations responsible for producing the above innovations. At issue here are the characteristics of those VNPOs which are active as innovators, as well as those engaged in non-innovative activity.

As discussed in the previous chapters on methodology, this stage of the study is an exploratory one of a field where there has previously been little empirical evidence. It is intended to structure the field of innovative behaviour by VNPOs and the characteristics of the innovators. This is an essential first step to a deeper understanding of the innovative role of VNPOs, but not sufficient for its full understanding. It does not have explanatory or predictive power. For this, more complex and detailed analysis of the process of innovation is required. This is pursued in subsequent chapters.

Detailed methodology of the mapping exercise

As outlined briefly in the earlier overall discussion of research methodology the chosen approach here was through a postal census of all VNPOs in each locality engaged in the field of the PSS. For the reasons discussed above, a key problem here was to establish a database of such organizations. This was approached by using the main local umbrella agency in each area (the RCC in Southshire, and the CVSs in the other localities), which kept a directory of voluntary organizations active in their locality.

Such an approach was not without drawbacks. Inevitably, these directories were incomplete for a range of reasons (such as their not keeping abreast of organizational birth and morbidity). Wherever possible, they were supplemented therefore by checks against other available sources of information, such as from other smaller dedicated umbrella groups, libraries, or even word of mouth. Whilst not exhaustive, this database was as extensive as possible.

The postal survey was then carried out in three tranches, one for each locality. In each area, pre-publicity was carried out, through the available newsletters of the local umbrella groups. This provided forewarning of the arrival of the questionnaire and added the support of the umbrella body to it, emphasizing its importance to the locality. Each questionnaire was accompanied by a supporting letter, which again explained the purpose of the survey, emphasized the support of the local umbrella body, and gave names and telephone numbers for any queries. The questionnaire was directed at the chief officer or chair of the organization, because of their role and knowledge of the strategic intent (or lack of it!) of their organization. Copies of the questionnaire are available from the author upon request.

Reminder letters were sent out to all non-respondents after three weeks. A second follow-up exercise to non-respondents was carried out after a further two weeks, comprising letters and/or telephone calls. This second follow-up exercise was targeted upon those organizations which were under-represented in the response group, compared to overall sample population in each area. This representativeness was on the basis of the organizational classification of voluntary organizations detailed above.

Based upon this classification, the characteristics of the total sample and of the response group are displayed in Tables 5.1 and 5.2. This shows the response group as broadly representative of the total sample population, though with a slight over-representation of *other-regarding* organizations, compared to *self-regarding* ones. This probably reflects the more likely presence of paid staff in the former group, with more time in which to complete a questionnaire.

In total, 376 organizations were surveyed across the three localities, and 196 replied. This gives a basic response rate of 52.1 per cent. However, the true response

Table 5.1 Characteristics of total sample

Client group	%	Orientation	%
Adult	63.3	Self-regarding	42.3
Children/family	17.8	Other-regarding	50.5
General	18.9	Intermediary	7.2
Total	100.0	Total	100.0

($n = 376$)

Table 5.2 Characteristics of respondents

Client group	%	Orientation	%
Adult	66.1	Self-regarding	36.5
Children/family	14.3	Other-regarding	56.7
General	19.6	Intermediary	6.8
Total	100.0	Total	100.0

($n = 196$)

rate is probably higher than this, for a number of reasons. These include the level of organizational morbidity amongst registered VNPOs (that is, some will have ceased to exist, although still continuing to be listed). Other work (Osborne and Hems 1996) has estimated the morbidity level of charities registered with the Charity Commission to be 23.0 per cent. If this were the case in this study, this would reduce the total sample size by 86 to 290, and increase the response rate to 67.6 per cent. In fact, the morbidity factor at these local levels may be less significant than for the register of the Charity Commissioners, because the local umbrella groups (one hopes) will be more abreast of developments in their sector. The true response rate therefore probably lies somewhere in the range of 52.1 per cent to 67.6 per cent.

This rate could undoubtedly have been increased by further chasing. However, given the exploratory nature of this stage of the work and the efforts made to ensure that the response group was representative of the overall sample, this was held to be sufficient. Additional effort was reserved for the subsequent case studies.

Each questionnaire was numbered upon receipt, and classified according to its target client group and orientation. These classifications were tested for reliability and validity as outlined above. The postal survey was then ready for analysis.

Mapping the innovative activity of VNPOs

Organizational perceptions of innovation

In the survey, each organization was asked whether it had developed an innovation over the last three years, and was asked to describe it briefly. The refusal in this questionnaire to define innovation at this stage was deliberate. It was important to gauge how VNPOs themselves perceived innovation, rather than to impose theoretical constraints at the outset. It was also felt to be far more useful to ask these organizations to offer an example of innovation rather than a definition. The latter approach might test their command of the English language, but would not necessarily give any picture of the type of activity involved.

As with any such survey, there will be an inevitable tendency for respondents to want to over-report the phenomenon being examined. This was acknowledged in the explanatory notes to the questionnaire and it was emphasized that the research was as interested in knowing when organizations had not been innovative as when they had been. However, it has to be recognized that over-reporting may still be an element of the responses.

Of the respondents, 51.8 per cent reported that they had been involved in developing innovative services, compared with 48.7 per cent who reported that they had not been so involved (see Table 5.3). Bellebury and Midwell reported the highest levels of innovation, 56.9 per cent and 54.0 per cent respectively, whilst organizations in Southshire reported a lower level of 46 per cent.

Table 5.3 Reported levels of innovative activity (by percentage)

Type of activity	Bellebury	Southshire	Midwell	Total
Innovative	56.9	46	54	51.8
Traditional	43.1	54	46	48.2
Total	100	100	100	100

The innovations reported varied tremendously. They included:

- support groups for the carers of adults with special needs;
- a volunteer scheme which combined adults with special needs with traditional volunteers, in order to meet the practical needs of dependent elderly people;
- a small residential care scheme for adults with learning disabilities, based upon principles of normalization;
- a marriage guidance council developing a sex-therapy service;
- setting up a *buddy* support scheme for people with AIDS;
- a support group for deaf people starting to teach sign language to hearing people as well as those who were deaf;
- an emergency accommodation facility for adolescents, as part of a community project for young people;
- a new branch of an existing organization;
- a new local lunch club for elderly people;
- a holiday play scheme for children with cerebral palsy;
- a social club for elderly people opening an extra day a week;
- an existing lunch club for elderly people offering a free Christmas dinner to its members; and
- an existing day-care facility which sought to encourage Black adults with special needs to attend.

In terms of the previous discussion of innovation, all the developments certainly involved *newness* of a greater or lesser degree. However, only a portion involved the *discontinuity* element of innovation, and some were clearly simple changes to, or developments of, an existing service. In itself, this initial information told little about the legitimate innovative activity of VNPOs. It did, though, speak volumes for the loose way in which the phenomenon was defined by the managers of these organizations – which itself raised research issues as to why this should be, for exploration in the later stages of the study.

One finding of import derives from this initial analysis, however. It clearly negated the description of innovation as a key characteristic of VNPOs as a whole. Even when invited to describe their role in developing an innovation, and with the aforementioned tendency toward over-reporting, still only just over half of the organizations surveyed reported innovative activity. The reality is therefore far more complex than the more routine and/or normative statements about the innovative capacity of VNPOs would have us believe. The complexity of this reality is unravelled in the subsequent stages of this mapping exercise.

The innovative activity of VNPOs

In order to make sense out of the raw data of this survey, it was necessary to impose some structure into it, derived from theory. That is, it was necessary to classify it against more objective and conceptually derived criteria, rather than the assertions of managers within the sector.

This task was approached by using the typology of organizational change derived previously. In order to do this, the information from each respondent who had identified his/her organization as having developed an innovation was classified along two dimensions: whether the innovation served the existing client group of that organization, or a new one (its *market*), and whether the innovation involved the modification of the existing services of an organization, or the development of a new service (its *mode of production*). The key in this approach was therefore the issue of *discontinuity* for the organization identified earlier, either in terms of the clientele that it was serving, or of the services that it was offering.

Intrinsic to any such classificatory activity is the issue of the validity of the approach used and its reliability in application. The reliability and validity of the information gathered through the questionnaire was verified for a subset of organizations at the later, case-study, stage when this information was double-checked with respondents during interviews. No problems were encountered in respect of these responses.

As argued earlier, the classification itself was derived from a theoretical framework which offered construct validity to it. In terms of its application, though, there is clearly an issue of the validity and reliability of the judgements of the researcher. These were tested as outlined previously and found to be satisfactory.

The results of this mapping exercise are presented in Tables 5.4 and 5.5. Table 5.4 focuses solely on that activity reported as being innovative by the respondents. The most significant figure here is probably the level of *developmental* innovation reported (type C). This is significant because, against the theoretical concept of innovation, this activity really is not innovative at all. It involves discontinuity neither in terms of the client group of the organization concerned nor in terms of the service that it is providing. This gives us an essential first distinction in looking at the innovative capacity of VNPOs, between their legitimate innovative activity and that which might more accurately be described as developmental activity. The former does involve real discontinuous change for the organizations concerned, whilst the latter is a development of the existing work of the organization.

It must be emphasized, again, that no normative distinction is being made here, of one of these being in some way better than the other. Rather, it is a question of giving greater texture to our understanding of the work of VNPOs and the managerial challenges that organizational change poses for them. However, it should be noted that the use of the classification of organizational change in social services derived for this study has allowed this greater texture to be uncovered.

Table 5.4 Classification of innovative activity (by percentage)

Type of activity	Bellebury	Southshire	Midwell	Total
'A' (total)	18.2	20.6	5.9	14.8
'B' (expansionary)	18.2	5.9	8.8	10.9
'C' (developmental)	24.2	20.6	35.3	26.7
'D' (evolutionary)	39.4	52.9	50.0	47.6
Service innovation (A+B+D)	*75.8*	*79.4*	*64.7*	*73.3*
Service development (C)	*24.2*	*20.6*	*35.3*	*26.7*
Innovations involving the development of new services (A+D)	*57.6*	*73.5*	*55.9*	*62.4*
Innovations involving a new client group (A+B)	*36.4*	*26.5*	*14.7*	*25.7*
Total	100.0	100.0	100.0	100.0

Table 5.5 Classification of overall organization activity (by percentage)

Type of activity	Bellebury	Southshire	Midwell	Total
Service innovation	43.1	36.5	35.0	37.9
Service development	13.8	9.5	19.0	13.9
Traditional activity	43.1	54.0	46.0	48.2
Total	100.0	100.0	100.0	100.0

The second point to be derived from Table 5.4 regards the focus of the legitimate innovative activity. The majority of this activity is concerned with developing new services (types A and D), as opposed to working with a new client group (types A and B). To an extent, this undoubtedly reflects the fact that wholly new client groups rarely come into existence – the example of people with AIDS is one of the few concrete examples of recent times. It is probably also a product, though, of the 'particularism' of VNPOs – that is, that they are invariably set up to meet the needs of a specific client group and are likely to remain loyal to that group, rather than moving into working with other existing client groups. Indeed, for the groups registered as charities, the vagaries of British charity law have actually made it quite hard for them to change the focus of their organization (Chesterman 1979).

The final general point to arise from this first analysis of the survey concerns the geographic pattern of innovation. Voluntary bodies in Midwell were more concerned with service development, and less with total innovation, than their peers elsewhere, whilst those in Southshire had a higher rate of total innovation. Far from being the constant in the activity of VNPOs which the more normative accounts would suggest, therefore, service innovation was a variable.

Moving on to Table 5.5, this brings innovative and developmental activity, as defined within the theoretical construct rather than upon self-definition, together with the *traditional*, or non-innovative, activity of the survey respondents. Overall, this shows innovative activity being reported by about a third of the respondents (37.9 per cent), and with almost half of them (48.2 per cent) reporting traditional activity alone. Once again, far from being the constant of voluntary activity that the more normative statements would assert, innovative activity is more of a variable. On the basis of this initial evidence, it is therefore no longer possible to assert that 'VNPOs are innovative'. As a whole, they are not. However, a significant minority of them are engaged in innovative activity. This therefore raises the next question to be addressed – that is, which sorts of VNPOs are innovators?

The attributes of innovative VNPOs

Having clarified that not all VNPOs are innovative, this mapping exercise must now explore the attributes of the innovators, and of their developmental and traditional peers. A number of basic questions were asked in the questionnaire, about the age and staff group of the organization, the locus of the innovation, the orientation of the organization, and the prime funders of the organization. Again, the validity of these responses was verified as part of the case-study procedures and found to be satisfactory.

Of interest here was whether there were attributes which were specific to innovative VNPOs, and which differentiated them from either the developmental or the traditional ones. This analysis was approached in two stages. At the first stage the distributional statistics were tested for key differences using the chi-squared test of difference. In these, the usual statistical convention was followed, and statistical significance was imputed to those findings with a value for 'p' of 0.5 or less (that is, that this finding was likely to occur by chance in less than 5 per cent of occurrences). The use of this test in social research is usefully discussed in more detail in Phillip *et al.* (1975).

In the second stage, these simple relationships were then tested further using the more sophisticated statistical approach of discriminant analysis. This is discussed in more detail below.

A basic question often asked about the innovative work of VNPOs is the extent to which it represents either the actual *first use* of an approach to social care, or the *first application* in their community or sector of an approach developed elsewhere. A more useful way to talk of this is probably in terms of the distinction between objective and subjective innovation (Kimberly 1981), discussed above, as this avoids any possible confusion between invention and innovation. Table 5.6 shows that the overwhelming bulk of both innovative and developmental activity

Table 5.6 Nature of innovative and developmental activity

Type of development	Genuine innovations	Service developments	Total
Subjective	61 (84.75%)	25 (92.6%)	86 (86.9%)
Objective	11 (15.3%)	2 (7.4%)	13 (13.1%)
Total	72 (100%)	27 (100%)	99 (100%)

was within the subjective domain. In fact the figures for objective innovation (and development) are probably overestimates, due partly to their proponents' keenness to emphasize their uniqueness and partly to the incomplete knowledge of this researcher in weeding-out these claims.

Differentiating innovative and developmental organizations

Tables 5.7 to 5.11 examine the key characteristics of innovative and developmental VNPOs. These are, respectively, their age, the balance between volunteer and paid staff, the size of the paid-staff group, the orientation of the organization, and the major source of its funding. Each table contains two distributions: one displays the percentage differences in relation to the two types of organization and the other the percentages in relation to the variable concerned.

Table 5.7 The age of innovative and developmental organizations

Age	Innovative organizations	Developmental organizations	Total
Under six years old	23 (31.1%)	3 (12.05%)	26 (26.3%)
Six years old or over	51 (68.9%)	22 (88.0%)	73 (73.7%)
Total	74 (100%)	25 (100%)	99 (100%)

Age	Innovative organizations	Developmental organizations	Total
Under six years old	88.5%	11.5%	100%
Six years old or over	69.9%	30.1%	100%
Total	74.7%	25.3%	100%

$Chi^2 = 2.6660$; $0.2 > p > 0.1$
Note: In Tables 5.7 to 5.16, the data is analysed first as a proportion of each type of organization and second as a proportion of the discriminating characteristic.

Table 5.8 Staff group of innovative and developmental organizations

Staff group	Innovative organizations	Developmental organizations	Total
Volunteers only	17 (23.0%)	14 (55.8%))	31 (31.0%)
Paid staff (and/or some volunteers)	57 (77.0%)	12 (46.2%)	69 (69.0%)
Total	74 (100.0%)	26 (100.0%)	100 (100.0%)

Staff group	Innovative organizations	Developmental organizations	Total
Volunteers only	54.8%	45.2%	100%
Paid staff (and/or some volunteers)	82.6%	27.4%	100%
Total	74%	26%	100%

$Chi^2 = 7.1909$; $0.1 > p > 0.05$

Table 5.9 Size of paid staff group of innovative and developmental organizations

Size of staff group	Innovative organizations	Developmental organizations	Total
Five paid staff or under	34 (59.6%)	2 (16.7%)	36 (52.2%)
Six paid staff and over	23 (40.4%)	10 (83.3%)	33 (47.8%)
Total	57 (100%)	12 (100%)	69 (100%)

Size of staff group	Innovative organizations	Developmental organizations	Total
Five paid staff or under	94.4%	5.6%	100%
Six paid staff and over	69.7%	30.3%	100%
Total	82.6%	17.4%	100%

$Chi^2 = 5.7181; \ 0.025 > p > 0.01$

Table 5.10 Orientation of innovative and developmental organizations

Orientation	Innovative organizations	Developmental organizations	Total
Self-regarding	10 (15.6%)	7 (25.9%)	17 (16.8%)
Other-regarding (including intermediary organizations)	64 (86.4%)	20 (74.1%)	84 (83.2%)
Total	74 (100%)	27 (100%)	101 (100%)

Orientation	Innovative organizations	Developmental organizations	Total
Self-regarding	58.8%	41.25	100%
Other-regarding (including intermediary organizations)	76.2%	23.8%	100%
Total	73.3%	26.7%	100%

$Chi^2 = 1.3808; \ 0.3 > p > 0.2$

Table 5.11 The major funding source of innovative and developmental organizations

Major source of income	Innovative organizations	Developmental organizations	Total
Voluntary income or fees	38 (44.2%)	15 (55.5%)	53 (46.9%)
Governmental funding	48 (55.8%)	12 (44.5%)	60 (53.1%)
Total	86 (100%)	27 (100%)	113 (100%)

Major source of income	Innovative organizations	Developmental organizations	Total
Voluntary income or fees	71.7%	28.3%	100%
Governmental funding	80%	20%	100%
Total	76.1%	23.9%	100%

$Chi^2 = 0.6589; \ 0.5 > p > 0.4$

Little was found to be of significance in differentiating these two groups. Developmental organizations did tend to be older than their innovative counterparts, but not at a significant level. There were only minor differences apparent in relation either to the orientation or major funder of these organizations.

The key significant variable appeared to be in the nature of the staff group of these organizations. Innovative VNPOs were significantly more likely to have at least one member of paid staff, whilst developmental organizations displayed no distinctive staff bias. Interestingly, though, in that subset of innovative and developmental organizations which all had paid staff groups, the innovative organizations were significantly likely to have smaller staff groups than the developmental ones.

The question that has to be asked at this stage is whether this staffing difference is a sufficiently significant factor, by itself, by which to differentiate innovative from developmental organizations. Although this is theoretically possible, it seems more likely that one of two other explanations (or a combination of them) is a more robust one. The first is that the presence of a (usually small) staff group in innovative organizations is actually a proxy for the presence of the level of resources required to fund innovative activity, combined with the level of informality that a small staff group usually offers. The second is that the significant factor may not be the overt staffing patterns of these two groups, but rather the organizational decision to describe itself as innovative in the original questionnaire. This may well have more to do with institutional or environmental factors encouraging this construction, rather than the nature of the organizational labour force. This point will be explored further in the case studies below.

Differentiating innovative and traditional organizations

Tables 5.12 to 5.16 display the key characteristics of the innovative and traditional organizations, along the same variables as in the previous sector. Greater differentiation and a stronger boundary is apparent between these organizations.

Table 5.12 The age of innovative and traditional organizations

Age	Innovative organizations	Traditional organizations	Total
Under six years old	23 (31.1%)	4 (4.8%)	27 (17.2%)
Six years old or over	51 (68.9%)	79 (95.2%)	130 (82.8%)
Total	74 (100%)	83 (100%)	157 (100%)

Age	Innovative organizations	Traditional organizations	Total
Under six years old	85.2%	14.8%	100%
Six years old or over	39.2%	60.8%	100%
Total	47.1%	52.9%	100%

$\text{Chi}^2 = 17.1481; \ 0.0005 > p$

Table 5.13 Staff group of innovative and traditional organizations

Type of staff	Innovative organizations	Traditional organizations	Total
Volunteers only	17 (23.0%)	63 (70.8%)	80 (49.1%)
Paid staff (and/or some volunteers)	57 (77.0%)	26 (29.2%)	83 (50.9%)
Total	74 (100%)	89 (100%)	163 (100%)

Type of staff	Innovative organizations	Traditional organizations	Total
Volunteers only	21.2%	78.8%	100%
Paid staff (and/or some volunteers)	68.7%	31.3%	100%
Total	45.4%	54.6%	100%

$Chi^2 = 35.0725; 0.0005 > p$

Table 5.14 Size of paid staff group of innovative and traditional organizations

Size of staff group	Innovative organizations	Non-innovative organizations	Total
Five paid staff or under	34 (59.6%)	18 (69.2%)	52 (62.6%)
Six paid staff or over	23 (40.4%)	8 (30.8%)	31 (37.4%)
Total	57 (100%)	26 (100%)	83 (100%)

Size of staff group	Innovative organizations	Non-innovative organizations	Total
Five paid staff or under	65.4%	34.6%	100%
Six paid staff or over	74.2%	25.8%	100%
Total	68.7%	31.3%	100%

$Chi^2 = 0.3509; p > 0.5$

Table 5.15 Orientation of innovative and traditional organizations

Orientation	Innovative organizations	Traditional organizations	Total
Self-regarding	10 (15.6%)	51 (54.2%)	61 (36.3%)
Other-regarding (including intermediary organizations)	64 (86.4%)	43 (45.8%)	107 (63.7%)
Total	74 (100%)	94 (100%)	168 (100%)

Orientation	Innovative organizations	Traditional organizations	Total
Self-regarding	16.4%	83.4%	100%
Other-regarding (including intermediary organizations)	59.8%	40.2%	100%
Total	44%	56%	100%

$Chi^2 = 27.9835; 0.0005 > p$

Table 5.16 Major sources of funding of innovative and traditional organizations

Major source of income	Innovative organizations	Traditional organizations	Total
Voluntary income or fees	38 (44.2%)	68 (80%)	106 (62%)
Governmental funding	48 (55.8%)	17 (20%)	65 (38%)
Total	86 (100%)	27 (100%)	171 (100%)

Major source of income	Innovative organizations	Traditional organizations	Total
Voluntary income or fees	35.8%	64.2%	100%
Governmental funding	73.8%	26.2%	100%
Total	50.3%	49.7%	100%

$Chi^2 = 68.5510; 0.0005 > p$

Young organizations, defined as under six years old, were significantly more likely to be innovators than their older counterparts. Moreover, the innovators were significantly more likely to employ at least one member of paid staff, whilst the traditional organizations were more likely to be volunteer-based. Other-regarding organizations were significantly more likely to be innovative, whilst self-regarding ones were more likely to be traditional organizations. Finally, there was a substantial difference in the funding patterns of these organizations. Where government was the major funder, a significant majority of VNPOs were innovators, whilst traditional organizations tended to be more reliant on voluntary income or fees.

This latter point is particularly interesting. Much of the 'hearsay' about VNPOs would suggest that those funded by the state would tend to be the more traditional ones, with the innovators having voluntary or commercial income as their major source of funds. This could be either because the expectations of the governmental funders, and/or conditions attached to this funding, tended toward traditional, mainstream activity, rather than innovation (Smith and Lipsky 1993), or because the isomorphic pressures within the field both encouraged governmental agencies to support traditional agencies which were similar to themselves and encouraged VNPOs to mimic the mainstream activities of governmental agencies (DiMaggio and Powell 1988). Contrariwise, the traditional market-based model of innovation would assert that voluntary income would encourage innovation, because of the independence that it would offer to VNPOs, and in particular that fee income would stimulate innovation, because of the market pressures and competitive environment that it implied (Porter 1985). The findings here do not support these assertions. On the basis of these findings, it is possible to hypothesize some different relationships, though without being able to 'prove' them on the basis of this evidence alone. First, that governmental income encouraged VNPOs to be innovators, either because of the comparative security that it offered them, compared to the precariousness of voluntary income (i.e. it encouraged *slack* innovation, in the Cyert and March (1963) formulation); or because governmental funders were expecting innovation from their fundees (who obligingly reported their

activity as such, to ensure their continued funding) and/or were seeking out innovators in their funding procedures. Second, and conversely, it may be that voluntary
income encouraged traditional activity because its precariousness required such
organizations to stay close to their existing activities rather than to innovate.
Similarly, because of the relatively small and (as yet) underdeveloped market for
social services (certainly at the time of this study), the precarious nature of fee income
for VNPOs may similarly lead them to be cautious, rather than to be innovators.

The statistically significant findings of these analyses are summarized in Table
5.17. It must be emphasized again that such analyses do not predict which VNPOs
will be innovators; rather they describe the type of organization involved in
innovative activity. That is, there are no causal relationships implied here. The
appropriate formulation is thus that, for example, 'innovators in the voluntary
sector tend to have at least one member of paid staff' rather than that 'because a
VNPO has at least one member of paid staff it is likely to be an innovator'. These
more causal and predictive questions are explored in later chapters.

Table 5.17 Summary of statistically significant relationships

Factor	Innovative vs. developmental organizations	Innovative vs. non-innovative organizations
Social environment	–	–
Age	–	x
Nature of staff group	x	x
Size of paid staff group	x	–
Orientation of organization	–	x
Major source of funding	–	x

Key: x = statistically significant relationship found

The potential boundaries of innovative VNPOs are illustrated diagramatically in
Figure 5.1. Again, these are not impermeable boundaries which means that, for
example, volunteer-based VNPOs cannot be innovators. This is clearly not the
case. However, it does illustrate the key, statistically significant, boundaries
between these different types of organizations.

The differences explored further, by Discriminant Analysis

Discriminant Analysis (Eisenbis and Avery 1972; Klecka 1980) is a statistical
approach 'for seeing the association between a large set of independent variables
and a dependent one' (Hedderson and Fisher 1993, pp. 141–142). It works by
classifying cases into one of a number of mutually exclusive groups, upon the basis
of such associations. In this case, it is particularly useful for differentiating the
relationships between innovative, developmental and traditional VNPOs, upon the
basis of the organizational characteristics (or variables) identified above. In this
study, the analysis was facilitated by use of the SPSS sub-program DISCRIMI-
NANT (Norusis 1988, 1990).

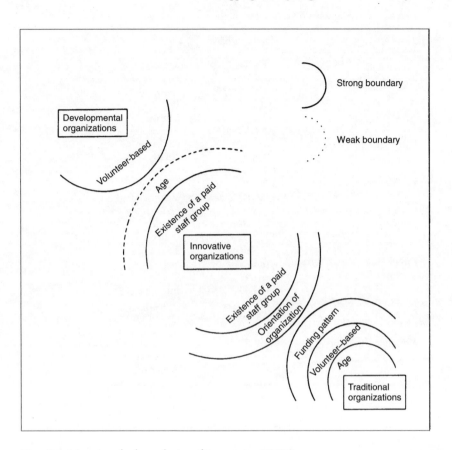

Figure 5.1 Mapping the boundaries of innovative VNPOs

Seven variables were taken for the basis of the discriminant analysis. Each was divided into a number of dummy variables. This was necessary for two reasons. First, some of the variables were nominal ones. However, DISCRIMINANT can work only with numerical variables, and so the nominal variables required translating into a series of numerical dummy variables to allow SPSS to distinguish between them. For example, the program would not differentiate between the different nominal categories contained within the variable *client*. It was therefore necessary to create a series of dummy binary variables for each of these subcategories (i.e. children, adults, and general).

Second, DISCRIMINANT is poor at dealing with numerical interval variables with a large range of values (such as staff size). Again, dummy variables were used here, this time to reduce the range of values to a smaller number of categories of greater significance (such as no paid staff, five or under paid staff, and six and over paid staff). These issues are dealt with in more depth in the works by Norusis cited above.

Table 5.18 The independent variables in the Discriminant Analysis

Variable	Dummy variables	Meaning
Age (in years)	AGE5	age < 6
	AGE20	5 < age < 21
	AGE21	20 < age
Area	AREA1	Bellebury
	AREA2	Midwell
	AREA3	Southshire
Client group	CLIE1	Children
	CLIE2	Adults
	CLIE3	General
Funding (major source)	FUND1	Government
	FUND2	Voluntary
	FUND3	Fees/charges
	FUND4	Bequests
	FUND5	Other
	FUND6	Trusts
Orientation	ORIN1	Self
	ORIN2	Other
	ORIN3	Intermediary
Paid staff (number of)	PAY0	None
	PAY1	Five or under
	PAY2	Six or over
Volunteers (number of)	VOL0	None
	VOL1	Ten or under
	VOL2	Eleven or over

The dependent variable, which the Discriminant Analysis was to analyse was the innovative (or otherwise) status of the organizations. This variable was called STATC. This was subdivided, as suggested above, into innovative, developmental, and traditional organizations, upon the basis of the work that these organizations reported in the questionnaires. The seven independent variables are detailed in Table 5.18.

The analysis proceeded in a stepwise manner, that is, removing a variable as its contribution to the analysis was identified. Because the dependent variable was separated into three subgroups, the analysis was set to produce two possible functions with which to discriminate between them (Hedderson and Fisher 1993). As previously, statistical significance was set at the 0.5 level.

DISCRIMINANT identified five of the independent variables as contributing at this level of statistical significance to the differentiation between the dependent subgroups. These were, in order of substance (i.e. the most significant was included in the analysis first and then removed):

PAY0,	PAY2
AGE5,	FUND3
FUND1,	

Table 5.19 Discriminating functions of analysis

Variable	Standardized canonical discriminant coefficient	
	Function 1	Function 2
FUND1	0.41981	0.02446
FUND3	−0.13758	−0.55909
AGE5	0.52097	−0.11977
PAY0	−0.54184	0.66502
PAY2	0.11451	0.93460

The two discriminating functions created from these variables were as in Table 5.19. The standardized canonical coefficients show FUND1, AGE5 and PAY0 to be the key variables (those with the highest discriminant coefficients) in the first function. FUND1 and AGE5 are both positive coefficients, whilst PAY0 is a negative one. This would suggest that the first function is discriminating upon the basis of the presence of governmental funding as a major source of finance and the age of the organization being five years or under, but negatively upon the absence of paid staff. By contrast the key variables in the second function are all positive. These are FUND3, PAY2 and PAY0. This function is thus discriminating positively upon the basis of the presence of these variables.

The significance of these functions is then shown in Table 5.20. The eigenvalue is a measure of the discriminating power of each function, that is how powerful it is, with a value of 0.40 or over being 'considered excellent' (Hedderson and Fisher 1993, p. 148). Thus function 1 is clearly a powerful one, with function 2 contributing only slightly to the analysis. This is confirmed by the percentage of variance in the analysis (that is, difference to be explained by the functions) accounted for by function 1, with over 80 per cent explained by this function. The high value of the Wilks lambda coefficient for function 2 is also revealing. This has a maximum value of 1.0 and varies in inverse proportion to the discriminating power of its function, once the previous function 1 has been removed from the analysis. In this case, this coefficient is high for function 2, indeed almost equivalent to 1.0, suggesting that most of the discriminating power is in function 1.

Table 5.21 shows the canonical discriminant functions at group means, for each function. The relevant point here is the range between these means, as indicating the direction in which these functions discriminate. These show that function 1 is a significant discriminant between the innovative and traditional groups of organizations (with a range from 0.81778 to −0.77328). Function 2, the weaker function, is the discriminant in relation to the developmental group of organizations. It is different from both the other groups but most strongly from the innovative organizations (0.71429 to −0.10258).

The relationship between these functions is displayed diagramatically in Figure 5.2, which gives a good visual view of the differences involved. Here the strength of

Table 5.20 The significance of the discriminating functions

Fcn	Eigenvalue	Pct of Variance	Cum Pct	Canonical Corr	After Fcn	Wilks' Lambda	Chi-square	df	Sig
1*	0.5407	83.48	83.48	0.5924	0	0.586349	92.354	10	0.0000
2*	0.1070	16.52	100.00	0.3109	1	0.903369	17.581	4	0.0015

* Marks the 2 canonical discriminant functions remaining in the analysis.

Table 5.21 Canonical discriminant functions at group means

Canonical discriminant functions evaluated at group means (group centroids)

Group	Func 1	Func 2
0	-0.77328	-0.10258
1	0.81778	-0.19444
4	0.20845	0.71429

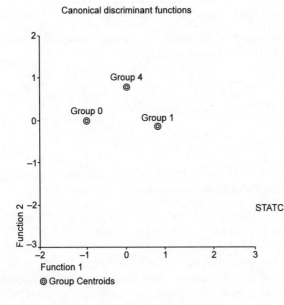

Figure 5.2 Territorial map of functions and variables

function 1 in discriminating between the innovative (Group 1) and traditional organizations (Group 0) can be seen clearly. By contrast, function 2 (the weaker function) provides little discrimination between these two groups, but does discriminate the developmental organizations (Group 4) from both of these previous groups.

Finally, Tables 5.22 and 5.23 show the predictive ability of the above functions. These compare the predicted group membership using these functions with the prior probability of correctly classifying membership upon the basis of chance. As would be suspected from the above analysis, the predictive ability in relation to the innovative and traditional organizations was high (on the basis of function 1), but that in relation to the developmental organizations (on the basis of function 2) was low. Nor was any pattern apparent in the destination of the failed classifications for this latter group of developmental organizations. These were split quite evenly between classification as traditional or innovative organizations (41.9 per cent to

Table 5.22 Predictive ability of discriminating functions

Organizational group	Number of organizations	Prior probability	Predicted by functions
Traditional	95	0.45	0.87
Innovative	70	0.38	0.70
Developmental	31	0.17	0.13

Table 5.23 Analysis of classifications in predictive matrix of Table 5.22 (by percentage)

Actual group	Traditional group predicted	Innovative group predicted	Developmental group predicted
Traditional	**87.4**	11.6	1.1
Innovative	27.1	**70**	2.9
Developmental	41.9	45.2	**12.9**

(Correct classifications highlighted in bold)

45.2 per cent respectively). This clearly reflects the relative power of the two discriminating functions.

Discussion of the Discriminant Analysis

The application of Discriminant Analysis has uncovered five variables of importance in discriminating between innovative, developmental and traditional VNPOs. These are governmental funding as a major source of finance for an organization, the use of fees and charges, being a young (under six years old) organization, the presence or not of paid staff, and the presence of a large staff group. On the basis of these variables it has been possible to construct two functions to discriminate between the three types of organizations. The first function was built around the variables of governmental funding, being a young organization, and the presence of a paid staff. The second function was built around the variables of fees and charges as the key source of income, the lack of a paid staff group and a reliance upon volunteers, and, paradoxically, the presence of a large staff group.

Upon further analysis it was found that the first function was far more powerful than the second one. It was subsequently identified also that this first function was especially good in discriminating between traditional and innovative VNPOs, whilst the second function was better at discriminating between the developmental organizations and the other two types. However, this second one was a much weaker function than the first one. The respective eigenvalues showed the first function to be significant, and the second to be below the usually accepted level of significance.

Taking the sign of the canonical coefficients into account, the first function correlated positively with governmental funding and being a young organization, and negatively with having no paid staff. When this function was compared to the organizational types, it was found to correlate positively with the innovative organizations and negatively with the traditional ones. This relationship was confirmed when it was used as a predictive tool, in relation to the categorization of the organizational types, where it was quite successful in predicting the pattern of innovative and traditional organizations.

Perhaps the most significant point about function 2 was its lack of discriminating power. It was strongly related to discriminating the developmental organizations from the other two groups, but could do so with very little efficiency or power (indeed a random choice would have proved more successful!).

This confirms the pattern uncovered in the earlier chi-squared analysis of the distributional statistics, that it is possible to differentiate between the innovative and traditional VNPOs upon the basis of their organizational characteristics (that is, that there are distinctive organizational groupings). However, it was hard to distinguish at all between the developmental organizations and the others. In terms of their organizational attributes at least, they were almost equally indistinguishable from the other two groups.

Conclusions

This chapter has been concerned with mapping and structuring the field of innovative activity by VNPOs. It began by discussing the characteristics of the innovations themselves, and ended by exploring the attributes of the innovators.

It found that *innovation* was used very loosely by the leaders of VNPOs, to cover a range of new(ish) activity, from opening a club an extra morning a week or providing the members of an organization with a free turkey at Christmas, to developing new services for people suffering from AIDS. However, using the definition and associated classification of organizational change developed for this study, it was possible to differentiate further between genuinely innovative activity, which did involve discontinuity in the services and/or the beneficiary group of an organization, and developmental activity, which improved an existing service to an existing beneficiary group of an organization.

The classification matrix developed for this study proved an essential tool in helping to separate out these developments from the genuine innovations, and identified this as an issue to be explored in more detail later in the study. Finally, it was also possible to identify a group of organizations which did not see it as feasible and/or appropriate for them to be involved in innovation. Rather, they concentrated upon providing their existing service, or range of services, to their existing beneficiary group. These were termed the 'traditional organizations'.

In terms of the innovators, and their traditional and developmental counterparts, this chapter has explored their attributes from two methodological directions, as part of its triangulation strategy. The first was through the analysis of distributional statistics, using chi-squared tests. The second method was the exploration of these organizational attributes in more relational terms, using discriminant analysis.

A strong level of mutual correlation was found between these two methodologies. Both found that it was possible to distinguish between innovative and traditional organizations on the basis of a set of organizational variables, but that it was much harder to distinguish between the developmental and the other organizations. This is clearly an issue for further exploration, below.

In terms of their organizational characteristics, these two approaches confirmed a boundary between innovative and traditional organizations based upon their funding patterns, staffing and age. Innovative organizations tended to be younger organizations, with at least one member of paid staff, and to have government as their major funder. Traditional organizations tended to be older, not to have a paid staff and to be more reliant upon fees and charges as their major source of funds.

With relation to the age factor, it is important to be clear about what is being revealed here. In one sense, it could be simply that young organizations are being seen as innovative because their very age means that anything that they might do would be a new departure for them. This was not the case here. Some organizations did report their own development as an innovation in itself, but this was where there had been no previous service available. Again, the support service for people with AIDS was a good example of this type of development. However, with the majority of organizations, perusal of the questionnaires made it clear that each reported innovation was a new impetus in relation to the existing services of these young organizations.

Finally, it is important to be clear about what is being identified here. These are *descriptive attributes* of innovative and traditional VNPOs. They must not be confused with *causal explanations*. They tell you what sort of VNPOs tend to be innovators. They do not tell you why. In order to explore these important causal issues, it is necessary to move on to the second stage of this study. This involves the use of cross-sectional case studies in order to test out four explanatory hypotheses about the innovative capacity of VNPOs.

6 Four causal hypotheses and a process

Introduction

Four causal explanations are frequently put forward to explain the innovative capacity of VNPOs. These have been outlined previously and are the organizational, cultural, environmental and institutional hypotheses. This chapter will explore these in more detail. As detailed earlier, this will be done through three cross-sectional case studies of innovative, developmental and traditional organizations, constituted across the three localities.

The approach taken was to construct the cross-sectional case studies with the aid of the typology of organizational change and innovation developed earlier (i.e. organizations which identified themselves as involved in creating total, evolutionary or expansionary innovations, the innovative organizations; as involved in developing existing services, the developmental organizations; or as being traditional service providers, the traditional organizations).

In theory this should have resulted in eight organizations from each locality: namely, three innovative organizations, one developmental and four traditional ones. This in turn would create three apparently unbalanced cross-sectional cases of nine innovative, three developmental and twelve traditional organizations. In fact, when the activity of the case-study organizations was explored in more detail, the original self-classification of their activity was found to need adjustment against the more objective template of organizational innovation and development constructed for this study. Specifically, whilst the self-classification of innovative activity was confirmed by this reclassification, there was elision between the self-classification of the developmental and traditional organizations. This strengthened the supposition developed from the postal survey that there was an element of social construction in the self-definition of these organizations, and particularly of the developmental organizations, as a result of an extraneous factor. That is, that they were describing their services as 'new' in some way because of an external impetus rather than the nature of the services themselves. This issue is explored further in the final hypothesis. The results of this reclassification are presented below, in Table 6.1. Table 6.2 then goes on to illustrate the diversity of organizations contained in the case studies. Table 6.2(a) describes the organizational types and Table 6.2(b) describes the organizational beneficiaries,

Table 6.1 Reclassification of the case-study organizations

Locality	Type of organization			Total
	Innovative	Developmental	Traditional	
Rural	3	2	3	8
Suburban	3	3	2	8
Urban	3	2	3	8
Total	9	7	8	24

Table 6.2(a) Summary of organizational type

Organization	Type of organization			Total
	Self-oriented	Other-oriented	Intermediary	
Innovative	1	5	3	9
Developmental	1	5	1	7
Traditional	5	2	1	8
Total	7	12	5	24

Table 6.2(b) Summary of organizational beneficiaries

Organization	Children and families	Adults with special needs	General	Total
Innovative	2	5	2	9
Developmental	2	3	2	7
Traditional	2	4	2	8
Total	6	12	6	24

Table 6.2 (c) Cross-sectional case study of innovative organizations

Locality	Type of innovation		
	Total	Expansionary	Evolutionary
Rural	A residential project for adults with learning disabilities (other-oriented organization) [1]	A volunteer project combining people with mental health problems with elderly people requiring practical support (local intermediary organization) [2]	A counselling service for couples with sexual difficulties (other-oriented organization) [3]
Suburban	A home-based respite support service for carers of adults with special needs (local intermediary organization) [4]	Toy library expanding its services to cover adults as well as children (other-oriented organization) [5]	Community support project for people with a hearing impairment (self-oriented organization) [6]

Locality	Type of innovation		
	Total	Expansionary	Evolutionary
Urban	A support organization for carers of adults with special needs changing its function to act as a local development agency in relation to community care (intermediary organization) [7]	Leisure project for adults with learning disabilities providing a service for older adolescents with such disabilities (other-oriented organization) [8]	Bereavement counselling service creating a group-work approach to counselling with an emphasis on self-help (other-oriented organization) [9]

Each organization is given a number here (and in Tables 6.2 (d) and (e)), used to identify them in this and the subsequent chapters.

Table 6.2(d) Cross-sectional case study of developmental organizations

Locality	Organizations		
Rural	A CVS improving its information dissemination service into isolated rural areas (local intermediary organization) [10]	A residential home for elderly people providing new day service accommodation (other-oriented organization) [11]	
Suburban	An organization providing practical support for people with material problems, improving their second-hand furniture service (other-oriented organization) [12]	Organization providing day services for adults with mental health problems developing new support groups (other-oriented organization) [13]	A pre-school play-group association improving its service for children with special needs (other-oriented organization) [14]
Urban	A support group for carers providing weekend meetings (self-oriented organization) [15]	A toy library improving its support services for mothers (other-oriented organization) [16]	

Table 6.2(e) Cross-sectional case study of traditional organizations

Locality	Organizations		
Rural	Organization providing volunteer support to people needing help (local intermediary organization) [17]	Organization providing counselling to individuals with problems (other-oriented organization) [18]	Organization providing social support to adults with hearing impairment (self-oriented organization) [19]

Table 6.2(e) (contd.)

Locality	Organizations		
Suburban	Organization to provide social support to adults with chronic health problems (self-oriented organization) [20]	Organization providing day care for children with learning disabilities (self-oriented organization) [21]	
Urban	Organization providing social support for elderly people (self-oriented organization) [22]	Organization providing community support for adults with sight impairment (self-oriented organization) [23]	Organization providing counselling to couples with relationship problems (other-oriented organization) [24]

whilst Tables 6.2(c)–(e) outline the individual organizations involved in the case studies.

All the organizations in the case studies were subject to:

- a structured questionnaire schedule, exploring their organizational and environmental framework, and incorporating the Abbreviated Aston Measures (Inkson *et al.* 1970) with other qualitative questions (for organizational leaders);
- a *workstyle* questionnaire based upon the Kirton Adaptation and Innovation (KAI) Inventory (Kirton 1976), to examine the orientations of key senior managers (for organizational leaders); and
- a semi-structured discussion of their work and objectives based upon a schedule of topic headings (for a range of informants).

For the organizations identified as producing innovative or developmental initiatives, these were supplemented by:

- a structured discussion with a number of informants about the innovative/ developmental process, based upon the model of the Minnesota Innovation Studies Project (Van de Ven *et al.* 1989);
- an unstructured discussion around the issues of innovation for that organization; and
- discussions with other key local actors (including those from the statutory and voluntary sectors, and service users where possible).

As detailed above, each hypothesis was then explored using a number of different approaches, in order to provide cross-validation.

The findings of these case studies are described in this chapter. Before proceeding to this discussion, though, it is important to provide further background for two of the research tools used here – the Aston Measures and the KAI Inventory.

THE ASTON MEASURES

These measures arose out of a major organization studies research project which was undertaken at Aston University in the 1960s and 1970s and which has been reported extensively elsewhere (Pugh and Hickson 1976; Pugh and Hinings 1976; Pugh and Payne 1977). They are tested and validated quantitative measures of the formal structure of organizations.

It is important to recognize, however, that the Measures have been subject to a number of criticisms over the years. A particular concern has been for their over-concentration upon the structural configurations of organizations to the detriment of their processual content. Starbuck (1981; see also Child 1984, for another important critique) has given an essential summary of their limitations. His critique is based upon two analyses. The first is that the design of the Measures was itself flawed: '[The researchers] selected certain phenomena to perceive and label as data, chose arbitrary schemata that matched their perceptions, and merely translated their prior beliefs into professionally legitimated language of data and statistical tests' (p. 82).

The second analysis is that, irrespective of the validity of the Measures themselves, they do not actually reveal anything of great import: '[Organizational structures] say little about the messages organizations exchange or the skills personnel exhibit. Organizations with similar structures may be plotting mass destruction or humanitarian services, may be going bankrupt or raking in large profits' (Starbuck 1981: 194).

This criticism has validity and it would be dangerous to use them in isolation. As with any artificially constructed measure, there are dangers that the measure can become confused with what it is supposed to be measuring. However, the advocates of the Aston Measures have also rallied against their critics. Pugh (1981) accepted in part the view of Starbuck that structure may not be the most important variable in organizational behaviour, but argued that this was to confuse the purpose of the Measures with a possible finding. The Measures were important, he argued, precisely because they allowed researchers to test whether or not there were important relationships to be explored. Moreover, Clark (1990) has well argued that, provided their limitations are taken into account, then they continue to be accepted within the field of organizational analysis as important 'instruments for operationalising and measuring key dimensions . . . of the structure of [an organization]' (p. 40). It is within this constrained view that the Aston Measures are used in this study.

Summarizing the utility of the Aston Measures, Pugh (1981) considered that 'it is abundantly clear that the original measures of structure and concept can be applied to a wide variety of diverse types of organizations with discriminatory power and meaningful results' (p. 145).

One area where they have been under-utilized, however, is in the study of VNPOs. In the original Aston studies, Donaldson and Warner (1976) did use them with occupational interest associations and Hinings *et al.* (1976) with church organizations. However, as far as the present researcher is aware (supported by informal discussions with Pugh in 1993) this study is the first to use them to explore the structural characteristics of VNPOs.

This is surprising, perhaps, given the number of assertions about the structural characteristics of these organizations, summarized in Knapp *et al.* (1990). However, Knokke and Prensky (1984) and Paton (1993) have both noted previously that there has been very little testing of a number of organizational assertions about VNPOs, the structural assertion being one of them. Consequently, this present study is the first to test this key assertion in an empirical setting.

In this study, the abbreviated form of the Measures was used. This is a simplified but still validated version of the original Measures, developed by Inkson *et al.* (1970), and which allows them to be used more easily in a complex research setting. They covered the dimensions of:

- *dependency* (of one organization upon others);
- *specialization* (of organizational tasks);
- *formalization* (of organizational roles);
- *autonomy* (of organizational decision making); and
- *workflow integration* (of organizational tasks).

The strength of this approach for this study is that these dimensions cover the key ones identified in the earlier literature review as being of substance in relation to the innovative capacity of VNPOs. However, it did necessitate the re- framing of the last dimension, that of *workflow integration*, into that of *professionalization*. It is suggested here that this approach is a valid one. The key issue of the previous dimension was the extent to which technology was unifying organizational tasks. In this formulation technology included 'the knowledge required for produ- cing...products' (Clark 1990, p. 28). In the newly formulated dimension, the issue is the unification of organizational tasks through professional training and the professionalization of an organization. In many respects it equates the profes- sional skills and knowledge of workers in these social-care services with techno- logical knowledge in a production process. The focus is thus the same and does have construct validity, in the sense that they are both measuring the same construct.

In each case, the paid manager (or chair, in an organization with no paid staff) was taken through a structured questionnaire covering each of these dimensions. This was then coded as detailed in Inkson *et al.* (1970), and analysis of variance carried out using the MANOVA program of the SPSS package of statistical techniques. The results of this analysis are discussed below.

THE KAI INVENTORY

This is a validated attitudinal questionnaire developed by Kirton (1976) and which continues to be used to explore the roles of organizational leaders in innovation (for example, Thwaites and Edgett 1991; Foxall 1994; Foxall and Hackett 1994). It consists of a list of thirty-two items rated on a scale of 1 to 5. Respondents are asked to rate themselves against each item. A rating of 1 means that the attitude described is one that they would find hard to hold whilst a rating of 5 indicates an attitude that they would find very easy to hold. Kirton (1976) found, in his applications of the test, that managers clustered around one of three approaches to organizational change:

- *organizational originality*, with a commitment to creativity;
- *methodical Weberianism*, with a commitment to 'precise, reliable and disciplined activity' (p. 625); and
- *Mertonian conformism*, with a commitment to 'proper respect for authority and rules' (p. 625).

Kirton argued that the first group were more able to deal with organizational discontinuity or changes in the 'rules of the game' (innovation), whilst the other two groups were able to deal with stability and/or gradual development. If such organizational leadership was important in the innovative capacity of VNPOs, therefore, one would expect the innovative organizations to have a tendency to present leaders in this first category. Again, the findings in relation to this analysis are presented below.

The organizational hypothesis

This hypothesis argues that the innovative capacity of VNPOs is a function of their formal structural characteristics – or perhaps their lack of them. If this hypothesis were to be proven, one would anticipate significant differences in the structural characteristics of the innovative, developmental and traditional organizations.

No such differences were immediately apparent from the conduct of the case studies. All the organizations were classified by the present researcher as being either an independent organization or part of a federation of organizations. This analysis was confirmed when respondents were asked similarly to classify the organizational origins of their own organizations. Nineteen (79 per cent) of the twenty-four organizations reported themselves as having been founded wholly independently and only five reported that any other organization had played a role in their foundation.

In terms of organizational decision making, all the organizations reported this to reside within the local unit, for a number of key organizational decisions (see box). Of the organizations 96 per cent reported these decisions to be taken by the management committee of the organization, often with a significant input from the officers of the organizations, or the paid manager; 4 per cent reported further that the paid manager had decision-making autonomy. This is not the same as saying that there were not informal or institutional influences on decision making. These are explored further later in this chapter. However, in terms of the formal organizational structure, there were no apparent differences in organizational autonomy between the three cross-sectional case studies.

Some differentiation was found when the complexity of organizational structures was explored, as seen in Table 6.3. Respondents were asked to specify the

---

Checklist of areas of organizational decision making explored in the case studies

- Allocation of organizational resources
- Staffing/personnel issues
- Capital expenditure (if appropriate)
- Structure of organizations
- Organization policy/procedures

Table 6.3 Levels of organizational tiers in the case studies

	Management committee plus volunteers [1]	[1] plus paid manager [2]	[2] plus other paid staff responsible to manager [3]	[3] plus other paid staff responsible to other managers
Innovative	1	3	5	0
Developmental	2	2	2	1
Traditional	5	2	1	0
Total	8	7	8	1

organizational tiers of their organizations. The innovative organizations did include more tiers than the developmental or traditional ones, whilst the traditional were the least 'tiered'. This would appear to correlate with the presence of a paid staff group in the innovative organizations discussed earlier.

What is most striking, however, is the extremely low level of organizational tiering in all the organizations. Only one had more than two tiers of paid staff in addition to a paid manager. The overwhelming picture is of small locally based organizations. As one respondent put it:

We like it small – we don't want to grow.

(Manager of Organization 13)

If all the case-study organizations were relatively simple structures, they also had relatively low levels of formalization, in terms of the extent to which their workings were formalized in documents. Eight organizations reported having written organizational policy documents, nine reported having written procedures, and eight reported having work schedules. The highest level of formal documentation came in terms of job descriptions – eleven organizations, or 46 per cent, reported having such a description for paid staff. Five organizations reported that they had no written information at all about their organizations. Only four organizations reported that they had any formal mechanisms for evaluating their work, in part or in whole.

Finally, as a measure of organizational specialization, organizations were asked to consider the extent to which any members of staff in their organizations specialized in one organizational task alone (Table 6.4). This was certainly more

Table 6.4 Specialization of organizational roles (categories not exclusive)

Role	Type of organization			
	Innovative	Developmental	Traditional	Total
Support services	2	1	0	3
Administrative	7	0	2	9
Service provision	5	4	2	11
Total number of organizations with specialist roles	8	4	3	N/A

common in innovative organizations than in the other two types, though half of these specialists were accounted for by people who specialized in administrative, rather than service-related, functions.

At this general level, then, whilst the interviews with the case-study informants provided a little evidence of differences between innovative, developmental and traditional organizations, these were of limited or small-scale nature. Innovative organizations did have more tiers of organizational structure, though all the organizations had lean structures. The innovative organizations did have more specialist job roles than the other organizations, though, again, the difference was relatively small and usually concerned administrative functions. As detailed above, these differences would seem to be related to the presence of paid staff in the innovative organizations.

However, the structural characteristics of the case-study organizations were not explored through these semi-structured interviews alone. These findings were also triangulated with evidence from more quantitative methods, by use of the *Aston Measures* of organizational structure. These analyses are displayed in Tables 6.5 to 6.9.

As a preamble, if these results are compared with those of the original Aston studies (Child 1973), then they do provide some empirical support for the contention that VNPOs, as a field, are far less formally structured than other fields of organizations. Beyond this most general point, there is no discernible structure to the pattern of organizations within the field of VNPOs. Little differentiation between organizations was apparent on the basis of organizational dependency and autonomy (Tables 6.5 and 6.6). The means were close together and with a wide-ranged 95 per cent confidence interval, which suggested a great deal of overlap between the organizational categories.

More variation was apparent in terms of organizational formalization (Table 6.7). However, whilst the literature might lead one to expect the innovative organizations to be the least formalized (and consequently most adaptable), it was the traditional organizations which were the least formal. Even here, though, the ranges, standard deviations and 95 per cent confidence intervals were large also, and presented a picture of a substantial overlap between the groups. There was insufficient variance to allow one to claim any statistical significance for these findings.

Table 6.5 Analysis of organizational dependency

Analysis of Variance

Source	D.F.	Sum of Squares	Mean Squares	F Ratio	F Prob.
Between Groups	2	0.8075	0.4038	0.0930	0.9116
Within Groups	21	91.1925	4.3425		
Total	23	92.0000			

Group	Count	Mean	Standard Deviation	Standard Error	95 Pct Conf		Int for Mean
Grp 0	8	2.8750	2.0310	0.7181	1.1770	to	4.5730
Grp 1	7	3.2857	1.3801	0.5216	2.0093	to	4.5621
Grp 2	9	2.8889	2.5221	0.8407	0.9502	to	4.8276
Total	24	3.0000	2.0000	0.4082	2.1555	to	3.8445

GROUP	MINIMUM	MAXIMUM
Grp 0	1.0000	7.0000
Grp 1	1.0000	5.0000
Grp 2	0.0000	7.0000
TOTAL	0.0000	7.0000

Note: In Tables 6.5–9 the following key applies:
Group '0' – traditional organizations,
Group '1' – developmental organizations,
Group '2' – innovative organizations.

Table 6.6 Analysis of organizational autonomy

Analysis of Variance

Source	D.F.	Sum of Squares	Mean Squares	F Ratio	F Prob.
Between Groups	2	0.7440	0.3720	0.3683	0.6963
Within Groups	21	21.2143	1.0102		
Total	23	21.9583			

Group	Count	Mean	Standard Deviation	Standard Error	95 Pct Conf		Int for Mean
Grp 0	8	0.2500	0.7071	0.2500	−0.3412	to	0.8412
Grp 1	7	0.4286	1.1339	0.4286	−0.6201	to	1.4772
Grp 2	9	0.6667	1.1180	0.3727	−0.1927	to	1.5261
Total	24	0.4583	0.9771	0.1994	0.0457	to	0.8709

GROUP	MINIMUM	MAXIMUM
Grp 0	0.0000	2.0000
Grp 1	0.0000	3.0000
Grp 2	0.0000	3.0000
TOTAL	0.0000	3.0000

Table 6.7 Analysis of organizational formalization

Analysis of Variance

Source	D.F.	Sum of Squares	Mean Squares	F Ratio	F Prob.
Between Groups	2	18.9444	9.4722	1.1907	0.3237
Within Groups	21	167.0556	7.9550		
Total	23	186.0000			

Group	Count	Mean	Standard Deviation	Standard Error	95 Pct Conf		Int for Mean
Grp 0	8	1.2500	2.8158	0.9955	-1.1040	to	3.6040
Grp 1	7	3.0000	2.6458	1.0000	0.5531	to	5.4469
Grp 2	9	3.2222	2.9486	0.9829	0.9557	to	5.4887
Total	24	2.5000	2.8438	0.5805	1.2992	to	3.7008

GROUP	MINIMUM	MAXIMUM
Grp 0	0.0000	8.0000
Grp 1	0.0000	6.0000
Grp 2	0.0000	8.0000
TOTAL	0.0000	8.0000

Finally, the most variation was found in the specialization and professionaliza-tion dimensions (Tables 6.8 and 6.9). Again, confounding the asserted importance of task flexibility for innovative organizations, it was the innovative VNPOs which had the highest degree of specialization and professionalized workflow in their staff structure, and the traditional organizations which had the least. Clear gradients were apparent for the means, with the innovative and developmental organizations closer together and the traditional ones somewhat separated off. Yet again, though, the range of values is widespread, as demonstrated by the standard deviations and 95 per cent confidence intervals. Nonetheless, the *F*-probability levels (which vary

Table 6.8 Analysis of organizational specialization

Analysis of Variance

Source	D.F.	Sum of Squares	Mean Squares	F Ratio	F Prob.
Between Groups	2	12.2123	6.1062	3.5872	0.0457
Within Groups	21	35.7460	1.7022		
Total	23	47.9583			

Group	Count	Mean	Standard Deviation	Standard Error	95 Pct Conf		Int for Mean
Grp 0	8	0.5000	0.7559	0.2673	-0.1320	to	1.1320
Grp 1	7	0.8571	1.2150	0.4592	-0.2665	to	1.9808
Grp 2	9	2.1111	1.6915	0.5638	0.8109	to	3.4113
Total	24	1.2083	1.4440	0.2948	0.5986	to	1.8181

GROUP	MINIMUM	MAXIMUM
Grp 0	0.0000	2.0000
Grp 1	0.0000	3.0000
Grp 2	0.0000	6.0000
TOTAL	0.0000	6.0000

Table 6.9 Analysis of organizational professionalization

Analysis of Variance

Source	D.F.	Sum of Squares	Mean Squares	F Ratio	F Prob.
Between Groups	2	76.6409	38.3204	3.2848	0.0574
Within Groups	21	244.9841	11.6659		
Total	23	321.6250			

Group	Count	Mean	Standard Deviation	Standard Error	95 Pct Conf		Int for Mean
Grp 0	8	4.0000	4.4721	1.5811	0.2612	to	7.7388
Grp 1	7	6.7143	3.3022	1.2481	3.6602	to	9.7683
Grp 2	9	8.2222	2.2236	0.7412	6.5130	to	9.9314
Total	24	6.3750	3.7395	0.7633	4.7960	to	7.9540

GROUP	MINIMUM	MAXIMUM
Grp 0	0.0000	13.0000
Grp 1	4.0000	12.0000
Grp 2	4.0000	12.0000
TOTAL	0.0000	13.0000

inversely with significance) were much smaller than in the previous analyses and suggest that these are statistically significant differences.

These patterns of variance were then explored further through Discriminant Analysis. Although the number of variables involved was too small to rely upon this approach in isolation, it provided further validation of the previous findings and was a further useful point of triangulation.

Using this approach, five variables were named (Table 6.10), and two discriminatory functions were uncovered (Tables 6.11–14). These functions are illustrated diagrammatically in Figure 6.1.

Table 6.10 Variable labels in Discriminant Analysis

Variable	Label
Dependency	DEPEN
Autonomy	CONC
Formalization	FORMALI
Specialization	SPECI
Professionalization	WORK

Table 6.11 Standardized canonical discriminant coefficient of Discriminant Analysis

	Function 1	Function 2
CONC	−0.03240	−0.03214
DEPEN	−0.033094	−0.17208
FORMALI	0.18378	0.69489
WORK	0.51479	0.71426
SPECI	0.56661	−1.03051

Table 6.12 Significance of discriminating functions

Function	Eigenvalue	% of variance	Culm. % of variance	Wilks lambda after first function removed
1	0.4294	81.7	81.7	N/A
2	0.0962	18.3	100	0.912264

Table 6.13 Within-group correlations between discriminatory variables and canonical discriminant functions

Variable	Function 1	Function 2
CONC	0.28577	0.00611
DEPEN	−0.01247	0.30229
FORMALI	0.45383	0.50938
WORK	0.82886	0.43034
SPECI	0.87369	−0.3793

Table 6.14 Canonical group functions evaluated at group means

Group	Function 1	Function 2
0 (traditional)	−0.72046	−0.22816
1 (developmental)	−0.11322	0.44889
2 (innovative)	0.72847	−0.14632

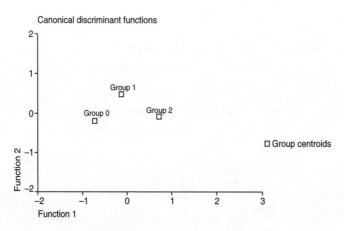

Group 0 – traditional organizations
Group 1 – developmental organizations
Group 2 – innovative organizations

Figure 6.1 Territorial map of discriminant functions and group centroids

Function 1 is clearly weighted toward the variables SPECI and WORK, whilst function 2 is weighted toward FORMALI. The eigenvalue of the first function, and the percentage of variance that it accounts for, shows function 1 to be a powerful one, with function 2 contributing only marginally to the analysis. This is confirmed by the high value of the Wilks lambda coefficient once the first function is removed.

Table 6.14 relates these discriminating functions to the *group means* of each dependent group. These show function 1 discriminating strongly between the traditional and innovative organizations and function 2 to be discriminating the developmental ones. This is illustrated diagramatically in Figure 6.1.

These discriminant functions give further support to the specialization of job roles and professionalization as being the key structural variables in understanding the innovative capacity of voluntary organizations, compared to traditional organizations. These are the two key variables in function 1, which is the more powerful of the two functions and discriminates most between innovative and traditional organizations, with developmental ones being situated between them. Function 2, which is very much weaker is less clear at identifying discriminatory variables, though formalization is the most clear-cut. However, this function adds almost nothing to our discriminating between the traditional and innovative organizations, though it does provide some support in differentiating the developmental ones. Once again, it has been seen that the developmental organizations are far more elusive to discriminate than are the other two organizational types.

The relative import of these functions can be seen when they are used as a predictive tool. Table 6.15 shows the functions to produce a significant improvement in predictive ability, compared both to the random predictions and to predictions based upon the foreknowledge of the numbers of each such type of organization – though again the predictive strength is less for the developmental organizations than for the other two types.

This pattern is confirmed further in Table 6.16. It proved quite hard to predict which organizations were likely to be developmental ones, reflecting the weakness of function 2. Moreover, when it came to the innovative and traditional organizations, the latter proved to be the easier to predict, suggesting that this group was the most cohesive and least diverse of the three organizational groupings, in terms of the structural characteristics of the organizations concerned.

Table 6.15 Predictive ability of discriminating functions

Organizational group	Number of organizations	Random probability	Prior probability	Predictability functions
Traditional	8	0.3333	0.3333	0.875
Developmental	7	0.3333	0.2917	0.429
Innovative	9	0.3333	0.375	0.556

(Overall success rate is 0.6250)

Table 6.16 Classification results of application of discriminant functions (%)

Actual group	Predicted group		
	Traditional	Developmental	Innovative
Traditional	*87.5*	12.5	0
Developmental	28.6	*42.9*	78.6
Innovative	11.1	33.3	*55.6*

Note: 'Perfect fits' are highlighted in italics

Conclusions about the organizational hypothesis

This section has explored the proposition that the innovative capacity of VNPOs is a function of their organizational structure. It has contained data from the semi-structured interviews with the chairs/paid managers of the case-study organizations (and other informants), together with two types of statistical analysis of quantitative information derived from use of the Aston Measures. Individually none of these sources is strong enough to be a sufficient test of this hypothesis. However, a high level of mutual cross-validation has been found between the three approaches. Little support has been found for the contention that the innovative capacity of VNPOs results from a distinctive pattern of dependency (or otherwise) by them upon other organizations, or from the formalization of their organizational tasks and structures, or from the autonomy of their organizational decision-making processes.

There has been rather more support apparent for the contention that the innovative capacity of VNPOs has a relationship with the specialization of their job roles and the professionalization of work processes within these organizations. The former point may at first sight seem surprising, given the emphasis of much of the organization studies literature upon the importance of multi-task job roles in encouraging innovative activity. However, this is less surprising when one examines the nature of the job specialization, with a large proportion of it being accounted for by administrative posts. It may well be that this specialization in administrative functions by some organizational members of staff either is acting as a proxy for resource availability or is significant because of the extent to which it frees up mission-related staff for more service-oriented tasks.

The importance of the professionalization of the work process also comes across, though less strongly and with less significance. Its precise contribution to the innovative capacity of VNPOs must wait upon the forthcoming analysis of the other hypotheses, to put it in its proper context. On the basis of the evidence so far, however, it is hard to disagree with the conclusion of Starbuck (1981) about the impact upon organizations of their structural features, quoted previously. Like his work, this study has suggested that 'organizational structure may have little to do with organizational behavior; structures may be organizationally superficial façades in front of behavioral processes' (p. 194).

The cultural hypothesis

This hypothesis is concerned with the impact of the internal environment of a VNPO upon its innovative capacity. On the basis of the previous literature review, it is suggested here that there are three components of the culture of an organization which need to be considered in this context. The first is size of the organization and the composition/motivation of its staff group. This is approached here by integrating material both from the postal survey and the previous material on the structural aspects of organizations, together with evidence gained from the semi-structured interviews in the case studies.

The second factor is the nature of the leadership of the organization. Here a validated attitudinal questionnaire, the *KAI Inventory*, was used to assess the attitude of organizational leaders to change. This has been discussed further above. This information was then combined also with evidence from the semi-structured interviews, and thrown into relief by discussion of the independent longitudinal case study discussed earlier.

Finally, the nature of communication within the case-study organizations is explored, in terms of the range and scope of the communication channels inside the organizations, the types of interpersonal structures within them, and their relationships with their governing bodies. This material is derived from the semi-structured interviews and is again compared to the independent longitudinal case study.

Organizational size of staff group

The postal survey provided some basic information on the size and make-up of the staff groups of the different types of organization in this study. Innovative organizations were significantly more likely to have at least one member of paid staff compared to the developmental or traditional organizations. They were also significantly smaller than developmental organizations and younger than traditional organizations.

In the previous section it was also noted that the innovative organizations had a limited tendency toward specialization and, to a lesser extent, to the professional integration of their workload. Analysis of the nature of the specialist tasks undertaken (Tables 6.4 and 6.8) showed that much of this specialist work was in relation to administrative or support work rather than service-oriented, for the innovative organizations. Table 6.9 also confirmed a tendency toward the professional bias of the innovative organizations. The traditional organizations showed an alternative weighting toward a volunteer workforce. However, the developmental organizations presented no clear pattern. A final component to this cluster of factors is the resource availability for each organization. The annual budgets for each organization are displayed in Table 6.17.

The pattern shows a higher level of resource availability for the innovative organizations than for either the developmental or the traditional ones, though the resource levels of all the organizations overall are low. Only two organizations

Table 6.17 Annual budgets of case-study organizations (1993)

Type of organization	Level of budget				
	£1000 or below	£1001–£10,000	£10,001–£100,000	£100,001+	Total
Innovative	1	4	3	1	9
Developmental	3	3	0	1	7
Traditional	6	1	1	0	8
Total	10	8	4	2	24

had budgets of over £100,000. This skewed income distribution of the voluntary sector has been confirmed elsewhere by the present author: 81 per cent of the organizations within the voluntary sector have incomes of under £100,000 and their combined weight accounts for only 11 per cent of the total income of the sector (Osborne and Hems 1995). Nonetheless, the picture is clear, within these parameters, of the innovative organizations being more resource-rich than their developmental and traditional counterparts.

What is not clear, however, is the nature of this relationship. Two possibilities are open. The first is the Cyert and March (1963) contention about the availability of resources giving organizations the capacity to innovate (slack innovation, or innovation as a result of the availability of resources). The alternative is that their innovative capacity is giving these organizations a 'competitive edge' (Porter 1985) over the other organizations and so allowing them to be more successful in resource acquisition (innovation as a spur to the acquisition of further resources). These factors will be explored in greater detail below.

With relation to their staff groups, a cluster of factors from this previous evidence does seem to differentiate innovative organizations from their developmental and traditional counterparts. Compared to the developmental organizations, they are more likely to have a paid staff group (though a smaller one than those developmental organizations with staff groups); are more likely to have specialist job roles for some staff, often in administrative/support functions; have a slight bias toward professional staff for service delivery; and are likely to have greater resource availability.

The pattern is similar for the differences between innovative and traditional organizations. The innovative organizations are significantly younger than traditional ones, are significantly more likely to employ paid and professional staff, and are markedly different in the development of specialist roles.

There does thus appear to be a cluster of staffing factors which are associated with the innovative capacity of VNPOs. These are the presence of a paid staff group, specialization of administrative and support functions, and sometimes a commitment to professionalization. However, neither the nature nor direction of this relationship is clear at this stage. Nor is it suggested that all these factors have to be present at the same time. An element of contingency is probable in this respect. As suggested earlier, the presence of a paid staff group may be a proxy for the level of resources required to support innovation – or the resource level may be a result of the innovative activity rather than a precursor of it.

Moreover, the impact of the professionalization of VNPOs is unclear. Two distinct views were expressed by the respondents in the study. On the one hand, some saw professionalization as a positive advantage, allowing the organization to be more effective in its work:

> Government funding for the scheme is helping us employ good staff . . . voluntary organizations like us are being professionalized and this is a good thing. Some others are thought old-fashioned and amateurish, though, and this is a problem for us.
>
> (Staff member of Organization 4)

> We're different from other organizations in [our federation] – we are more professional and forward-looking. They carry on doing the same things . . . we don't have much to do with them.
>
> (Manager of Organization 9)

The link that the first respondent drew between professionalization and government funding is interesting and will be returned to below. Contrary to these views, however, other innovative organizations saw their *lack* of a professional basis as the key to their innovative activity, often linking professionalism in other voluntary organizations and in the state to bureaucracy and inflexibility:

> We're committed to the needs of our people, not like the professionals in [national voluntary organization]. They just want to take over.
>
> (Chair of Organization 6)

> Our motivation is different from the social workers in the Social Services Department. They may be qualified but they are just administrators and bureaucrats. We're not like that. We're committed.
>
> (Manager of Organization 1)

The impact of the staff group does appear therefore, not to be unimportant, but to be contingent upon other factors, possibly such as funding patterns and personal beliefs. As with the other suggestive findings uncovered thus far, this point raises as many questions as it answers. These are explored in more detail below.

Organizational leadership

This was approached in two ways, by an attitudinal test and by the semi-structured interviews. First, as noted above, the KAI Inventory was used to assess the attitude of organizational leaders to organizational change. In fact, no clear pattern emerges between the three types of organizations in the case studies. One-way analysis of variance was carried out, using the ONE-WAY sub-program of SPSS.

The results are displayed in Tables 6.18 to 6.20. As can be seen from Table 6.18 there were no significant differences between the leaders in each organizational group with regard to 'organizational originality', as expressed by the group means. The 95 per cent confidence intervals overlapped strongly, whilst the variance between groups, measured by the *F* probability (0.3786) was considerably above the outer significance level of 0.05.

Table 6.18 Originality and organizational leadership

Analysis of Variance

Source	D.F.	Sum of Squares	Mean Squares	F Ratio	F Prob.
Between Groups	2	55.7754	27.8877	1.0200	0.3786
Within Groups	20	546.8333	27.3417		
Total	22	602.6087			

Group	Count	Mean	Standard Deviation	Standard Error	95 Pct Conf		Int for Mean
Grp 0	8	31.7500	3.1053	1.0979	29.1539	to	34.3461
Grp 1	6	35.6667	3.3862	1.3824	32.1131	to	39.2203
Grp 2	9	32.6667	7.2629	2.4210	27.0839	to	38.2494
Total	23	33.1304	5.2337	1.0913	30.8672	to	35.3936

GROUP	MINIMUM	MAXIMUM
Grp 0	27.0000	36.0000
Grp 1	33.0000	42.0000
Grp 2	24.0000	44.0000
TOTAL	24.0000	44.0000

Table 6.19 Weberian methodicalism and organizational leadership

Analysis of Variance

Source	D.F.	Sum of Squares	Mean Squares	F Ratio	F Prob.
Between Groups	2	171.5821	85.7911	1.5134	0.2443
Within Groups	20	1133.7222	56.6861		
Total	22	1305.3043			

Group	Count	Mean	Standard Deviation	Standard Error	95 Pct Conf		Int for Mean
Grp 0	8	31.7500	4.7734	1.6877	27.7593	to	35.7407
Grp 1	6	35.3333	8.3586	3.4124	26.5616	to	44.1050
Grp 2	9	38.1111	8.8380	2.9460	31.3176	to	44.9046
Total	23	35.1739	7.7027	1.6061	31.8430	to	38.5048

GROUP	MINIMUM	MAXIMUM
Grp 0	24.0000	36.0000
Grp 1	22.0000	46.0000
Grp 2	27.0000	49.0000
TOTAL	22.0000	49.0000

Table 6.20 Mertonian conformism and organizational leadership

Analysis of Variance

Source	D.F.	Sum of Squares	Mean Squares	F Ratio	F Prob.
Between Groups	2	145.7216	72.8608	3.4374	0.0521
Within Groups	20	423.9306	21.1965		
Total	22	569.6522			

Group	Count	Mean	Standard Deviation	Standard Error	95 Pct Conf		Int for Mean
Grp 0	8	14.1250	3.6815	1.3016	11.0472	to	17.2028
Grp 1	6	14.8333	7.0261	2.8684	7.4600	to	22.2067
Grp 2	9	19.5556	3.2059	1.0686	17.0913	to	22.0198
Total	23	16.4348	5.0885	1.0610	14.2343	to	18.6352

GROUP	MINIMUM	MAXIMUM
Grp 0	9.0000	21.0000
Grp 1	7.0000	23.0000
Grp 2	14.0000	25.0000
TOTAL	7.0000	25.0000

There is also a lack of significant relationships with regard to methodical Weberianism (Table 6.19), again with a great deal of overlap between organizational leaders from the three groups. However, interestingly, there is a pattern in relation to Mertonian conformism (Table 6.20) which borders on the significant (the *F* probability being 0.0521). However, the relationship is the inverse of what one would expect, if the attitudes of organizational leaders were pre-eminent in the development of the innovative capacity of VNPOs. It is the leaders of the *innovative* organizations which showed the greatest tendency toward conformism and those in the *traditional* ones which were the least conformist! Finally, as has frequently been the pattern in the case studies, the leaders in the developmental organizations spanned the spectrum.

This lack of a clear relationship between types of organizational leadership and innovative capacity was confirmed in the semi-structured interviews, when the leaders of the organizations were offered five descriptions of potential leadership roles, and were asked which was the most significant one for them. The five roles were:

- ensuring that their organization ran efficiently (administration);
- supervising the work of the other staff in the organization (line management);
- encouraging the staff of the organization to take on as much responsibility as possible for their own actions (delegation);
- building up and working through local networks (networking); and
- providing leadership and inspiration to the staff of the organization (leadership).

Table 6.21 Self-classification of managerial style

Organizational type	Type of managerial style				
	Administration	Line management	Delegation	Networking	Leadership
Innovative	4	0	1	2	2
Developmental	1	1	1	2	2
Traditional	5	1	1	1	0
Total	10	2	3	5	4

The first result, not suprisingly, was that most respondents said that it was quite hard to do this exercise. They often had to take on many different roles in different situations. They saw their job as being a multi-task one. When pressed about which role most closely matched their own most of the time, the respondents replied as detailed in Table 6.21. The multiplicity of roles that organizational leaders had to carry out in VNPOs was well captured by the manager of one innovative organization:

> Even if the [new] idea didn't originate with me, I would have to enthuse others, set up contacts and arrange meetings, carry out administrative functions for weeks, months or even years.
>
> (Manager of Organization 2)

No one type of leadership was clearly related to innovative capacity. This should not necessarily be seen as surprising. Because of these organizations' small size, managers in VNPOs face a range of competing demands and pressures, and are required to take on a multiplicity of tasks and roles to ensure that their organizations survive, let alone develop new services. The management role may therefore be less specialized than in the public and for-profit counterparts. There is little evidence here that a particular type of management style is a sufficiently influential factor, *by itself*, to develop the innovative capacity of VNPOs.

Organizational life

Staff in the case-study organizations, whether paid or unpaid, invariably also undertook multi-task roles. The relative lack of specialization in organizational roles, and especially in service-related ones, has been noted earlier; where there was organizational specialization this was frequently in administrative and support roles rather than in the *mission-critical* service-related roles.

The communication channels of all the organizations were also extremely short. They typically led from a local management committee either direct to the volunteers/members/staff of the organization, or to a paid manager and then to the other staff of the organization.

The role of this local management committee could be an important factor in the development of the innovative capacity of VNPOs. It was earlier identified as the formal repository for organizational authority. A possible explanation for innovative capacity could thus be that this decision-making task was perceived as a more proactive and far-sighted role in the innovative organizations than in the other types of organizations.

In fact, in most of the organizations the management committee was commonly described by staff or volunteers as 'reactive', responding to the instructions of the key officers of the committee (usually the chair, secretary, treasurer or paid manager). Even where the committee was active, it was invariably in partnership with the significant staff of the organization:

> The Management Committee always has the final say, but usually advised by the paid worker concerned.
>
> (Manager of Organization 2)

> The Management Committee takes all the action – on the basis of my suggestions.
>
> (Treasurer of Organization 23)

This raises the critical point of the role of individual agency in the release of the innovative capacity of a VNPO. A large part of the organizational literature has emphasized this role, either in terms of the role of the 'hero innovator' (Schein 1985) or of the proactive manager making things happen (Kamm 1987).

Indeed, these case studies did find that key individuals were essential to the service innovations and developments described here, and this finding has been confirmed by other, longitudinal, case-study research by the present author (Osborne 1996). However, although such forceful individuals were essential to the fulfilment of innovative capacity, it is untrue to see them as a component of the innovative organizations alone. They were also found in the developmental and traditional organizations. In these organizations they were not acting as 'hero innovators', but were carrying out other essential organizational functions, such as advocacy or fund-raising. Their various roles are specified in Table 6.22.

What comes through here is the interplay between the individual agency of a key actor in an organization and their personal beliefs, which would constrain and/or enable this activity. This interplay between individual action and personal beliefs will be explored further below, when the institutional hypothesis is examined.

Such individual agency does seem to be a *necessary* condition for the fulfilment of the innovative capacity of VNPOs. In all the innovative organizations it was possible to identify such a forceful individual. However, by itself, it is not *sufficient* to produce innovation. It may also be directed in a range of different directions, dependent upon organizational needs. The factors which might affect this direction are discussed further below. At this stage it is possible to highlight the importance of this factor but also to note that its impact upon the innovative capacity of VNPOs is contingent upon other organizational factors. The direction and impact of such individual agency is clearly dependent upon these other factors.

Table 6.22 Individual agency in the case-study organizations

Organization	Key individual roles
Innovative organizations	
1	The manager of the project was the driving force behind it, both philosophically and entrepreneurially.
2	The organizer of the volunteer centre took on a facilitator role in enabling the innovation to happen. The commitment of the project worker was essential to its success.
3	This service had been mooted for some time but only crystallized because of the commitment of a specific counsellor. The manager of the service provided crucial support.
4	The organizer of the CVS was essential in supporting this development, whilst the project worker shaped its focus and development.
5	This project was struggling to survive, despite being a 'good idea'. A key part of the problem was that the chair of the group had many other commitments and could not devote enough time to it, whilst no other member of the group was prepared to 'champion' it.
6	The chair of the organization provided philosophical commitment to the service involved and a belief in its superiority to the services offered by other organizations.
7	The manager of the organization had come from the for-profit sector and was committed to acting in a proactive and entrepreneurial way to ensure the survival of his organization.
8	The manager of the organization was also its founder, with a firm conviction in the superiority of the service that it offered to any other available services.
9	The manager and the project worker were both committed to high professional standards and to being proactive in finding ways to respond to need.
Developmental organizations	
10	This was struggling to survive. That it did was credit to the energy and determination of its manager, but this left little time to devote to some of the (intended) new directions. Other organizations it was involved with all had different agendas for the project concerned here, and no one person championed it solely. It thus struggled to survive.
11	The home was administratively well run. The role of the individual was less apparent here.
12	No one individual was important here. The organization took a collectivist view of action, on the basis of religious belief.
13	The manager of the project was committed to raising funds for the survival of the project and had little time to devote to service development. His efforts ensured organizational survival.
14	The organizer of this association was a dynamic individual but with a huge geographic area to cover. Much of his time was taken up with fulfilling his other responsibilities.
15	The organizer was a very active individual involved in a number of different voluntary organizations. His commitment was to the traditional forms of services, however, and this commitment was as influential as any equivalent other commitment to innovation.

Table 6.22 (contd.)

Organization	Key individual roles
16	The manager of this project was responsible for a multitude of administrative and organizational tasks which she performed very efficiently. She described herself as someone who had been an innovator in the past but now felt all her energy to be taken up with ensuring organizational survival in an uncertain environment.
Traditional organizations	
17	The chair of the organization was a dynamic individual with an unswerving commitment to the types of support that the organization already offered.
18	The chair of this organization provided a committed Christian basis to the service, but had no major role as an organizational change agent.
19	This group was reliant upon three committee members to organize its meetings and activities. Without them it would have collapsed.
20	Again this organization was reliant upon its chair and secretary for its existence. It would have collapsed without them.
21	The organizer of this project was a highly dedicated person who took a key role in the activities of the project. She was committed to the existing model of service through the personal experiences of her son.
22	The manager of this project had a tremendous amount of ability and energy. However, it existed in financial jeopardy and her energies were devoted to ensuring its survival.
23	The treasurer of the organization had been the imagination behind its founding. It continued to survive almost wholly because of her efforts.
24	The organizer of this project had an immense amount of energy. However, she was highly involved in the national activities of the federation of which it was a part, and so had part of her time to devote to local activity or development.

Conclusions on the cultural hypothesis

This section has examined the hypothesis that the innovative capacity of VNPOs is a function of their organizational culture, as evidenced by their staff group, leadership and internal organizational life. A number of factors have been identified which might lead to innovation in VNPOs. However, none of them, by themselves or as a group, has been shown to be influential enough to act as a convincing explanation of their innovative capacity. It does seem that the influence of these internal factors, as with the structural ones before, is contingent upon other ones, such as the external environment or the institutional framework of an organization. It is to these external factors that this study must now turn.

The environmental hypothesis

The third of the four hypotheses argues that the innovative capacity of VNPOs derives from the distinctive nature of their relationship to their environment. In fact, by reference to the earlier literature review, it is possible to dis-aggregate this hypothesis into four distinctive 'sub-hypotheses'. The first is that the key environmental stimulus is the relationship of the organization to its service users, or its 'end-users'. The second is that it is a function of the strategic approach of, and relationship to, its environment taken by the organization. The third is the importance of the inter-organizational field and of inter-organizational communication in stimulating the innovative capacity of VNPOs. Finally, the fourth sub-hypothesis concerns the impact of the external funders of VNPOs upon their innovative capacity. Each of these sub-hypotheses will be reviewed in turn.

The relationship of VNPOs to their service users

This was explored in the semi-structured interviews with the respondents in the case studies, both through three specific question areas on this issue and by the use of open-ended questions. Little variation between the three case studies was found in the relationship of the organizations to their service users. All expressed a clear user-orientation. The innovative organizations were perhaps more inclined to provide user-defined, rather than solely standardized services, but the contrast was one of shade rather than sharpness (Table 6.23).

Table 6.23 Organizational relationships to their service users

(a) Type of services provided to users

Type of organization	Standard services	User-defined	Total
Innovative	3	6	9
Developmental	2	5	7
Traditional	4	4	8
Total	9	15	24

(b) Specified 'end-user' of services

Type of organization	Services to at least some individual users	Services to other organizations only	Total
Innovative	9	0	9
Developmental	7	0	7
Traditional	8	0	8
Total	24	0	24

(c) Accessibility of service to users

Type of organization	User can refer themselves	Entry through another organization only	Total
Innovative	7	2	9
Developmental	6	1	7
Traditional	7	1	8
Total	20	4	24

This pattern was confirmed in the open questions:

> Our Association shapes what it offers to members, responding to individual needs at a particular time.
>
> (Chair of traditional Organization 23)

> We're totally responsive to our members and evaluated by our members . . . we provide what people who attend want.
>
> (Manager of developmental Organization 13)

> [The organization] offers help to all bereaved people, whatever their age, sex, nationality or belief . . . Each person is treated as an individual – bereavement has no rules, and what might work for one person is not necessarily right for another . . . During 1990 much discussion took place with the Management Committee about the ever growing waiting lists . . . Twenty people who had requested the service were still waiting for contact from us and the great number was felt to be unacceptable.
>
> (Case worker of innovative Organization 9)

Whilst the general impression of VNPOs as being responsive to their clients was confirmed, therefore, no pattern was apparent to suggest that the innovative organizations had an especial relationship here.

The strategic approach of the organization to its environment

Miles and Snow (1978; see also Astley and Van de Ven 1983) in their seminal work analysed the extent to which organizations have a choice in the way that they interact with their environments. Organizational fields do not act mono-lithically, they argued; rather each organization in that field seeks its own fate. They developed four *gestalts* by which to classify the specific approach of an organization to its environment, and these were used to classify the approaches of the organizations in this study. The gestalts and overall pattern are summarized in Table 6.24, whilst the individual responses are also summarized in Table 6.25.

The differing strategic approaches of the innovative and developmental VNPOs, compared to the traditional ones, is striking. The latter were almost entirely committed to the *defensive* gestalt, of maintaining a commitment to the 'status quo' of their services, and were deeply suspicious of external attempts to change this. They viewed the changing environment with dismay.

As has been the pattern previously, the developmental organizations showed no distinct overall pattern, but presented a mixture of responses to their social environment. By contrast, the innovative organizations were positive and proactive in their strategic approach. In some cases this was exhibited by an embracing of a dynamic approach to their environment as a whole, whilst in others it was more a

Table 6.24 The Miles and Snow gestalts and their pattern in this study

Gestalt	Key features	Types of organization		
		Innovative	Developmental	Traditional
Defender	Limited product/service line, with an emphasis on stability and efficiency	0	2	7
Prospector	Broad/changing product and service line with a dynamic approach to its environment	4	0	0
Analyser	Has a standard range of products/services, but also searches for new ones	5	3	1
Reactor	Makes inconsistent choices; a 'non-strategy'	0	2	0

Table 6.25 Summary of organizational strategies

(a) Innovative organizations

Prospectors	*Organization 1* had a range of services that it offered to its user group and was actively seeking new ways in which to respond to need and to secure its market niche.
	Organization 4 was based within a CVS which offered a broad range of social care services, and which regularly reviewed the environment for unmet needs which required attention.
	Organization 7 had explicitly changed its function to take advantage of funding opportunities, and was working on a range of issues in the community care field.
	Organization 8 had developed a range of day occupation services for adults with learning disabilities, and was constantly seeking new ways in which to develop its services.
Analysers	*Organization 2* provided a standard range of volunteer opportunities, but was always open to discussing new ways to work/areas to work in.
	Organization 3 provided traditional 'couples' counselling for those with a relationship problem, but also was willing to explore new forms of service delivery.
	Organization 5 provided a standard toy library for children with special needs, but also was prepared to consider new opportunities for it to develop different services.
	Organization 6 provided a core day service for people with a hearing impairment, but was also willing to consider how to develop this service further in new areas.
	Organization 9 provided traditional individual bereavement counselling, but also was developing new approaches to counselling to respond to identified unmet need.

(b) Developmental organizations

Defenders	*Organization 10* was only just surviving as a CVS, and could provide only a bare minimum and limited range of standard CVS services.
	Organization 11 was a traditional residential home for elderly people with an emphasis on stability and efficiency. The development reported here was very much an improvement to the existing service paradigm.

Table 6.25 (contd.)

Analysers	*Organization 12* provided a core second-hand furniture service for deprived families, but was prepared to explore new ways in which it could help its chosen client group.
	Organization 14 was a pre-school play-group association which carried out the core range of services and support provided by such associations, but it was also exploring new types of support to offer where money was available.
	Organization 16 was a toy library providing a standard range of toy lending services, but it was also diversifying into other ways to support families and parents in need.
Reactors	*Organization 13* provided a mix of standard and user-defined day services, but with no apparent guiding principles. It reacted to immediate stimuli.
	Organization 15 provided support groups for carers of adults with special needs, but with no discernible pattern. The main factor appeared to be the 'ad hoc' decisions of the group co-ordinator at any one time.

(c) Traditional organizations

Defenders	*Organization 17* was a volunteer centre committed to providing volunteer drivers alone – which it did very effectively. It was suspicious of external attempts to change this role.
	Organization 18 was a small counselling organization which stuck rigidly to its traditional model of individual counselling, despite declining numbers. It found it hard to adopt to a changing environment.
	Organization 19 was a self-help group which ran a standard range of social activities, but with no willingness to try new approaches ('we know what we like'), even though it was declining in numbers.
	Organization 20 was another self-help group which was proud of its range of activities, but did not deviate from them – even when encouraged to do so by external agents.
	Organization 21 was an organization which provided a standard range of social support activities for its established clientele with a learning disability.
	Organization 22 was an organization which provided social support to elderly people. It had a standard set of services which it provided very well.
	Organization 24 was a large counselling organization for couples with relationship problems. It relied upon a standard range of traditional one-to-one counselling activities.
Analyser	*Organization 23* provided regular social activities for its members, but it also explored different ways in which to offer this service, though within the traditional paradigm of the organization.

case of maintaining a core of standard services, but with a willingness to explore alternative models of service delivery.

This pattern was further confirmed by the responses of these organizations to a question about their overall service pattern (Table 6.26). Whilst the traditional organizations were largely committed to maintaining their existing level of services, there was a similar commitment to increasing their range of services from almost all of the innovative organizations.

The difference in approaches was graphically illustrated in short passages from two of the open-ended interviews:

Table 6.26 Direction of service change pattern

Type of organization	Decreasing the overall range of services	Maintaining the overall range of services (including substitution)	Increasing the overall range of services
Innovative	0	2	7
Developmental	0	4	4
Traditional	0	7	1

We provide transport here – it's what we do. Some other [organizations] have tried to get us to change, to say that people need different things now, but it's what we do.

(Driver for Organization 17, a traditional one)

Networking is very important for us. It's the way that we find out what is going on and what's needed. How else could we do it?

(Organizer of Organization 4, an innovative one)

Clearly the innovative organizations were taking a far more proactive role in their changing environments and seeking ways to develop in these environments. As was noted previously, in the review of the organization studies literature, organizations which are innovators have been found to view change as an opportunity, whilst the more traditional ones see it as a threat. This was undoubtedly the case here.

The inter-organizational field

The initial descriptive accounts of their environments by informants suggested that the innovative VNPOs operated in far more complex social environments, in terms of their organizational interactions, than did the traditional organizations. There were two ways to look at this phenomenon: in terms of environmental complexity and of organizational linkages.

The environmental complexity of the case-study organizations was evaluated by discussion with the organizational leaders about the key inter-organizational relationships which they needed to maintain, in order to achieve 'mission-critical' goals. *Simple environments* were defined as those where an organization had a minimal need to interact, or only at a very superficial level (such as simply taking telephone referrals from other organizations for volunteer drivers, as in the case of Organization 17). *Medium environments* were those where organizations needed to interact at a significant level with one other organization, in order to achieve their 'mission-critical' goals. Finally, *complex environments* were those where organizations needed to interact with at least two, and often more, organizations in order to achieve these goals.

The pattern in this analysis showed significant differences in the organizational environments (Table 6.27). The innovative organizations inhabited far more complex organizational environments than the traditional ones, and with once again no

Table 6.27 Environmental complexity of case-study organizations

Type of organization	Complexity			
	Single	Medium	Complex	Total
Innovative	0	4	5	9
Developmental	1	4	2	7
Non-innovative	6	2	0	8
Total	7	10	7	24

clear pattern for the developmental organizations. The difference in perspective is graphically illustrated by two brief quotes from respondents. When discussing their contacts with other organizations, a member of one of the traditional organizations dismissed the importance of working with other organizations in this wider organizational environment:

> No, we don't work with other organizations – no other groups offer what we do.
>
> (Member of Organization 20)

Conversely, the organizer of one of the innovator organizations saw such relationships as essential to their work:

> I used to work with these people [as a teacher]. I know them and they can talk to me about their needs. I also know the people in the [statutory] agencies. We work together.
>
> (Organizer of Organization 8)

A similar picture emerged when the case-study organizations were asked to describe how they related to their wider environment (Table 6.28). Again, three alternatives were identified: *isolation*, where there was a minimal linkage between the organization and its environment; *direct*, where the linkage was directly from the organization to its wider environment; and *network*, where the linkages were complex and involved the conscious negotiation of inter-organizational relationships. The pattern of these linkages in Table 6.28 confirms those from the previous tables.

Table 6.28 Organizational linkages to their environments

Type of organization	Types of linkage			
	Isolation	Direct	Network	Total
Innovative	0	4	5	9
Developmental	0	4	3	7
Traditional	5	3	0	8
Total	5	11	8	24

Again, the traditional organizations emphasized their isolation from the wider environment, whilst the innovators emphasized their linkages, and a majority of these talked of the importance of their networks of inter-organizational relationships as being essential to achieving their organizational goals.

Examples of typical networks for the traditional and the innovative VNPOs are shown in Figures 6.2 and 6.3 The traditional organizations display simple, rather linear, networks – if indeed they can be called such. These typically involved the receipt of referrals, and sometimes funding, from (usually) a statutory agency, and the provision of services to its identified clients. As with Organization 24, the SSD did sometimes have a further link through a representative on the management committee – though (as was found in this case), they rarely attended meetings.

The networks of the innovators are considerably more complex, though. Not only do the organizations rely upon the statutory ones for referrals and funding, but they saw these as an important source of information about unmet or newly identified needs and about gaps in existing services, as the above quotations suggest.

The links with the local community were similarly far more proactive for the innovative organizations (with local churches being an important source of linkages for many VNPOs, though not all). The organizations themselves often sat upon inter-agency forums and planning groups, and saw these as an important part of their work, necessary to achieving their mission-critical goals. The organizations in the innovative case study cited three reasons for the importance of these. They allowed them to contribute to the shaping of statutory services, to provide input about unmet needs (and to learn from others), and to build potential alliances with other agencies or organizations about future developments.

Interesting relief upon the issue of these networks was given by one of the developmental organizations. In many respects, this was similar to its innovator counterparts, in that it saw network activity as a key role for itself and actively sought to create such inter-organizational linkages in order to develop new services. However, this organization (a CVS) was a comparatively new one, only just surviving, and had no credence with other organizations in its locality as a significant actor. This lack of network linkages thus severely limited its ability to fulfil its innovative potential.

> I have very little time. I need to develop more contacts locally – they are important for my work, but all my effort is taken up with producing the newsletter. It's very frustrating.
>
> (Organizer of Organization 10)

> The CVS is under-resourced. It's not very effective . . . [it] doesn't lack goodwill but what it does lack is the resources and contacts to carry the words into action.
>
> (Manager of a major established local voluntary agency involved in working with Organization 10)

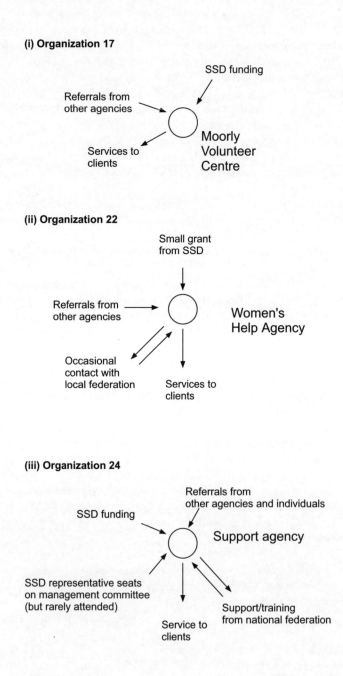

Figure 6.2 Examples of network patterns of traditional organizations

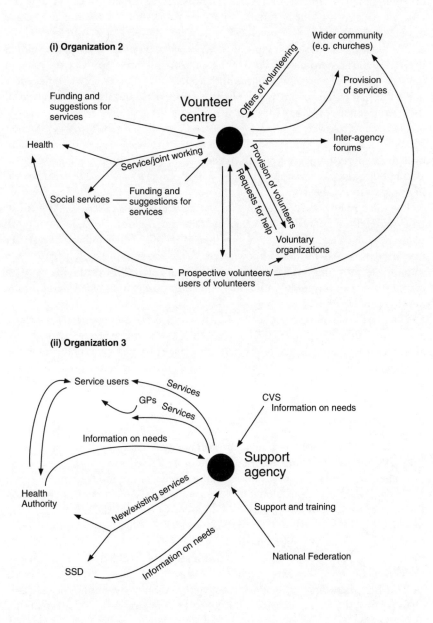

(i) Organization 2

Wider community
(e.g. churches)

Funding and
suggestions for
services

Vounteer
centre

Offers of volunteering

Provision
of services

Health

Service/joint working

Inter-agency
forums

Social services

Funding and
suggestions for
services

Provision of volunteers

Requests for help

Voluntary
organizations

Prospective volunteers/
users of volunteers

(ii) Organization 3

Service users

Services

GPs

Services

CVS
Information on needs

Information on needs

Support
agency

Health
Authority

New/existing services

Support and training

SSD

Information on needs

National Federation

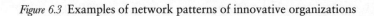

Figure 6.3 Examples of network patterns of innovative organizations

These inter-organizational networks identified above performed a number of different functions for the innovative organizations. In our discussions, seven different roles were uncovered that these networks played for the innovative organizations in these case studies.

The first of these was *to provide a general service context*. For example, organization 8 derived its purpose from the failure of the statutory services to provide meaningful day occupation services for adults with learning disability. It was therefore now filling this gap as part of a network of service providers, and within the context of the overall service provision for such adults.

The second role was *to provide legitimization for the work of the organization*. A good example of this was Organization 7. This was explicitly sponsored by the SSD to provide support to other VNPOs in the development of community care services. Without these links it certainly would not have been seen as a credible organization in its organizational field.

The third role was *to provide sources of ideas for new service developments*. At its most basic this could simply be by the exchange of demographic information, but more often it involved agencies working together to identify either important areas of new needs or areas of unmet known needs ('service gaps'). The linkages to the statutory agencies played a key role with Organization 2 in identifying areas of unmet need both for adults with a mental health problem and for elderly people needing practical support.

The fourth role of these network contacts was *to facilitate the inter-agency planning of new services*, often co-ordinated by the VNPO. A good example of this was the multi-agency planning team which developed the service provided by Organization 4.

The fifth role was *to help in resource acquisition*, by providing a conduit for information about funding sources to be disseminated and for funding linkages to be made. This was the case with Organization 8.

The sixth role was *to act as a key factor in the actual implementation of an innovation*. The sexual counselling service of Organization 3 was initially reliant upon the existing network of contacts of this organization with the health authority, and particularly with GPs, for disseminating information about its service and for providing referrals. These were an essential precursor to the success of this innovation.

Finally, the inter-organizational networks could provide an important role in *the sustenance of an innovation*. A negative example of where this did not happen was provided earlier by Organization 10. A more positive example was Organization 2, where multi-agency commitment to the new service was a key to its survival and success. These organizational roles are summarized in Table 6.29, in relation to each of the organizations explored in the cross-sectional case study of innovation.

A further interesting piece of negative confirmation of the importance of these inter-organizational relationships and networks was provided by the toy library (Organization 5). This organization was failing, largely because its 'traditional' service, a toy library for *children* with special needs, had been established outside of the existing network of service providers, and without the legitimizing support of the SSD (which went on to found its own similar resource). Because of this the organization was in danger of extinction. In an attempt to prevent this happening,

Table 6.29 Roles performed by the inter-organizational networks in the case-study organizations

Organization	Function						
	Service context	Legitimacy	Sources of new ideas (new needs/ service gaps)	Service planning	Resource acquisition	Implementation	Sustenance
1	X	X			X		X
2	X		X	X	X	X	X
3			X		X	X	
4	X		X	X	X	X	X
5	X						
6	X		X		X		
7	X	X	X	X	X	X	X
8	X	X			X	X	X
9					X	X	X

the organization tried to diversify its activity to provide leisure support for *adults* with special needs. Once again, however, it was not properly linked into the existing service delivery network. This meant that it lacked legitimization with these pre-existing service providers (it was seen as a child-care organization inappropriately trying to work with adults – which is precisely what it was); and was not clear on the actually existing unmet needs. Consequently, it did not have the contacts to help with the implementation of its innovation or with its sustenance. In a very real sense, it was the lack of a network of inter-agency connections that led to the failure of this innovation, and possibly of the organization itself.

Finally, it is important to emphasize that these networks derived their importance from being the *outcomes* of other activity, rather than their production being an activity in its own right. Such networks were the representation of ongoing successful working relationships and derived much of their import from this. It is marked that where 'networking' was pursued as an activity in its own right it was noticeably less successful, both for the organizations and innovations concerned (as was the case with Organization 10, above). It is the content of these networks that is significant, not their form (this point has been explored further in other work involving the present author; see PSMRC 1991 and Osborne and Tricker 1994).

In conclusion, this section has found the inter- organizational fields of VNPOs to be a key factor in their innovative capacity. They can provide the service context and legitimization of a service, the means through which needs are identified and new services planned, and the medium for their implementation and sustenance. In this respect they confirm the work of Camagni (1991a) upon the importance of such networks. To use his words, they provide the 'innovative milieu' for the growth of service innovations.

However, significantly, what has been lacking from the above discussion of the environments of innovative VNPOs is the concept of the *competitive* environment. As discussed previously in the literature, a key component of the model of innovation in the organization studies literature and developed from the study of for-profit organizations, has been the explicit link between competition, innovation and profitability (see, in particular, Porter 1985 and Nelson 1993, above). According to Porter, innovation 'is important to competitive advantage in all industries, holding the key in some' (p. 42).

In this model, a competitive environment provides the spur to innovation and defines the direction and nature of any innovative developments. These developments, in turn, give the organization a 'competitive advantage' through which to gain a price and/or market-share advantage over its competitors.

In this study both the competitive environment and the concept of a competitive advantage have been absent. One has to query, therefore, what is the driving force behind the innovative capacity of VNPOs in a non-profit environment.

The environmental factors discussed here do indeed appear to have provided the 'milieu' within and through which VNPOs can fulfil their innovative capacity, but it does not seem to have provided the stimulus, as the for-profit model above would argue. In these circumstances, it is therefore necessary to ask some further questions about why VNPOs should act in an innovative manner.

These questions do have their parallel elsewhere in organization theory. Huxham (1993; Huxham and Vangen 1996), as discussed above, has explored why VNPOs should collaborate in the absence of the spur of competition to do so (which is again the driving force for collaboration with for-profit organizations), and has produced a model of *collaborative capability*. This study must ask similar questions if it is to produce a useful model of *innovative capacity*. The beginning of this search starts below, with the exploration of the funding environments of the case-study organizations.

The funding patterns of VNPOs

An initial estimate of the importance of this factor was seen in Chapter 5. No substantial difference was found in the funding patterns of the innovative and developmental VNPOs (Table 5.11). However, there was such a difference in the funding patterns of the innovative and traditional VNPOs (Table 5.16). On the one hand, the traditional organizations were significantly more likely to be dependent upon voluntary income or fees. On the other hand, the innovators comprised over 70 per cent of those organizations in this study citing governmental funding as their major source of finance. This pattern was also confirmed in the Discriminant Analysis, where the major source of funding was a key component of the discriminating function between innovative and traditional organizations.

The case studies provided further evidence and validation of this pattern, with the innovative organizations weighted toward governmental funding as either the major or secondary source of income and the traditional organizations weighted toward voluntary income. Few were reliant upon fees. The developmental organizations continued to present a mixed picture (Table 6.30).

Given this picture of the importance of governmental funding to the innovative organizations, one might hypothesize that the quest for governmental funding was

Table 6.30 Funding patterns of case-study organizations

(a) Innovative organizations

Status	Source of funding			
	Governmental	Voluntary	Fees	None
Major source	5	3	1	0
Secondary source	3	3	1	2

(b) Developmental organizations

Status	Source of funding			
	Governmental	Voluntary	Fees	None
Major source	5	1	1	0
Secondary source	2	4	1	0

(c) Traditional organizations

Status	Source of funding			
	Governmental	Voluntary	Fees	None
Major source	2	6	0	0
Secondary source	0	6	0	2

analogous to the competitive environment of the for-profit organizations in the organization studies literature. In terms of being in competition with other organizations for government funding, however, this was not the case. None of the innovative case-study organizations was in direct competition with other organizations for funds. Even where contractual income was involved, this was on the basis of negotiated rather than competitive tendering.

Moreover, only one of the organizations was in indirect competition with other VNPOs, in the sense that it was reliant upon grant-aid and so was one of a number of organizations seeking such support, which was itself cash-limited. However, the key relationship here was perceived by that organization to be between the local authority and itself, rather than with other potential competitors for the 'pot' of grant-aid.

A further complication to this funding relationship was unearthed when the role of the local authority within each area was explored further. Although each of these authorities was responding to the development of the mixed economy of welfare and was taking up the role of the enabler and co-ordinator of the social-care market, each was doing so in a different way. Elsewhere (Osborne 1997), this author has explored these modes of service co-ordination, using the *ideal types*, in the Weberian sense, of market, hierarchy and clan. It is apparent from this further analysis that local authorities are not acting in one universal way to co-ordinate service delivery, and in particular are not relying solely (or at all, sometimes) upon the market/price mechanism. This was apparent in only one locality in the study (Bellebury). Moreover, even here, it was in a highly imperfect form. Apart from competition for the mainstream forms of service delivery (such as residential care for elderly people), the market rarely comprised more than one, or at most two, potential service providers. Hardly a market at all.

This is an important insight into such funding relationships and deserves further exploration. What is important here is that, for most service areas involving innovation, direct competition between rival VNPOs was not a feature. In Southshire, hierarchical committees were used to co-ordinate need and resources, and with service providers as a part of this structure. In Midwell, the term 'clan' was used to identify those organizations which were a part of the service provision system and those which were not, on the basis of shared normative values. In Bellebury, the market mechanism did indeed provide a formal framework for negotiation (in the sense of service specifications and tenders, and of contractual award and evaluation). However, even here, the process involved negotiated, and not competitive, tendering.

Discussion with the Commissioning Officer for the SSD covering Bellebury revealed this interaction between rhetoric and reality. The key policy document covering its work with VNPOs stated that its aim was 'to develop a mixed economy of care which will increase choice for consumers and improve the quality of services *through increased competition*' [my emphasis]. However, the relationship portrayed by the Commissioning Officer was different:

> [We] want to buy services from outside and our policy is to support the voluntary sector. It provides something that the Social Service Department cannot do – people don't want Social Services, they want voluntary organizations... For the private sector we look at unit costs, but it's different with voluntary organizations. They bring us their costs and ask for funding and then we negotiate with them... It's a co-operative partnership.

Clearly then, if the funding source of VNPOs is an important factor in their innovative capacity, it is not in the anticipated sense of providing a surrogate market to stimulate innovation through competition. It is operating in more sophisticated ways. These are explored further below.

Conclusions

This section has reviewed the case-study evidence about the importance of the external environment in stimulating the innovative capacity of VNPOs. Little was found to differentiate the relationships of innovative organizations toward their end-users. However, important environmental factors were uncovered, not least in the strategic relationship of innovative organizations to their environment compared to traditional ones, the complexity of their environments, and the key sources of funding. It has been suggested that this environment provides the *milieu* in which the innovative potential of VNPOs can be realized, but not because of the competitive nature of this environment. Rather it concerns the extent to which these organizations are prepared or able to be open to this milieu in achieving their mission-critical goals. To borrow an image from systems theory, it concerns the extent to which voluntary organizations are *open* rather than *closed* systems, reliant upon interaction with their environments in order to achieve their 'mission-critical' goals, and so open to influence from this environment (Scott 1992).

Still, though, this milieu does not provide a convincing explanation, by itself, of why certain VNPOs evinced an innovative capacity and others did not. Moreover, there has been so far in this study a lack of any real pattern to explain the position of the developmental organizations in all this. In an attempt to make some sense of this, the final sections of this chapter will explore this issue further in relation to the institutional hypothesis, and discuss the role of process in the construction of the innovative capacity of VNPOs.

The institutional hypothesis

This hypothesis concerns the impact of institutional forces upon both the commission and the interpretation of action within an organizational field. The nature of such institutional analysis was discussed earlier. On the one hand this concerns the often covert *rules of the game* which can enable and/or constrain the actions of organizations within their organizational field. On the other hand it concerns the way that action is constructed and interpreted by the key stakeholders within such an organizational field.

Within the field of non-profit studies, as noted previously, Pifer (1967, 1975) prefigured this argument in his development of the concept of the *quango*, as a VNPO whose direction is set (and changed) by the priorities of government rather than its own mission. Carter (1974) has argued also for the importance of innovation as social construct for VNPO, as a way of establishing their hegemony over governmental organizations.

However, such arguments were wholly empirical ones, with little reference to theory. At the other extreme of the spectrum has been the work of key writers within the organization studies literature. Their contribution, by contrast, has been almost wholly theoretical, with little empirical testing. The pre-eminent contribution has been that of DiMaggio and Powell (1988) who have argued for institutional forces as a key feature of *organizational isomorphism* for VNPOs; as they became part of organizational fields dominated by the more powerful (and resource-rich) governmental organizations, so their work and direction became inevitably constructed by these powerful organizations. Singh *et al.* (1991) and Tucker *et al.* (1992) have developed this argument in relation to VNPOs, and have contended that they are especially vulnerable to such institutional forces. This literature has been discussed in more detail previously, in the section of Chapter 2 upon organization theory.

As that previous discussion noted, whilst the organization studies literature has developed this institutional argument in relation to VNPOs in general, it has not developed it in the specific case of innovation. That will be attempted here.

Evidence for the examination of this hypothesis will be drawn from the structured and semi-structured interviews held with the staff and beneficiaries of the case-study organizations, as well as with other key informants at national and local level. Inevitably, institutional arguments involve a concentration upon values and upon processual issues. Thus, a qualitative approach is highly appropriate (Bryman, 1988). Issues of reliability and validity have been approached by using both data triangulation (multiple respondents for each organization, and archival or documentary sources where appropriate), as well as a number of feedback loops, both to confirm the accuracy of information being obtained and to test out the developing argument. The former involved both verbal feedback during interviews, and the circulation of written summary records to the case-study organizations to check their accuracy. The latter involved group feedback meetings in each locality.

The core of the institutional argument relates to the interrelationship between the environmental field that an organization operates in and the impact of this upon the formal structure and actions of an organization. In many respects this is the corollary of the argument of Starbuck (1981), previously highlighted in the discussion of the structural hypothesis. It is well summarized by DiMaggio and Powell (1991):

> The new institutionalism locates irrationality in the formal structure itself, attributing the diffusion of certain departments and operating procedures to inter-organizational influences, conformity, and the pervasiveness of cultural accounts, rather than to the functions they are intended to perform.
>
> (p. 13)

Lane (1993) goes on to define institutions as

> the humanly created constructs in the interaction between individuals. They are the rules and norms resulting in formal and informal rights and obligations which facilitate exchange by allowing people to form stable and fairly reliable expectations about the actions of others.
>
> (p. 166)

The central question of such analyses is upon the adaptive processes through which organizations survive, and the internal and external pressures which produce these processes.

The concern here is to explore the role of such institutional pressures within the cross-sectional case studies of this research, using this model of Lane. He argues that one must fulfil three conditions in order to build an institutional argument successfully: specify the key institutional forces involved, detail how they affect decision making, and provide an explanation for their force.

The institutional hypothesis: what are the institutions?

The first step in the approach of Lane (1993) to institutional analysis was to uncover the institutions themselves. These were explored on three levels in the present study. These are the *meta-environmental* level, concerned with the overall societal framework for service delivery within the PSS sector; the *macro-environmental* level, concerned with the forces operating within the organizational field of an organization; and the *micro-level*, concerned with forces operating within particular VNPOs.

Meta-environmental level factors

At the most general level these comprise the societal context of the PSS and the societal changes that impact upon the provision of the PSS. These include in particular the assumptions built into national legislation about VNPOs, and the actual impact of this legislation.

Undoubtedly the most significant such meta-environmental factor has been the ideological sea-change away from the welfare state consensus of the 1960s and 1970s, with its assumption of governmental hegemony in service planning and delivery, and toward the *mixed economy of care* (Wistow *et al.* 1994, 1996), as discussed previously. The reasons for this sea-change are complex and have been well analysed previously (Mischra 1984; Ascher 1987) and need not concern us here. What is relevant here is that it represented a major shift in the institutional paradigm, both for the PSS and for VNPOs.

As noted in Chapter 1, the paradigmatic shift for local government has been away from the concept of the unitary planning and provision of public services to local communities and toward that of the *enabling state* (Rao 1991). For the PSS this shift was embodied in two key documents of the late 1980s, the Griffiths Report and the Department of Health White Paper, *Caring for People*. These promoted the idea of SSDs as

> designers, organizers and purchasers of non-health care services and not primarily as direct providers, making the maximum possible use of voluntary and private sector bodies to widen consumer choice, *stimulate innovation* and encourage efficiency. [my emphasis]
>
> (Griffiths 1988, para. 1.3.4)

The White Paper went further in detailing the benefits that the then government considered as arising from such a shift:

> Stimulating the development of non-statutory service providers will result in a range of benefits for the consumer, in particular: a wider range and choice of services; *services which meet individual needs in a more flexible and innovative way*... and a more cost-effective service. [my emphasis]
>
> (Department of Health 1989, para. 3.4.3)

Wistow *et al.* (1994) are quite specific about the extent of the paradigmatic shift that this involved, in terms of both local government in general and the PSS in particular. They argue that whilst the Griffiths Report could be seen to look back to and to be written within the tradition of community development, as epitomized by Abrams *et al.* (1989), the White Paper marked

> *a major break with previous policies for the personal social services*... The emphasis shifted from mobilizing informal and community resources to developing a social care market ... Its inevitable consequence was that market development and market management would become key responsibilities for social services departments. Not only were these responsibilities for which, as indicated above, departments had little or no relevant experience but, as many subsequently argued, they were incompatible with the (previous) nature and value base of social care. In studying the development and management of the mixed economy we are, therefore, not only exploring how social services departments defined and understood new roles, but also how they began to prepare for a process of substantial change in their organizational culture. [my emphasis]
>
> (Wistow *et al.* 1994, p. 22)

If this was the general context of the changing institutional framework for the PSS, it had a particular import for the role of VNPOs in the PSS. From being a marginal and optional element of the social care sector, in terms of service provision, they became increasingly expected to provide a whole range of mainstream social care services. This expectation was enshrined within the National Health Service and Community Care Act 1990 (hereafter called the NHSCC Act). However, in taking on this role VNPOs were not expected to provide more choice simply by dint of their plurality, compared to the perceptions of monolithic local government. They were further expected to bring new qualities to the provision of the PSS. One such quality was their capacity for innovation. This perception was confirmed by a Conservative government minister in the 1992 general election campaign, in his definition of the desirable characteristics of VNPOs for the provision of public services: 'The [voluntary] sector has particular qualities which enable it to show more pioneering zeal, to operate more flexibly, and to work very often nearer to real and cost effective objectives' (NCVO 1991, p. 1). Indeed, as discussed previously, such perceptions of the innovative capacity of VNPOs were embedded in the founding of the welfare state, and the later development of Social Services Departments in 1970 (Beveridge 1948; Ministry of Health 1959).

To an extent, these assumptions were of less weight to VNPOs at that time, because governmental funding was a less significant source of income to those organizations. However, as Osborne and Hems (1995) have shown, the importance of governmental funding has increased dramatically for these organizations over the last fifteen years. As the importance of this funding has increased, so similarly has the importance, and impact, of the assumptions underlying it.

The assumption of the innovative capacity of VNPOs is highly significant in this policy context. *Innovation* itself was increasingly being seen as a policy goal in the PSS in its own right. The King's Fund Institute (1987), for example, argued for the centrality of innovation to community care policies, though with never quite defining what was meant by this. In more polemical vein, Smale and Tuson

(1990) at the National Institute of Social Work argued that innovation should become 'almost synonymous with social work. (Good) practice is the promotion of innovation and change, sometimes through the way resources are distributed and delivered, and sometimes through the way people relate to each other and manage problems' (p. 158).

As the concept of the mixed economy of care developed, so did the importance of the perceived innovative capacity of VNPOs. The Home Office *efficiency scrutiny* of governmental funding of VNPOs (1990) asserted strongly that government should continue to fund them (albeit in a more focused way), in part because they continued to be in the 'forefront' of developing new service approaches and of meeting new needs. Similar assertions were also made by both the Conservative and Labour parties in the run-up to the 1992 general election (NCVO 1991; Labour Party 1990).

Finally, it is important to recognize that VNPOs have not themselves been passive vessels in these institutional seas. As was highlighted in the earlier discussion of institutional analysis, they are constrained by them, but are also active in their construction. Gladstone (1979) was a forceful advocate upon behalf of the sector of the hegemony of VNPOs over the state, whilst the Wolfenden Committee (1978) argued hard for innovation as being a key contribution of VNPOs to society. The major intermediary organizations representing the sector have continued also to assert the importance of this archetypal characteristic (for example, Burridge 1990).

In summary, the last decade has seen the coming together of two streams of thought to create a new societal paradigm for the work of VNPOs in the PSS. These have been the development of the concept of the mixed economy of care and the ongoing theme of the innovative capacity of VNPOs.

The significance of this confluence should not be underestimated. As was noted earlier, the for-profit literature possesses an inherent assumption of the links between innovation and success in a market economy. By linking the provision of the PSS to a market framework this suggested a new and central role for VNPOs in this emerging paradigm. To understand the influence of this upon the actual management and work of VNPOs, it is necessary to move below this meta-level of analysis, to the macro- and micro-levels.

Macro-environmental level factors

The macro-level institutional factors are those which are actively part of the organizational field of an organization in its own locality. As noted earlier, Singh *et al.* (1991) and Tucker *et al.* (1992) have both emphasized the pre-eminent influence that funders can have upon VNPOs in these environments, because they can define both the criteria for receipt of funding and also those for the evaluation of subsequent performance. Precisely because of the meta-level emphasis, above, of the importance of innovation in social care and of the perceived innovative capacity of VNPOs, such expectations were frequently incorporated into the macro-level institutional pressures, from both national and local funders.

At a national level, the Department of Health planted innovation firmly as a ground-rule into its award of grants to VNPOs, under Section 64 of the Health Services and Public Health Act 1968 ('Section 64 grants'). Having completed the identifying information upon your organization, the first section of the application form for a project grant under this scheme states that, for a project to be considered, 'It *must* be innovatory and for a local project of national significance' [my emphasis]. This is amplified in the Guidance Notes for completion of the application form:

> A national project must be clearly designed by a national voluntary organiza-
> tion to further the Department's policy objectives by testing an innovatory idea
> or by helping to develop a particular pattern of service . . . A general scheme
> grant towards an innovatory local project may *exceptionally* be made by the
> Department in the following circumstances:
> (a) pump-priming to meet exceptionally high initial costs (b) where a project
> spans a number of local or health authorities . . . (c) where an innovatory local
> experiment has potential national significance . . . (d) where the Department
> on its own initiative wishes to test certain proposals for client care.

Similar conditions are found also in the application procedures of the Inner City Partnership (ICP) scheme of the Department of the Environment.

Latterly, the Department of Health has also adopted the 'outcome funding' model (Williams and Webb 1992) of the Rensselaerville Institute as an explicit way through which to promote innovation, and other policy goals, in the PSS. This was so, for example, in relation to the *Drugs and Alcohol Specific Grant, 1994–95* (it also retained the consultancy group, the *Innovation Group*, through which to administer the scheme).

A similar commitment to innovation as a key criterion for funding voluntary activity was found in two national charitable foundations interviewed as part of this study. Both had explicit criteria about innovation in their funding procedures, which prescribed what sorts of projects they were willing to fund.

This picture of a strong institutional bias toward an innovatory role for VNPOs in social care was found also at the local level. The SSD in Bellebury had a specific policy document on working with VNPOs. In line with the documents discussed above, it declared that they have 'a capacity to innovate, experiment and test new ideas', and that a key criterion for funding such groups should be the extent to which they could be 'pioneer(s) in service development, acting to develop new models of care which [could] act as examples to other providers'. A similar stance was taken in the strategic plan for 'investing in the voluntary sector' adopted by the Chief Executive's Department of Midwell. Innovation was identified as one of four priority issues to receive funding from the local authority, in relation to VNPOs.

The Council in Southshire had perhaps a more circumspect view of the volun-
tary sector, which emphasized the categorical constraints upon local government as much as the nature of VNPOs: 'The public sector is just as innovative as voluntary organizations . . . but the Social Service Department has statutory responsibilities,

which limits its ability to innovate. This is where voluntary organizations can come in and be innovative' (Assistant Director of Social Services for Southshire).

It would be wrong, however, to understand the macro-level stimuli for the innovative capacity of VNPOs solely as a reflection of the meta-level paradigm. There were also important imperatives which operated at the macro-level alone. The most substantial of these was undoubtedly the need for resource holders to allocate scarce resources in the PSS. In this context, innovation was not so much a policy goal as a gatekeeping device to preserve and allocate these scarce resources.

Officers of one central governmental department, for example, explained that they did not use a strict definition of innovation. Rather, the term was used loosely to allow them to support and 'help [VNPOs] to do things that we would like them to do'. Similarly the Research Director of one of the large charitable Foundations said that the definition of innovation 'can vary if we want it to. We use a lot of discretion in the matter.'

This approach was by no means appreciated by many VNPOs. It drew an angry response from one of the voluntary sector respondents in this study:

> Things have to be innovative for the [funding body], whether they are needed or not. It's just dressing things up as innovative to get money. What we want is an appropriate response to an appropriate problem . . . which meets the needs of the community – but we have to dress things up as innovative for them. The process is tortuous.
>
> (Field worker of an intermediary organization)

Finally, the perceptions of other VNPOs in each locality can be equally important in constructing the institutional field at a local level. In Southshire, because of its size there was an 'intermediary body of intermediary bodies'. It comprised all the CVSs and other umbrella groups in the county. In 1992–93, as part of its contribution to the development of the first Community Care Plan in Southshire, it issued a position statement on the voluntary sector in Southshire. Amongst other characteristics, this asserted that VNPOs were 'adaptive and innovative'.

Micro-environmental level factors

These are the institutional factors operating within VNPOs, and can come from a variety of sources. Three significant such micro-level institutional forces were uncovered in this study: personal beliefs, organizational missions/values, and organizational history.

PERSONAL BELIEFS

A significant source of institutional pressure upon VNPOs could be in the personal beliefs of their staff, and particularly of their managers. These would inform the expectations and potentiality of an organization. They could mean that key individuals anticipated that VNPOs should be innovative and so framed such expectations in their management of the organization. These beliefs were often framed within the vision of the 'heroic' VNPO battling the 'dragons' of bureaucracy. For one manager this meant that she was committed to 'finding something that needs doing, cutting through red tape in bureaucracy and just doing it' (Manager of Organization 4). For another manager, it was not so much a question of a personal commitment, but rather an adherence to a particular philosophical approach – the Steiner philosophy in this case – which predisposed him to expect his organization to be innovative: 'How do you start? It's a leap in the dark. You need to believe that you are right and have something new to offer. Our [philosophy] provided us with that' (Manager of Organization 1).

ORGANIZATIONAL VALUES/MISSION

The innovative organizations betrayed a strong institutional bias toward innovation as being a key/core task for their organization. In a few cases this overlapped with the personal philosophical basis for action described above: 'We're driven by the values of [the Steiner philosophy] – we want to develop services which emulate these schools but in the community. This needs change' (Staff member of Organization 1). Usually, though, innovation was part of the values embodied in an organization at a less philosophical, though equally important, way. For some, this operated at a strategic level and was critical to their organizational purpose and mission: 'innovation is our core task . . . we are proactive in responding to need' (Manager of Organization 7).

For others it seemed to be more of an operational principle, such as method of staff motivation: 'Innovation is vital for [our organization] – bereavement is a forgotten area, so you need innovation for stimulation. It keeps you and your counsellors going – the work is so hard . . . ' (Manager of Organization 9).

It is also important, however, to recognize that these organizational values could equally have a negative impact upon the predisposition of an organization to be an innovator. Innovation could be selected out as an organizational goal. Often this was because the organization had a core task to which it was committed, and which was perceived as not requiring organizational change: 'We just have one purpose, so we don't need to develop any new services' (Manager of Organization 18). 'We don't need to change – we provide an ongoing service. We provide transport and we're good at it' (Manager of Organization 17).

ORGANIZATIONAL HISTORY

A final micro-institutional force acting upon the innovative capacity of VNPOs was the 'shadow of the past' – their own history. Where organizations had established a tradition of innovative activity, then the expectations were often for this to continue in the future. In many cases this determined the perceptions of the staff of an organization itself: 'We were set up originally as a demonstration project, so we have always been innovative. We just carry on doing what we are good at' (Manager of Organization 7).

In other cases, it could interact with the macro-level factors, such as by effecting the expectations of funders: 'The Social Services know our work. We are seen [by them] to be an innovative agency' (Manager of Organization 8).

Finally, as with organizational values, the past history of an organization could also act as a 'dead hand', militating against innovative effort: 'We could provide different things but we don't. We provide the same things on an ongoing basis. It's what our members want and have always wanted. It's what they have always had' (Treasurer of Organization 19).

Summary

This section has discussed the types of institutional forces at work upon VNPOs in the case studies, at the meta-, macro- and micro-levels. These are summarized in Table 6.31. Clearly, these factors do not operate independently of each other. As noted above, for example, organizational history can well affect the expectations of funders, as could central governmental perceptions. Moreover, it is important to recognize that one of these factors, by itself, is probably not sufficient to release the innovative potential of VNPOs. At the most simplistic level, if this were so, then because the *meta*-level forces affect all such organizations, this would imply that all VNPOs would have the same response to them. This is not the case. Similarly, the values of an organization, by themselves, are no guarantee of innovation, if for example they are at odds with the expectations of the significant funders of that organization. Again, an institutional analysis stresses the interdependence and interaction of organizations and their environment, rather than a simple or mechanistic environmental determinacy.

As Granovetter (1985) has argued, organizations are embedded in their environments to the extent that they are influenced by and influence these environments, and by the extent to which this interaction both enables and constrains the activities of an organization. It is this interaction between the factors at the three levels which is important, rather than solely the factors operating at any one level.

A key determinant of this interaction can be the extent to which the factors operating are in congruence or not with each other. A good example of this was Organization 1. Despite an organizational commitment to seeing itself as an innovator and as at the forefront of community care developments (it had even

Table 6.31 The institutional forces at the meta-, macro- and micro-levels

Meta-level	societal changes
	central governmental perceptions
	legislation
Macro-level	expectations of funders
	expectations of other VNPOs
Micro-level	personal beliefs/values
	organizational missions/values
	organizational history

received an endorsement on its most recent brochure from Sir Roy Griffiths himself), it received an unexpected setback when it was refused a Section 64 grant by the Department of Health, on the grounds that it was 'not sufficiently innovative'. Here the institutional forces of the two levels were clearly not congruent. This issue is explored further in the final section of this chapter.

The impact of institutional forces

The first stage in the approach of Lane (1993) to unpacking institutional forces was to describe them. This has been done. The second stage was to examine their impact. That is the intention here. This will be discussed first in general terms and then in relation to each group of organizations in the case studies.

Table 6.32 sets out the institutional forces acting upon each group of cross-sectional case-study organizations, at the three levels. For the macro- and micro-levels, the forces are specified. The approach is different for those at the meta-level. These are the same for all the organizations. Here the issue is the response of these organizations to these forces. Each is denoted as a favourable, negative or ambivalent response, or as no response discernible.

In summary, a pattern is apparent here, with a clear institutional bias toward innovation at the micro-level for almost all the innovative VNPOs. For many this was reinforced by similar pressures at the macro-level. Similarly all but one of these organizations had at least a neutral attitude to the meta-level influences.

The one exception was Organization 5, which felt more negative about the meta-level changes and where no significant institutional factors could be uncovered operating at any of the levels. This was an organization which had tried to innovate to survive, because of the erosion of its traditional service base. However, this was a good example of not being congruent with the expectations of the macro-level. The service developed was not seen as an important one by the SSD, for example, which had developed its own service. Because of this lack of congruence, the organization was in danger of collapse.

Finally, amongst the developmental organizations, the institutional forces for innovation were quite weak, whilst for the traditional organizations the institutional framework ran counter to innovative activity, at the macro- and micro-levels, whilst there was a lack of a positive response to the meta-level changes.

The innovative organizations

The institutional factors explored above affected the innovative organizations in one of three ways. The first was in how and whether new social needs were perceived to require an innovative response. A good example of this was Organization 9, a bereavement counselling service in Midwell. This had latterly encountered a significant growth of its waiting list of clients requiring counselling. Within a different institutional framework, this could have been perceived as a threat of work-overload by its staff, and led to a 'siege' mentality (Osborne 1992). Alternatively it could have been seen as a bridge to 'more of the same' – that is, ammunition to be used in gaining more of their existing resources (i.e. more counsellors). However, this growing waiting list was interpreted instead as needing a new response which could deal with needs in a new way (as well as reducing the waiting list!). This was through the use of group therapy sessions. The link between the initial waiting list 'problem' and its innovative response was made clear in the 1993 Annual Report of the group:

> Home visits were made to those on the waiting list with the view to them joining a therapeutic support group. No national guidelines were available for support groups so, therefore, [we] developed a system for group work which has been accepted by other branches of [the Federation] when opening such groups. Since support groups were first formed 175 have taken advantage of them showing that the Support Group System is a cost effective service.

This was a model example of how to turn what could have been viewed as an administrative problem into an innovative advantage, and which has subsequently met the express needs of a growing number of people, on a national basis.

The second way in which the institutional factors could affect the innovative organizations was in sensitizing them to the needs of their funders. In the case of Organization 7, it had been established by the SSD as an umbrella group for community care in Midwell, following the withdrawal of their support for the local Council for Voluntary Service. It therefore relied upon the SSD for its legitimacy and had to be sensitive to its needs.

The third way in which the institutional factors could affect the innovative organizations was in how they perceived and portrayed their own services. Many of the staff of these innovative organizations made wry observations that funding applications were often a game: if the local authority wanted to fund an innovative service then this is what you described to them, irrespective of the actual nature of the service. Two of the organizations had their funding agreements up for renegotiation in the next twelve months, and were currently in discussion with their management committees as to how best to present their projects, to demonstrate their innovativeness. 'It's all about perception', said one manager; 'it's a marketing exercise really', said another.

In conclusion, for the innovative organizations, the overall institutional framework created a predisposition both to see innovation as a core activity for the organization, and to see their activities in an innovative perspective. As outlined above, this often came from a combination of micro-level organizational factors together with the expectations of funders.

The developmental organizations

The developmental organizations threw a particularly interesting light upon the impact of the institutional forces. The defining characteristics of these organizations had proved elusive in the earlier stages of this study. They were thrown into more positive relief by this approach.

Table 6.32 Responses of case-study organizations to their institutional environments

Organization	Meta-level factors	Macro-level factors	Micro-level factors
(a) Innovative organizations			
1	(+)	Securing of funding from local authority essential to its survival, with innovation seen as a key indicator of organizational success in this forum.	Philosophical basis predisposed to innovation; belief of staff in the superiority of the organization to statutory ones, with innovation as a key indicator.
2	(?)	Perceived by SSD to be meeting key service gaps; seen as important agent for bringing diverse agencies together.	Personal belief of staff of the organization in VNPOs being more flexible and adaptive.
3	(0)	Encouragement of national federation to uncover new ways of meeting personal relationship problems.	Personal commitment of counsellor to developing the service as an important one for the agency.
4	(−)	Host organization perceived as source of innovation and encouraged by social services to develop new services; money specifically earmarked for this type of project; belief of key purchasers in social services in the innovative potential of VNPOs.	Belief of host-agency organizer in the ability of the agency to innovate; organizational mandate to seek out unmet needs and develop new ways of meeting them.
5	(−)	A lack of any macro-level factors.	Personal beliefs of organizer.
6	(?)	Local authority seeking to develop the mixed economy of care, by encouraging independent service provision.	Belief in the superiority of their organizational staff; belief that they were best placed to respond to unmet need.
7	(+)	Funded by social services to stimulate innovation in the community.	History of innovation, and commitment to it as an important goal.
8	(+)	Perceived by social services as key source of innovation.	Personal belief of manager in the ability of the organization to develop new services.
9	(0)	Need to meet funding criteria of social services.	Innovation important for staff development.
(b) Developmental organizations			
10	(0)	Pressure for voluntary sector to lead the way in developing new services, especially in the light of pending local government reform . . .	. . . *but* organization has neither the resources nor the 'clout' to take on such a role.
11	(0)	Expectation of consistent quality services from funders.	Belief in improving quality of existing services.

Table 6.32 (contd.)

Organization	Meta-level factors	Macro-level factors	Micro-level factors
12	(0)	None discernible.	None discernible.
13	(−)	Social services has emphasis on funding innovative services ...	... *but* organization sees itself as providing specialist (therapeutic) ones.
14	(?)	None discernible.	None discernible.
15	(0)	None discernible.	None discernible.
16	(0)	None discernible.	Belief of organizer in the strength of the existing mode of operation of the group.
(c) Traditional organizations			
17	(−)	None discernible.	Pride in the specialist service that they already provide, and no desire to change it.
18	(0)	None discernible.	Innovation not felt to be needed because the organization concentrated upon one specialist type of service.
19	(0)	None discernible.	Beneficiary group believed to want continuity, not change.
20	(−)	None discernible.	Pride in what they have done before and desire to continue with this approach.
21	(?)	None discernible.	Beneficiary group believed to want continuity, not change.
22	(?)	Expectation of continuance of existing service from funders.	Importance of continuity with services provided previously.
23	(?)	None discernible	Beneficiary group is felt to be different from others and in need of a service which deals with their special needs, and the importance of the continuity of these specialist services.
24	(?)	Expectation of mainstream service from funders.	Innovation seen as marginal to organizational mission.

Key for the meta-level factors:
(+)   positive response to these factors (seen as being a good trend in social care)
(−)   negative response to these factors (seen as being problematic or as having a negative effect upon social care)
(?)   ambivalent response to these factors (mixed feelings toward the meta-level factors)
(0)   neutral to these factors or no discernible response.

First, there were three organizations which had originally classified themselves as 'innovative' in the postal survey, but which were reclassified subsequently as developmental organizations in this study. These three organizations were each suffering crises of legitimacy in their own ways. One was a generic support group for carers which found its traditional niche being undermined by the growth of specialist carers' groups. Here a claim of innovation was an attempt to carve out a new niche for itself, particularly in relation to the local authority and its continuance of funding. The second organization was similar, in that it was a generalist support group for people in need, again feeling threatened by the growth of specialist groups in the area of community care. The final organization was a newly established CVS which was struggling both to survive, particularly in financial terms, and also to gain credibility in terms of the field of established VNPO. Its claim to innovation was thus an attempt to establish its legitimacy for both these constituencies.

Second, there were four organizations which had originally classified themselves as not having been involved in innovative activity. Upon further examination in the case studies, this was found to be a valid classification. However, three of these organizations included service developments which might have been posed as an innovation by another group in search of legitimacy (such as developing a new play group for children by a Play Group Association, opening a modernized day-care facility at a residential home for elderly people, and starting a parenting skills group as part of a toy library). That they were not portrayed as innovations lay partly in the fact that these groups saw themselves as mainstream service providers, and not innovators, and partly in the fact that all three had secure long-term funding which did not require them to demonstrate such innovative activity. These factors were nicely illustrated by the co-ordinator of Organization 16: 'We used to develop new services but we don't now – we provide a fixed level of service – our funding is stable now and in the future – we have secondments from the local authority for fixed services.'

The fourth organization in this group was slightly different. Although it did need further legitimacy from the local authority (it was in danger of closure) and it certainly provided services which could have been portrayed as innovative, it failed to take this opportunity. This apparent failure to act in its own best interests by this organization was rooted in the perceptions of its staff about their own work. They had received funding from both the health authority and the SSD, though by far the greatest sum (and most significant in terms of survival) was from the latter. However, the staff of the project were largely from a health background (such as community nurses). They continued therefore to pose their services within the institutional paradigm of health rather than social care. This dissonance of institutional paradigms was putting the survival of the project in doubt: 'We used to be a health venture, then a joint one, then health withdrew. Now the funding is Social Services ... We're uneasy about this. Social Services seem to want social support, but we don't provide this, we're therapeutic' (Staff member of Organization 13).

The traditional organizations

These too were subject to institutional pressures, but in different directions. For six of them, their historical legacy was so strong that they could think of doing nothing else, and indeed had no real desire to do any other form of activity. For four other organizations, however, this legacy was problematic. Organizations 19 and 23 were both in danger of dying out because they remained committed to the type of activity that they had always provided. Yet this was manifestly not attracting into the groups new, younger members, who had different needs and wanted different services. Like the proverbial rabbits in the headlights, they waited their inevitable fate, unable to move this dead hand of history from their shoulders.

For the other two organizations in the group, the issue of legitimacy with their funders was of prime importance, though in these cases the expectation was of the continuance of a standard service: 'Our funding is stable – what's important is continuing to provide the same service' (Secretary of Organization 22).

Why do the institutional factors work?

Thus far in this chapter, it has been possible to demonstrate both that institutional factors have been uncovered at work in these case studies and the types of impacts that they had upon the organizations involved. It is argued here that this exploration has offered good evidence for the importance of these institutional factors in predisposing organizations toward either innovative or traditional activity, or toward the construction of their activities as innovative or not.

The final part of the approach of Lane adopted in this chapter was to explain how the institutional factors operate. This question is worthy of a further more detailed study in its own right. However, drawing both upon the existing literature and upon the evidence in this study, certain core elements are evident.

The issue of the innovative capacity of VNPOs is perhaps something of a paradox. As was illustrated in the literature review, within the non-profit studies literature, it has something of the status of a legend, though with little empirical foundation. By contrast, in the organizational studies literature, this issue is noted by its absence. Much of the literature is devoted to the innovative capacity of for-profit organizations, and comparatively little of it is addressed to the public sector, let alone VNPOs. Indeed, where it has been addressed, it has invariably assumed the links between a competitive market and innovation. It has thus been in terms of how to make them more like for-profit organizations, and consequently as more likely to be innovators (for example, Osborne and Gaebler 1993). Almost no attention has been turned to explaining the innovative capacity of VNPOs within their own terms. Such an approach has as much to contribute to mainstream organizational theory as it does to the non-profit literature.

This study has made a start upon developing such a contribution. As noted earlier, the for-profit literature emphasizes the workings of the market, and in particular competition, as being the prime mover in the development of innovation. Firms innovate to obtain a competitive advantage over their rivals and so to increase their profits. Inevitably such action involves risks – that is, innovation can be costly, or fail. Firms therefore make a judgement upon the need to innovate upon the basis of this balance between profitability and risk.

However, for VNPOs, that impetus is not there, for two reasons. First, by definition, they are not profit-*distributing*, so that there is no direct financial incentive for innovation. The risks and costs of innovation have no financial benefits to offset them, nor a profit–loss 'bottom line' by which to evaluate their impact.

Second, even with the developing mixed economy of care, there is still only a limited amount of direct competition between VNPOs to provide services. Often contracts are negotiated on a one-to-one basis between the local authority and a chosen VNPO. The recent change of government in the UK has also undermined the commitment to competition as the solution to poor-quality public services, if it has not negated it entirely.

Despite these apparent theoretical limitations, innovation by VNPOs was clearly demonstrated in this study. If one is going to develop a theory of such innovative capacity of VNPOs one therefore needs to look beyond both the assertions of the non-profit literature and the concentration of the organizational studies literature upon the significance of the profit motive.

It is argued here that a *one-factor* explanation is neither possible nor desirable. It belies the complexity of real life. A far better approach, rather, is a contingent one (Lawrence and Lorsch 1967), which sees a number of factors as potentially contributing to the *innovation mix* for VNPOs, and as releasing their innovative capacity. A major factor here, as has previously been suggested in more general terms by Singh *et al.* (1991) and Tucker *et al.* (1992), is the search for *legitimacy*. This is the benefit that innovation can bestow upon a VNPO – be it legitimacy in the eyes of their beneficiaries, their staff, their peers, or perhaps most significantly, their funders.

It is in this search for legitimacy that institutional factors become so crucial, for it is they which construct the meaning of the activity of an organization. This legitimacy may be in terms of maintaining adherence to the organizational history, in terms of predisposing the organization to seek innovative solutions to problems, or in terms of how it seeks to construct the meaning of its activity to the key stakeholders and funders. The demonstration of innovative activity can frequently be a key performance indicator in demonstrating organizational effectiveness to these stakeholders, either because it fulfils their ideological preconceptions about the superiority of VNPOs as service providers or because it is seen as achieving the already nebulous and ill-defined governmental policy objective for innovation in community care services.

Of course, innovative activity is not the only way in which to gain legitimacy. Providing a specialist service, being a campaigning organization, or providing a key mainstream service could be equally valid. Indeed, some of the traditional organizations eschewed innovation quite purposefully, in exchange for one of these other sources of legitimacy.

A key question left, therefore, is why some organizations choose innovation as a route to legitimacy, whilst other organizations choose other routes. This is where it is necessary to bring this institutional impetus toward innovation together with the other key factor in the *innovation mix* uncovered in this study, the relationship of an organization to its environment. This provides the context for the relationship between the different levels of institutional factors uncovered here, as well as with the other environmental and organizational factors uncovered earlier. The innovative capacity of VNPOs is thus forged in such a crucible. To reveal the nature of this process, the last section of this chapter turns to the process of innovation uncovered in the case studies. Following on from this, a final chapter will bring all the elements of this study together in an initial model of the innovative capacity of VNPOs, as well as testing some of its key components out against a number of *hard* cases.

The process of innovation

This last section addresses the processes by which innovations were brought to fruition in the cross-sectional case-study VNPOs. It will commence by outlining briefly the methodological approach to these processes and issues. This will be followed by a short discussion of the ways in which 'innovation' was defined by the innovative organizations in the study. It will then highlight key processual issues drawn out of the case studies, before drawing conclusions.

Methodological approaches to the process of innovation

The process issues in the case studies were drawn out by structured and semi-structured interviews with the managers and staff of the relevant VNPOs, and by the collection of archival or documentary evidence, where available. In order to undertake an analysis of the process issues involved, use was made of matrices both to analyse and to display the processual data. This approach was invaluable in highlighting key factors in the innovation process(es) and in aiding 'pattern-matching' between case-study organizations (Miles and Huberman 1984).

Operationalizing 'innovation' in the case-study organizations

Although all the organizations talked confidently about their innovative role, it was apparent from the interviews that the same phenomenon was not always being described. At the most basic level, it was true that innovation was always seen as involving 'new ideas' (co-ordinator of Organization 3). This was most articulately put by the manager of Organization 4, who emphasized the issue of discontinuity, as does our *template* definition, in differentiating innovation from service development: 'It's breaking new ground – doing something that people haven't done before. *It's starting something new, not just developing something that's already there.* It's something new – it's meeting a need in a different way' [my emphasis]. Despite this basic agreement, though, the organizations did put different emphases on the factors involved. For one organization, the core of this 'newness' was in defeating the 'dead hand' of bureaucracy: 'It's new – surprising, different. It's using one's initiative. *It's something [that] needs doing and cutting through the red tape and bureaucracy and doing it*' [my emphasis] (Manager of Organization 8). For another organization, though, a key feature of this newness was in the element of providing a service not available in the area: the classic 'gap-filling' role: 'It's providing a service not in this area before – filling a gap in services' (Co-ordinator of Organization 3).

Finally, for yet another organization, the key feature was the genuine 'newness' of an innovation, which was differentiated from the diffusion of innovations from elsewhere: 'It's setting up a new service, a creative response to need – *not just copying a service from elsewhere*' [my emphasis] (Manager of Organization 1).

Clearly, then, although there was agreement over the importance of newness in innovation, and in its discontinuity compared to service development, there were different emphases on this. As will be apparent below, these sprang from the different processes involved in the development of an innovation and from significant contextual factors. Within the broad definition of innovation developed previously, therefore, this initial exploration would seem to suggest a cluster of associated processes, rather than a single unitary one.

Six themes uncovered

The processes of innovation in the case-study organizations are displayed in Table 6.33. Each process is explored within a standard matrix. The horizontal dimension concerns the chronological development of the innovation, from its prehistory to its posited future. The vertical dimension draws out pertinent issues, across four 'streams' identified below. (This approach is adapted from that of Van de Ven and Poole 1988.)

Table 6.34 summarizes the six key themes arising out of these analyses. The first of these is implicit in the differences displayed between each process of innovation, and has already been raised above. This is that there is no *one* process of innovation. Innovation is not a mechanistic process which develops in a purely instrumental manner, as some of the more crass models from the for-profit literature would have (for example, Carson 1989). Rather, its development is embedded in the interplay between a number of factors, which interact and give meaning to each other. In this study, the four factors isolated are the actual 'historical' events of innovation, the actions of key individuals, the internal (organizational) context of innovation, and the external (environmental) context.

Again, these are not discrete streams but rather interact to give each other meaning. For example, with Organization 1, the decision in the events stream by the parents group to try to develop for their adult siblings a quality alternative to the statutory provision was given further meaning by the development of the NHSCC Act. This legitimized their ability to do so, in the overall service context. Similarly, with Organization 7, its need to find a direction for itself when its status as a demonstration project ended had resonance with the search of the SSD for an alternative intermediary organization, as its relationship with the existing CVS soured (leading to its eventual closure). Finally, in Organization 5, a key factor in the failure of its innovation, and the possible closure of the organization itself, was the lack of any internal organizational forces to balance the creative, but unfocused, thinking and actions of the lead organizer. She became a classic *loose cannon*, with no checks or balances on her actions.

Table 6.33 The processes of innovation

Stream	Background/ trigger issues	Development	Implementation	The future
(a) *Organization 1*				
Events	1985. Meeting of parents of children attending Steiner School, concerned over the lack of a satisfactory adult provision. Decide to 'emulate the quality of life experienced in a Camphill School'.	1985–90. Selecting a site; building their credibility; capital fund-raising.	1990 onwards. Building credibility in locality, and developing their relations with SSD; revenue fund-raising.	Financial security essential. For this to be achieved, it needs integration into range of community social services locally, and to develop the day service to include local non-residential users.
Key individuals	Future project director is key articulator of core values upon behalf of group (not a parent but committed staff member who was approached by parents)	Future project director makes a 'leap of faith' to leave his paid employment, to develop project: 'You can't recruit or fund-raise on an idea. You need an actual service in being.'	Project director holds core values.	Project director and key SSD officials.
Internal context		Employment of professional fund-raiser.	Recruitment of appropriate committed staff.	Development of appropriate staff: staff training.
External context	Development of community care legislation gives added legitimacy to project.	Development of national support, using Steiner networks, to aid fund-raising.	Poor relationship with SSD needs addressing – mutual negativity. This affects ability of project to gain revenue funding from community care resources of SSD.	Improved relationship with SSD.

(b) *Organization 2 ('Needy people helping needy people. We didn't set out to innovate anything, just to meet needs ... it's not an innovation really, just a solution to a couple of problems.')*

Events	1988–89. Agency organizer meets with professional staff representing other community agencies, in a local series of community	1989–90. Project established as part of VB; speedy development.	Hampered by poor-quality supervisors initially. Took off with appointment of new project supervisor.	Doesn't want to grow too big. Maintain impetus and quality of service.

Table 6.33 (contd.)

Stream	Background/ trigger issues	Development	Implementation	The future
	lunches. Out of these arose discussion of unmet needs, to be brought together by volunteer bureau (VB).			
Key individuals	VB organizer as catalyst for discussions: 'honest broker'; importance of informal network of contacts from community lunches.	VB organizer.	Appointment of new project supervisor – enthusiast.	VB organizer and project supervisor.
Internal context	VB looking for ways to sustain itself; financially insecure.		(Un)reliability of volunteers; problems of trying to meet two needs – which has 'first' preference?	What would happen if VB closed down?
External context	Importance of existing informal contacts between front-line professionals – short-circuited existing (long) planning mechanisms.	Informal network formalized into steering committee.	Service seen as legitimate by SSD – given core funding ('more secure than the Bureau itself!'). VB seen as legitimate player by SSD – 'It gets things done'.	Becoming embedded in part of service delivery system.

(c) *Organization 3*

Events	National federation had supported sex therapy since 1976. Previous attempt to set up local service in 1985 failed when counsellor left. 1989: idea resurrected locally with appointment of new committed counsellor.	1989–92. Research carried out by counsellor into need; training.	1992 onwards. Slow take-up; marketing to other agencies is needed.	Training of an additional sex counsellor to lessen dependency upon existing therapist.

Stream	Background/ trigger issues	Development	Implementation	The future
Key individuals	Counsellor appointed in 1989 (advocate and enthusiast), and office manager who supported and encouraged her throughout the development of the service.			
Internal context		Sources of funding explored.	Impact on other counselling services of 'loss' of this counsellor to sexual therapy service (opportunity cost).	Sexual therapy service to become a useful marketing device to Health for funding for the agency as a whole. It legitimizes it as a necessity.
External context	Encouragement from national federation.	Provision of training.	Key role of Health in legitimizing service and providing network for referrals (Health Promotion Unit and GPs), plus funding.	Further funding likely from Health, which sees the innovation as a key service.

(d) *Organization 4*

Stream	Background/ trigger issues	Development	Implementation	The future
Events	Ongoing role of local CVS to explore unmet need and to establish projects to meet them. 1988. Project established elsewhere in region.	1990. CVS agrees to develop project in locality, at behest of SSD. Pilot scheme established.	1992. Mainstream project established.	Expansion of service area/size of project.
Key individuals	CVS organizer – self-professed 'networker'. Held in high esteem by SSD.	Enthusiastic worker appointed.	Close collaboration between CVS organizer and project worker.	Continued collaboration between agency staff and CVS.
Internal context		Project dependent upon CVS for initial organization.	Problem of reliability of volunteers.	Need to establish independent identity from the CVS.

Table 6.33 (contd.)

Stream	Background/ trigger issues	Development	Implementation	The future
External context	SSD keen to see this project disseminated throughout region. Saw CVS as key organization to do this – 'our venture capital'.	Importance of link to CVS in establishing the credibility of project. SSD encourages and supports the development.	Need to develop credibility with other voluntary agencies, and not just SSD – facilitated by links with CVS.	Needs secure funding for the future and external credibility of project in its own right.

(e) *Organization 5*

Events	Toy library short of members and of funding; needs to search for a new role. Attempts to 'migrate' to support for adults.	Little consultation with other agencies.	Letters/fliers sent out. Little take-up.	Failure of project and possible closure of toy library.
Key individuals	Branch organizer as creative thinker, but not implementor or doer. Few other active members, on consistent basis.	Branch organizer takes responsibility for development and implementation of the project, with limited success.		
Internal context	Lack of active membership. Existing beneficiaries growing up and not being replaced by new ones.	Over-dependence on one person.		
External context	Lack of support from other agencies.	Little attention by project to service network as a whole.	SSD has own leisure resource for adults. Does not support toy library initiative.	Lack of legitimization and support/ funding.

(f) *Organization 6*

Events	1989. Local deaf association identified gap in service provision for deaf adults at 19 – no suitable living accommodation. Subsequent need for day service also identified.	1990. National voluntary organization (NVO) opens residential service. Perceived as 'annexation' of local need by national agency, for own purposes.	1991. Day service opened. Key issues of transport and of integration with other social services.	Need to maintain existing service, and to put continued pressure on the SSD for other services.

Stream	Background/ trigger issues	Development	Implementation	The future
Key individuals	Organizer of parents group (vicar for deaf community) is advocate/holder of valuers. Active in meetings and lobbying.	Organizer acts as catalyst for parents group to develop and to take the lead in service development. Further lobbying required.	Organizer is key figure in implementation. No other paid workers – sessional only.	Need to develop committed group away from dependency upon one person.
Internal context		Parents take up ideas of day service – NVO excluded.	Independence from other organizations maintained, so not to repeat earlier annexation by NVO.	Need to develop number of active members in the project, to 'share the load'.
External context	NVO involved initially – but viewed suspiciously by parents, seen as interested in 'empire building'. Alternative parents group set up.	Links to school provision through parents group important – it provided awareness of unmet needs.	SSD prepared to support service as meeting a gap. Responds to pressure produced from lobbying activity of organizer.	Need to develop secure funding in the medium term, probably from the SSD.

(g) *Organization 7*

Events	1986–87. Agency set up as carers project, as one of series of DoH demonstration projects on community care. 1989. DoH projects reach end of life. 1990. Change of function for agency, to community care intermediary upon behalf of SSD.	1990 onwards. Short developmental period, leading to transformation of organization from one function to the other.	Acts as mediator between SSD and VNPOs on community care.	Develop further links into local voluntary sector – seen by some organizations in this sector as puppet of SSD.
Key individuals		New manager appointed with business background which comes to be defining characteristic of agency – 'We're preparing VNPOs for the market place.'		
Internal context		Change of staff, to undertake new function.	'One-person organization.'	Develop further staffing to lessen reliance on one person.

Table 3.33 (contd.)

Stream	Background/ trigger issues	Development	Implementation	The future
External context	Souring of SSD– CVS relationship.	Closure of CVS. SSD instrumental in re-formulation of agency, which becomes embedded in needs of SSD.	SSD legitimizes agency as 'voice of the local voluntary sector'.	Continued funding to do a job upon behalf of SSD. Needs to establish wider credibility with local voluntary sector.

(h) *Organization 8 ((1) 'We're setting up new services that are people-centred, a creative response to need. We're not just spreading innovation for elsewhere – we're creating new user-led service.' (2) '[My job] is dreaming up the idea, writing it down, informing others of the service, looking for a suitable venue, chasing the grant application, contacting families . . . and organizing transport.'*

Stream	Background/ trigger issues	Development	Implementation	The future
Events	1986–87. Lack of good services for young adults with learning disabilities leaving educational system perceived by group organizer. Existing services standardized and service-led.	1987. Discussions with parents/ carers and SSD.	1988. Project established in part of Midwell.	Diversification of work of project to cover new needs/ expand over whole of area, not just existing wards.
Key individuals	Organizer as visionary and entrepreneur: 'hero(ine) innovator'.	Continued central role for organizer of project.	Organizer surrounded by number of volunteers and sessional workers.	Need to expand paid staff of project.
Internal context		Project is small – centres around organizer. This produces dichotomy of organizational flexibility vs. over-dependence on one person. Management committee established by organizer to broaden base of project.		
External context	Lack of needs-led day occupation services for adults with learning disabilities. Passing of NHSCC Act.	SSD positive about project. Fits in with community care legislation. The project takes on an implementation role for them. Project becoming embedded in local service network. Importance of link to school; organizer is a former teacher there, and knows beneficiaries/parents. Link to local church helped in getting key resources – such as premises for the project.		Continued funding required from the SSD into the future, as no other sources utilized.

Stream	Background/ trigger issues	Development	Implementation	The future
(i) *Organization 9*				
Events	1988. Agency established in Midwell. 1990. Pressure of numbers on waiting list causes reappraisal of agency policies.	1990: planning for group-based approach to service delivery.	1990. Implementation.	Project essential part of strategy of agency to convince SSD of need for future funding for agency.
Key individuals	(Paid) organizer sees this branch of overall federation as professional, compared to other branches which rely on volunteers only.	Organizer joined by qualified nurse. Both take proactive role in group development.	Organizer and nursing colleague take prime role in implementation.	Desire to develop network of groups which are self-supporting.
Internal context	Changing perception of need in relation to waiting list pressure. Some needs (learning to make friends again) are seen as better dealt with in groups.	Importance of small agency size, where easy to make changes.	Focus on quality service by management committee and staff.	Survival of the agency.
External context	Lack of model elsewhere in the national federation as to how to respond creatively to growing waiting list.	Joint funding from SSD and Health.		

The second theme of the case studies is the importance of a chronological approach to understanding innovation. It is not a 'steady state' but rather evolves over time. This has been argued previously in the important work of Pettigrew (1990), and was confirmed here.

Two issues need to be emphasized in this theme. First, a chronological perspective needs to embrace what psychologists would call an 'A–B–C' approach. This specifies the antecedents of a behaviour, the details of the behaviour itself, and its consequences (Osborne 1986).

Thus, innovations have a prehistory and this is essential to understanding the subsequent shape of their development (see also Osborne 1996 for further development of this point, in the context of a longitudinal case study of a VNPO and

Table 6.34 Summary of processual themes across the case study of innovative organizations

Organization	Nature/type of innovation	Type of organization	Time-scale	Role of key individuals	Environmental factor(s)	Role of network	Institutional factors
1	New organization and new service to area	Paid staff plus volunteers	Long	Organizer as holder of values and entrepreneur	Service gap; changing legislation	National legitimacy and fund-raising	Strong institutional link to existing Steiner network; worked against link to SSD (involvement in this study as legitimizing tactic)
2	New service for existing organization and to area	Paid organizer only; financially precarious	Short	Organizer as 'honest broker' in network; supervisor as enthusiast	Service gap; bureaucratic/ long-winded planning process for statutory agencies	Embedded in existing service network of professionals; 'short-cutting' bureaucratic planning structures	VB legitimized by service system as key player; VB needing to secure funding from SSD
3	New service for existing organization and to area	Paid staff plus volunteers	Long	Counsellor as advocate; organizer as enabler	Service gap	Implementation network	Legitimization by national federation; innovation as way to gain funding
4	New organization and new service for area (diffused from ajoining area)	CVS organizer plus project co-ordinator and volunteers	Medium	CVS organizer as entrepreneur and 'networker'; project co-ordinator as enthusiast	Previously successful scheme nearby, which SSD wanted to replicate; service gap	CVS as key organization in voluntary sector and for SSD	Project instigation from SSD; CVS as its 'venture capital' – an appropriate role in service development

5	New service for organization, but already existing in area	One co-ordinator	Short	Sole source of organizational inspiration/action	SSD had other resources to use; lack of role for toy library	Lack of good network contacts	Weak; lack of support from SSD
6	New service for area in existing organization	One paid co-ordinator plus member – volunteers	Medium	Advocate plus lobbyist	Distrust of existing national organization for deaf people; service gap	Supportive network of deaf community plus carers	Weak; isolation of deaf community
7	Transformed organization and new service for area	Paid organizer only	Short	Transformer of organizational/sectoral values; entrepreneur	Poor relationship between SSD and CVS; service gap as consequence of changing legislation	Embedded in SSD service network	Organization as getting legitimacy from SSD: 'creature' organization
8	New organization and new service for area	One paid organizer	Medium	'Hero innovator'; visionary/advocate for the service	Service gap	Embedded in SSD service network; church network also important in implementation	Legitimacy plus funding
9	New service for organization and for area	Two paid staff	Short	'Hero innovators'; professional approach	Service gap	Implementation support from links with statutory agencies	Implementation of professional approach; project as part of funding strategy re statutory agencies

innovation). With Organization 6, for example, a great deal of the fierce independence involved in its development was as a consequence of the perceived nefarious actions of another national VNPO, in the 'prequel' to the development of the innovation itself. Similarly, the failure of the innovation by Organization 5, and its own probable closure, was a consequence of its long-standing inability to engage with its local service and institutional contexts.

The second issue is the variable time-scale of innovation. For some, such as Organization 2, innovation was quite a rapid process, with decisions made and acted upon over quite a short space of time. For others, such as Organization 3, the prehistory of the innovation was far longer than its development and innovation.

The third theme is the essential role that key individuals play in the development of innovations. This appears in part to reflect upon the importance of individual agency in the development of innovation – individual action is necessary. It also reflects the fact that many local VNPOs are small in any case; thus the impact of individuals upon these organizations is in any case far greater.

Yet again, there is no one role taken on by individuals in these processes. They can act as classic 'hero innovators', as the holders of core values, as enablers, or as service advocates/lobbyists (see the individual project summaries for examples of each of these roles). The precise role is determined and constrained by the context of the innovation.

Moreover, it is worth reiterating the findings from the cultural hypothesis, investigated earlier. The presence of powerful individuals is no guarantee of innovation; there are many other, equally valid, organizational roles that they can undertake, besides innovation. Their presence is a necessary, but not a sufficient, condition for innovation.

The fourth theme has already been alluded to above, and that is the importance of appreciating the external context of the organizations and the innovations concerned. As was seen both in the literature review and in the exploration of the environmental hypothesis, organizations do not act in a vacuum, but in relation to their environmental context. There was further cross-validation of this in these processual analyses (such as in relation to Organizations 1 and 2). Just as a responsiveness to their environment was found to be a significant characteristic of innovative organizations, so this responsiveness is equally influential upon the actual process of innovation.

The fifth theme is the mechanism through which this environmental responsiveness impacts upon the organizations and innovations concerned. This is the network of contacts surrounding these organizations. Again, this point was raised in the environmental hypothesis, in relation to the complexity of the networks of the innovative VNPOs compared to the simplicity of the traditional ones. There is further cross-validation of this in these processual analyses (the process of innovation in Organization 2 is a good example of this theme).

However, these networks do not play a single role. Just as the relationship between an organization and its environment can vary, so can the functions carried out by the network(s) which mediate this relationship. Thus, in these cross-sectional case studies, networks could be a source of ideas for innovation (Organization 2), a source of funds and other resources to facilitate innovation (Organization 1), a support network to help with difficulties of bringing an innovation to fruition (Organization 4), a source of legitimization for the innovation (Organization 8), or a mechanism through which to implement the innovation itself (Organization 3).

The final theme is the impact of the institutional context upon the process of innovation. This theme came across over and over again as the crucial one in the process of innovation. This might be because other agencies were essential to legitimizing the credibility and validity of an innovation (Organizations 1 and 5), because the innovation was being used as a tool through which to enhance the legitimacy of its host agency (Organizations 3 and 9), or because the host organization was so *embedded* in the dominant service system that it was essentially an agent of this system (Organization 7). The operationalization of this institutional framework was apparent in the funding patterns of the innovators. The innovation could be triggered by the award of funding (Organization 7), or funding could be a later reward for a service recognized as a successful innovation (Organization 8).

Earlier, the question was posed as to why a VNPO should want to innovate, given the risks and costs, in the absence of market competition and a profit motive. An important component of the answer lies in this institutional framework of VNPOs. This study has shown Singh *et al.* (1991) and Tucker *et al.* (1992) to be quite correct in analysing the vulnerability of such organizations to this institutional framework. Because they rely upon other organizations for their funding, and often for their wider societal legitimization (certainly in terms of the service delivery system) then they are especially vulnerable to the expectations of these powerful organizations. As was demonstrated in the previous section, for these powerful (often governmental) organizations, innovation is a core component of their expectations because of its status as a policy initiative, its role as a gatekeeper in allocating scarce resources amongst or across a range of organizations, and its status as 'conspicuous productivity' (Feller 1981) – a way through which to demonstrate their efficient use of public money in the absence of more objective criteria.

Interestingly, the most graphic examples of this institutional effect are seen in the two organizations which struggled most with it. For Organization 5, its failure to appreciate the institutional context of service provision led to the failure of its innovation – and possibly its own demise. More complexly, Organization 1 had sought and gained its national legitimization from its Steiner philosophy and network of contacts. This was immensely important in its initial raising of capital resources to start the project. However, in adopting this approach it neglected, even condemned, the institutional requirements of local government. This created real problems when it needed to switch to revenue funding and raising, principally from them. It was perceived as not meeting the institutional requirements of these agencies and as not being sufficiently innovative. Indeed, its initial impetus for involvement in this study was an attempt to gain approval as an innovative project from another perceived key player (the foundation funding the present study), and so to enhance its institutional support and likelihood of revenue funding.

Conclusions

This section has explored the processual issues involved in the innovations within the cross-sectional case studies. A high level of cross-validation has been found with the influential issues highlighted in the causal hypotheses examined previously. Whilst those hypotheses highlighted the factors which contributed to the innovative capacity of VNPOs, though, this section has examined their impact upon the realization of this capacity. Taken together, these elements provide the basis of an initial model of the innovative capacity of VNPOs. This model is developed fully in the next chapter, and its key elements are tested through a limited number of selected *hard cases*.

7 The innovative capacity of VNPOs

The intention in this chapter is to pull together the findings reported so far and to develop an initial model of the innovative capacity of VNPOs. This will then be tested further against a number of 'hard cases' to assess its robustness. It will end by highlighting its contributions to the literature; by discussing its implications for the management of the innovative capacity of VNPOs, both by their own managers and by local government; and by pointing the way to future research needs.

Toward a model of the innovative capacity of VNPOs

The story so far . . .

The driving force behind this book has been the increased prominence given to the innovative capacity of VNPOs in the development of public policy. Specifically it was prompted by the role envisaged for VNPOs in the PSS, as part of the development of the mixed economy of welfare. The intention was to explore the empirical substance of this capacity and to explore the key causal hypotheses about the source of this capacity. In doing so it was also intended to test the relevance and contribution of organization theory to our understanding of this innovative capacity of VNPOs, as well as what contribution their study could offer to organization theory in return.

Our story began by developing a clear understanding of the nature of voluntary activity. It differentiated between voluntaryism, as an organizing societal principle of voluntary action, volunteerism, as individual action freely chosen, and voluntarism, as the basis of organized, collective, voluntary activity. It made the point that, although voluntarism drew from the other two principles, it also had its own discrete conceptual roots. In particular the point was made that voluntarism has no necessary connection with volunteerism. On the basis of this conceptual clarity, this second chapter then reviewed current terminology about organized voluntary activity and concluded that VNPOs was the most appropriate term for such activity. This section concluded by establishing a definition of a VNPO, which drew upon the work of Salamon and Anheier (1994) and which focused upon organizational issues for its impact.

The third chapter reviewed the varied literatures about innovation. It began by exploring the extensive literature about innovation contained within organization studies. This was used to develop a clear definition of innovation, an understanding of the range of factors associated with both innovations and innovators, and an overview of the process of innovation. The importance of discontinuity in activity was raised in particular in relation to innovation. This chapter also explored some of the wider areas of organization studies which could contribute to helping to understand the innovative capacity of VNPOs. In particular the potential contributions of contingency, systems and institutional theory were highlighted.

This chapter then reviewed the literature about both the innovative capacity of VNPOs, and about innovation in the PSS. A key issue for both was the lack of any real definition of the phenomenon under investigation. The former literature was found to be long on assertions and normative formulations about this capacity but short on either empirical evidence or causal models about it. The formulation of Knapp *et al.* (1990) of this innovative capacity as a *legend* seemed particularly apposite: a kernel of truth certainly existed but it was shrouded with stories and implications which this kernel could not support. The latter literature was found to contain a wealth of descriptive material but only a very few studies of either analytic or prescriptive content.

This chapter ended by using the organization studies literature to give some greater clarity to understanding both the innovative capacity of VNPOs and its extent in the PSS. A typology of organizational change in social policy implementation was developed, drawing upon the work of Abernathy *et al.* (1983). This was especially useful in helping to differentiate between *organizational innovation*, which involved the discontinuity discussed above, and *organizational development*, which incrementally improved a service but within the existing service paradigm. This, it was argued, would help give a sharpness to the debate about innovation which had been lacking previously.

The fourth chapter outlined the methodology of the research which underpinned this book. It was argued that, because of the lack of research about the innovative capacity of VNPOs, it would be necessary to combine an initial inductive approach to mapping the extent of innovation by VNPOs in the PSS with a subsequent deductive one to exploring causal hypotheses about this activity. The issue of the locus of the study was also raised and it was argued that the use of three cluster, or locality, studies would provide local detail and allow environmental factors to be explored. Concretely, it was proposed to combine an initial survey of innovation by VNPOs in these loci with three cross-sectional case studies of innovative, developmental (i.e. incremental), and traditional (i.e. non-innovative) activity. This chapter ended by considering the reliability and validity of this study. It emphasized the need to use both methodological and data triangulation (Denzin 1970) in order to establish these conditions.

Chapter 5 reported the findings of the survey of voluntary activity in the PSS reported by VNPOs in the three localities. It began by describing the types of activity which were reported as being innovative by the organizations in this study, and emphasized that this activity ranged from the clearly innovative, in terms of the definition used in this study, to activity which simply modified or extended existing provision (such as opening a club an extra day a week).

On the basis of this discussion, and by the further application of the typology of organizational change developed previously, it was possible to specify three different types of organizational activity. These were *innovative* activity, which developed a new service for an organization and/or served a new client group (the key issue here being one of discontinuity with the previous activities of an organization); *developmental* activity, which developed or modified an existing service to an existing client group of the organization; and *traditional* activity, which maintained the existing services of the organization to its existing client group. When the activity reported in the survey was re-analysed in this way, it was found that around a third of the organizations surveyed reported legitimate innovation. This provided the first empirical mapping of the extent of innovative activity by VNPOs.

Following on from this mapping, this chapter also explored the main organizational attributes of the innovators compared to their developmental and traditional counterparts. These were explored using both chi-squared tests of statistical significance with the distributional statistics and the more sophisticated and relational approach of Discriminant Analysis. This exploration found it hard to differentiate between the innovative and the developmental organizations on the basis of their organizational attributes. However, important differences were uncovered by the chi-squared tests between the innovative and traditional organizations. The subsequent Discriminant Analysis brought these into relation with each other, by establishing a discriminant function which differentiated strongly between these two types of organization. The key variables involved were the presence of a paid staff group, the impact of governmental funding as a major source of organizational income, and the organization being a young one. This chapter ended by discussing the import of these findings. It emphasized that whilst they provided an important description of the organizational attributes which differentiated innovative VNPOs from their traditional counterparts, they had two significant limitations. First, they were not prescriptive attributes, in the sense that only organizations with such characteristics were innovative. This was manifestly not so. These, and other, attributes were contingent upon other factors for their import. Second, these attributes were not causal factors. They described the types of organizations which were typically innovators, but they offered no clue as to why this might be so. In order to answer this second question, it was therefore necessary to turn to the second part of this study, the cross-sectional case studies.

These case studies were developed in Chapter 6. They evaluated four possible causal hypotheses to explain the innovative capacity of VNPOs, which had been developed from the literature review in Chapter 2. These were that it was a function of their organizational structure (the organizational hypothesis), of their internal organizational culture (the cultural hypothesis), of their external environment and their relationship to it (the external organizational hypothesis), or of their institutional context and relationships (the institutional hypothesis). These were evaluated in turn.

Little was found to support the organizational hypothesis in its own right. Once again it was hard to locate any substantial differences between the innovative and developmental organizations. It was found that innovative organizations could be differentiated by their higher level of job specialization and of professionalization, but the relationship was weak and its import unclear. It was suggested that the higher level of specialization was accounted for mostly by administrative posts, which could have freed up the time of service-related staff for mission-critical activity. However, it was not clear whether professionalization was important for the impact upon staff of such training or as a proxy for organizational resources. It was concluded that, by itself, the organizational hypothesis could contribute only a little to explaining the innovative capacity of VNPOs, and that this evidence needed to be considered in relation to the other findings for a proper understanding.

There was also found to be limited support for the cultural hypothesis. It did confirm that a cluster of internal characteristics did describe the innovative organizations: that is, the presence of a paid staff group, the specialization of administrative tasks, and a tendency toward professionalization of service-related tasks. It also found that individual agency (in the sense of a strong individual committed to innovation as a process or to a specific innovation) was an important factor in the development of innovation.

However, none of these was found to be sufficient to explain the innovative capacity of VNPOs. Individual agency, in particular, was reliant upon other factors to give it its purpose and meaning; such single-minded individuals could be found in traditional or developmental organizations, but performing different functions.

The external environmental hypothesis proved to be more fruitful. Not only were innovative organizations found to inhabit more complex environments than traditional or developmental ones, they also exhibited a greater receptivity and responsiveness to their environments. The challenges of their changing environments were often perceived as opportunities for development rather than, as often for the traditional organizations, being perceived as threats to the status quo.

This relationship was understood further by placing it in the context of systems theory (Scott 1992). This allowed innovative organizations to be seen as open systems, which were reliant upon elements of their environment in order to achieve their organizational purpose, whilst traditional organizations were better understood as closed, natural, systems which were more self-sufficient onto their organizational purposes and which put a higher degree of import unto the survival of the organization in its pre-existing form. It was also conjectured that it was this environmental relationship which the earlier organizational and internal environmental factors were contingent upon for their import. Finally, it continued to be difficult to get any clear picture of the causal factors which differentiated the developmental from the other two types of organizations.

The final hypothesis was the institutional one. This concerned the effect of the institutional framework of an organization upon its work. This was dis-aggregated to the meta-, macro-, and micro-institutional levels. The meta-level concerned the overriding societal framework for the role of VNPOs in the PSS and the impact of government perceptions and legislation on these organizations. The macro-level concerned the impact of their locality on VNPOs and particularly the effect of key resource holders in their localities, such as local government. The micro-level factors concerned institutional forces operating within VNPOs. These included the personal and professional beliefs of their staff, the past history of the organization, and its organizational mission and culture.

These institutional forces were found to have a powerful effect upon the innovative capability of VNPOs. The current meta-level forces provided a context which legitimized, and indeed promoted, the innovative role of VNPOs in the PSS. At the macro-level this was operationalized through the funding policies and procedures of the key funders of such organizations, as well as through the mutual perceptions of the network of VNPOs of which any one organization might be a part. Finally, at the micro-level, the role of these institutional forces was reinforced by the self-perceptions of an organization and its members. These could predispose an organization to be more or less receptive to the meta- and macro-level forces acting upon it.

These institutional forces operated in several ways. They might predispose an organization to expect to act in an innovative manner or to be proactive in seeking out or responding to unmet social needs, on the basis of its past history, the personal values or beliefs of its staff, and/or the nature of its organizational philosophy. They could also predispose their key stakeholders and funders to have expectations of innovation by these organizations. This, in turn, could result in 'legitimate' innovation by these organizations, but it could also lead them to interpret or portray their organizational activity as being innovative, irrespective of its actual nature, in order to meet the institutional expectations placed upon them. This was apparent with a number of the developmental organizations, which portrayed service developments as innovations precisely because of these institutional pressures.

Indeed, it is important to recognize that institutional forces had as great an impact upon the developmental and traditional organizations as upon the innovators. It was seen that the developmental organizations often occupied an ambiguous position, where the expectations of their funders required them to portray their services as being innovative, irrespective of their true nature. The traditional organizations could be more immune to the external institutional forces, either because of a stable funding base with a non-innovative bent, or because of strong micro-level, internal forces, which held them committed to their existing mission and service mix.

Finally, the process of innovation was examined in this study. No one process was uncovered, but rather a cluster of processes, contingent upon a number of factors. Individual agency was found to be an essential part of this process, though in a number of different ways and performing a number of different organizational functions, dependent upon the innovation concerned. Individual agency was often the mechanism through which the micro-level institutional forces were operationalized within a VNPO. Equally too, though, such individual agency could be directed toward other organizational goals, such as campaigning or advocacy.

If this individual agency was a necessary condition for releasing the innovative capacity of VNPOs, it was not a sufficient one.

The macro-level external environment was also a key variable of the process. This could be important both in providing the context to frame and give meaning to the innovation process, and also in providing the medium in which the innovation developed. Of especial importance here were the networks of contacts between the innovative VNPOs and their local environment which could provide a source of innovative ideas, a source of support, both in terms of finance and the legitimacy of the innovation, and/or a core component of the operationalization and implementation of an innovation.

The final factor in the process was again the meta-level institutional framework. This framework was argued to be the essential incentive to innovation, in the absence of a competitive environment and profit motive, so essential to innovation in the for-profit sector. It was this framework which was the spur to release the innovative capacity of VNPOs.

It is important to emphasize, as Granovetter (1985) has suggested, that these institutional forces both *constrained* and *enabled* the activity of VNPOs. They *constrained* it in the sense that innovation was often an expectation of such organizations, so much so that it was frequently an essential element of their funding criteria. This led VNPOs to select certain types of activity above other types or to portray their activity as innovative, irrespective of its actual nature.

They *enabled* it in the sense that they carved out a distinctive niche for VNPOs against both governmental and for-profit organizations. Thus VNPOs had much greater opportunity to innovate than governmental organizations, because the *categorical restraint* (Knapp *et al.* 1990) limited the ability and/or opportunities for government to innovate. By contrast, their independence and ascribed institutional role gave VNPOs a freedom to innovate which government did not possess. Similarly it also enabled their role in contrast to for-profit organizations. It provided VNPOs with a source of funding for innovation which was not open to for-profit organizations. Moreover, the market for the PSS is too small to offer many opportunities for such organizations to cull greater profits through innovation and so militates against these firms taking the risks that innovation carries.

... and toward a model of the innovative capacity of VNPOs

These factors are brought together in Figure 7.1. This offers an initial model of the *innovation mix* – the way(s) in which the innovative capacity of VNPOs can be brought to fruition by the interaction of a number of variables in this mix. This sees the VNPO as an open system, dependent upon interacting with its environment in order to achieve its organizational mission. This environment (and the organization itself) is structured by, and contingent upon, the institutional framework.

The issues of contingency (Lawrence and Lorsch 1967) and of embeddedness (Granovetter 1985) are essential to this model. This is not to say that anything goes, however. The institutional framework is the essential component of this mix. It is

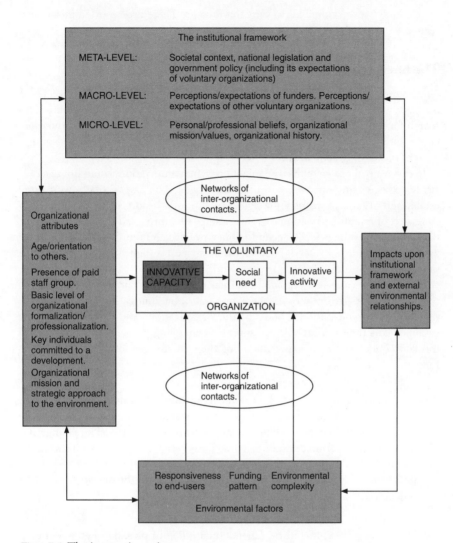

The institutional framework

META-LEVEL: Societal context, national legislation and government policy (including its expectations of voluntary organizations)

MACRO-LEVEL: Perceptions/expectations of funders. Perceptions/ expectations of other voluntary organizations.

MICRO-LEVEL: Personal/professional beliefs, organizational mission/values, organizational history.

Networks of inter-organizational contacts.

Organizational attributes

Age/orientation to others.

Presence of paid staff group.

Basic level of organizational formalization/ professionalization.

Key individuals committed to a development.

Organizational mission and strategic approach to the environment.

THE VOLUNTARY

INNOVATIVE CAPACITY → Social need → Innovative activity

ORGANIZATION

Impacts upon institutional framework and external environmental relationships.

Networks of inter-organizational contacts.

Responsiveness to end-users   Funding pattern   Environmental complexity

Environmental factors

Figure 7.1 The innovation mix

this which the other key elements of this model – the attributes of a VNPO and the key environmental factors in a locality – are contingent upon for their import, and which in return give substance to the institutional structure of a locality.

Moreover, within either the organizational attributes or the environment factors, there are a number of sub-components (such as organizational age or orientation in regard of the organizational attributes). Which of these come into play depends upon the overall interaction of the elements of the model.

This model is an important development in understanding the innovative capacity of VNPOs and its resolution. In order to test its bounds, the final stage of this study was to subject it to some hard cases. These are reported in the next section.

The hard cases

The bounds of this model were tested by a selected number of 'hard cases'. These are cases which seemed to fall outside its parameters, and so tested its validity. This search for 'disconfirmation' is as essential a part of theory building as is the more confirmatory approach, as it tests directly the validity of the underlying assumptions of the study (Salancik and Pfeffer 1977).

In this study these were five organizations where innovation would not necessarily be expected and one where it might have been. The first two cases were large established organizations of some age and with little history of innovation. Both were part of established national organizations. One provided residential care for deaf adults with other special needs and one provided community-based child-care services for children in need. Neither would suggest a high degree of innovative potential, on the basis of their previous work.

In both these cases it was changes in their institutional framework which led to the innovations. In both cases the emphasis upon innovation was mandated downwards by the national body of the organization, and in both cases the rationale was the same. It was a response to changing governmental policy and the consequent changed expectations of their main (frequently governmental) funders:

> All our fees are paid centrally to our organization and then passed down to us . . . I've been here for twelve years but all the major changes have been in the last five years, because of changes in government policy . . . The change has been top-down, from our national director of residential services – it's what the social workers in local authorities want now. (Senior manager of residential home for adults with profound deafness, talking about the development of an independent living facility at the establishment.)

> We're being encouraged by our national office to provide new 'integrated' services for children . . . Basically this means whatever the [Social Services] Department will pay for! (Regional manager of national child-care charity, talking about developments in his region.)

This institutional change required a service change for the organizations, so that they could continue to be congruent to their key funding environment. This was not an easy change for either organization, which had established ways of providing traditional residential services. One of the organizations in particular reported a number of staff changes because the existing staff group could not adjust to the new way(s) of working, whilst both emphasized that training was essential to the transition from traditional to innovative activity.

The third organization was also an older organization with a large staff group. It provided a community resource centre for young people with problems, such as homelessness, drug abuse or delinquent behaviour. Here, the age of the organization was not so much a 'dead hand' upon it, but rather a source of prehistory. For much of its past it had had to develop innovative services in order to secure funding – this had been a key funding criteria. It now had more secure funding through a service agreement with the local authority. However, this history of innovative activity had built up a momentum and expectation amongst the staff, and innovative responses to newly expressed needs were the expectation of these staff.

Another important factor was that, although the organization itself was relatively old, it had a high turnover of staff. The centre manager believed that this was beneficial, because new staff brought new ideas and approaches into the centre. Thus, the organization provided a framework with a bias toward innovation, within which the change of staff provided a flow of new perspectives and of innovative ideas: 'We expect our staff to have new ideas, and we have young staff coming in all the time. They're eager and keen and want to make a mark – they're committed to change' (Manager of resource centre).

The next two VNPOs were volunteer-based ones, which one would not have necessarily expected to be innovative as a result of the model outlined above. Both were carers' groups. The key factor here was that the SSD had been instrumental in setting up both organizations. To a great degree they were in effect expressions of the innovative activity of the SSD, rather than a source of innovation themselves.

This was confirmed when their activity subsequent to their establishment was viewed. Both had quickly become quite conventional in providing a range of standardized activities and services for their members. They had neither the time nor the inclination to continue to exert an innovative capacity. It was the establishment of these groups by the SSD which had been the actual innovation, rather than their subsequent activity.

The final organization was one which had significant funding from the local authority and which might therefore have been expected to be an innovative organization. It was a local information centre for people with a physical disability. This case, however, made plain that it was not solely *governmental* funding alone which stimulated innovation, but rather *the expectations of funders*, whoever they might be. In this case the expectations of the local authority were limited to the provision of an information service and little else. The centre conformed to these expectations: 'We get a grant from the Social Services to [provide information services]. That's it. We don't have any other contact. It's a pity – we know what the needs are but we are not used' (Co-ordinator of information centre).

These six hard cases have demonstrated both that the innovative capacity of VNPOs cannot be stimulated and released in a mechanistic way, and that the model developed here is sophisticated enough to be able to encompass this complexity and render it comprehensible. It has demonstrated that the stimulation of innovation is not conducive to the recipe book approach – that is, it is not a case of mixing a number of key ingredients together and then awaiting the innovation cake to rise. Rather, what is important is the interaction of these elements, which are themselves contingent upon the key environmental and institutional contexts. Organizations with apparently traditional attributes, as in some of these hard cases, can become innovators in the right institutional and local environment.

Innovation is thus a function of this interaction, rather than of any one single factor. In this sense it conforms very much to the contingency model of organizational dynamics discussed previously. What is essential is that the organizations involved operate as open systems, which are responsive to these factors, and indeed reliant upon them to achieve their mission-critical ends. This then allows the institutional framework and the key environmental factors to interact with organizational attributes. These attributes only gain their meaning from this interaction. In a sense, there is no such thing as an innovative VNPO *per se*, nor is it an essential (normative) characteristic of voluntary action. The innovative capacity of VNPOs is both stimulated and produced, and constrained, by these environmental factors and institutional frameworks surrounding voluntary action.

It could be argued that such an approach reduces the complexity of organizational life to a relatively small number of organizational contingencies. However, these shone through again and again in this study, in their impact upon the innovative capacity of VNPOs. Pfeffer (1981) has warned elsewhere against the spurious search for complexity in organizational analysis:

> It is clear that if the bounded rational managers ... of some of our theories really had to cope with worlds as complex as implied by the numerous measures and models applied to understand these worlds, they could face an impossible task. Yet somehow managers function, organizations operate, and work gets done ... In our fascination with complexity, we overlook the potential for finding simpler models to describe the world ...
>
> The field has lost sight of Occam's razor and the rule of parsimony. The law of requisite simplicity suggests that the premises underlying many of our theories are correct and that some relatively straightforward concepts properly applied can account for much of what occurs in organizations. We need to look for a small set of powerful concepts that are relatively simple in their application and measurement. The complexity of our models and measure has well exceeded the complexity of the phenomena we study.
>
> (pp. 411–412)

It is argued here that the initial model uncovered by this study provides just such a set of concepts for understanding and exploring the innovative capacity of VNPOs.

Finally, a helpful approach to evaluating the utility of such an emerging model as this one is provided by Deutsch (1966). This approach has been used recently by, amongst others, Salamon and Anheier (1992a, 1992b). Deutsch argues that a useful model needs to combine an appropriate mix of four factors. These are: (i) its *relevance* to the topic under consideration and the empirical evidence which relates to it; (ii) its *economism* compared to alternative models; (iii) its *predictive powers*, in terms of its *rigour* (its potential to offer insights to each step of its analysis), its *combinatorial richness* (the range of alternative scenarios that can be generated from it) and its *organizing power* (its ability to be generalized across different situations and data); and (iv) its *originality*, in that it contributes something new to the body of knowledge within which it is located.

Whilst Deutsch emphasized that no model could meet all these criteria, it is argued that the initial model described here scores strongly against these criteria. Its relevance can be seen to the extent that it encompasses the substantial concepts to have been unearthed in this study and incorporates them within an integrated conceptual framework, and its economism has already been emphasized above.

The predictive power of the model is perhaps more of a potential than a reality at this time. It has shown itself able to offer insights into both the structure and the process of innovation by VNPOs, and to have the ability to incorporate different organizations and localities. Its ability to offer predictive advice to voluntary-sector and local authority managers in the PSS is considered below. Further work is required now to test it across different organizational industries and fields. Finally, the originality of the model is strong. It is the first such model of the innovative capacity of VNPOs, whilst it also offers an insight for organization theory into the spurs to innovation in a non-market environment.

Implications for theory and research

This study has explored the role of VNPOs in innovation in the PSS. In conclusion, it is argued here that it has made two significant contributions to our knowledge base – an empirical and a theoretical contribution.

The empirical contribution

A key factor to arise out of the initial literature review was the paucity of empirical evidence against which to test the breadth of assertions about the innovative role of VNPOs. This study has provided just such an empirical basis.

This contribution has had two dimensions to it. First, and most generally, it has developed a classification of organizational change, derived from theory, through which to validate the innovative, or otherwise, activity of VNPOs – and indeed other organizations involved in the implementation of social policies. This classification has been able to distinguish such innovative activity from developmental and traditional activity. It has also enabled the nature of the *newness* and *discontinuity* of this innovation to be captured, and has dis-aggregated its *service* and *client* components for analysis. Second, the study has provided a mapping of the extent and nature of innovative activity by VNPOs, and has explored a number of organizational characteristics which describe the innovators, compared to their developmental and traditional peers.

The theoretical contribution

As well as providing an empirical description of the innovative VNPOs, and their innovations, it has developed an initial causal model of the innovative capacity of VNPOs. This model has emphasized the contingent nature of the fulfilment of this capacity, and specified the key factors upon which it is contingent. This model can be viewed from two perspectives.

NON-PROFIT THEORY

As was apparent in the literature review, the field of non-profit studies has suffered from a lack of attention to organization theory (Knokke and Prensky 1984; Paton 1993) which is only now being rectified, particularly in the United States.

This study has drawn significantly from organization theory in approaching the innovative capacity of VNPOs and their role in social policy. It has drawn in particular from the innovation studies sub-literature. This has allowed a clearer definition and understanding of innovation to be developed than was previously the case in the non-profit field, or indeed in the wider study of social policy. It has also derived useful insights from other branches of organization theory, and in particular from systems theory, contingency theory and institutional analysis. This study thus has demonstrated the contribution that organization theory can make to the study of VNPOs. This is by no means a unique contribution, but rather one of a wave of such contributions being made at present. Where it is unique is in its focus upon *innovation* by VNPOs.

ORGANIZATION THEORY

Despite the breadth of material written about the study of innovation, a gap has been apparent in the lack of an appreciation of innovation in a non-market environment. The existing literature has invariably emphasized competition and the profit-spur to innovation. Singh *et al.* (1991) and Tucker *et al.* (1992) have offered some pertinent insights into the impact of the institutional environment upon the field of social care and of VNPOs respectively. This study has built upon and developed these insights further, and has used the institutional paradigm to understand and analyse innovation within a non-profit environment. It has argued that it is the institutional framework, which both legitimizes innovative activity and offers the possibility of organizational legitimization through innovation. Just as Huxham (1993; Huxham and Vangen 1996) had developed the theory of collaboration in the absence of competition, so has this thesis developed the theory of innovation in the absence of competition.

A second, more limited, contribution has been a refinement of the concept of institutional isomorphism, as developed by DiMaggio and Powell (1988). They emphasize the pressures to organizational uniformity within any institutional field, and congruence between the organizational structures of the major and minor players in such a field. They argue for three types of pressures to such uniformity –

coercive, mimetic and normative isomorphism. In contrast, this study has shown not so much a pressure to conform to such *structural uniformity* but rather a pressure to *congruence with the prevailing expectations* within the institutional field. Whilst DiMaggio and Powell argue that interaction with significant 'higher-order collectivities' will lead VNPOs to mimic their characteristics, this has suggested otherwise. It has suggested that these former organizations can set a separate institutional agenda which will have an equal impact upon the work of VNPOs. It is thus possible to hypothesize a fourth type of isomorphism, where the pressure is not to structural uniformity in an organizational field, but rather conformity with the expectations of the major stakeholders about the roles and tasks that other organizations in this field should undertake. This might be termed *instrumental isomorphism*. This is an interesting point and deserves further exploration.

The need for further research

Inevitably, no research study is complete. This study itself opens up as many questions and venues for future research as questions that it has answered. Six areas are of particular import.

First, it was noted at the beginning that this book was entering an area which had had little previous research done in it. Thus the search for a model was initially akin to the proverbial search for a needle in a haystack. Having developed an initial model, it now needs further rigorous testing and refinement. This work should focus upon

- allowing the legitimacy of the model to be tested further, by replication studies;
- developing focused hypotheses to be constructed upon the basis of the model in order to refine some more of its detail (further work on the process of the release of innovative capacity would be useful, for example, perhaps building upon the work of Barley and Tolbert 1997); and
- testing the generalizability of the model across other service fields besides the PSS (Tucker *et al.* (1992) have suggested that institutional forces are a strong influence in such fields, so it would be instructive to explore their impact in other areas of public and social policy, such as that of the environment).

Second, comparative studies would be important to test the national bounds of the model. It is important to know the extent that this is a general model, capable of wide application, or if it is bounded by national characteristics. The present author has already begun such comparative work, in Hungary and Canada, and is presently discussing the possibility of further such work, in Japan and the United States.

Third, specific parts of the model would benefit from further attention. A systems approach has been used in an exploratory way, in order to help understand the innovative capacity of VNPOs. Further work is needed to develop this approach in a more analytic manner. Similarly, whilst the importance of networks has been highlighted, as key conduits of contact between organizations and their environments, only a start has been made in mapping them. Further work with the tools of network analysis (Knokke and Kuklinski 1982) would enable more detailed explorations of these networks and their internal dynamics.

Fourth, a typology of organizational change has been developed which has been used as a template for classifying the activity of VNPOs. It too has also been used largely descriptively. However, it offers the potential to explore key differences and approaches between different types of innovative organization – for example, between those organizations producing evolutionary as opposed to expansionary innovation. This needs further attention to fulfil its potential.

Finally, this study has suggested a development of institutional analysis, by focusing not so much upon structural convergence as upon congruence to the prevailing expectations within an institutional field. Again, this deserves more detailed exploration than has been the case here.

Lessons for the management of the innovative capacity of VNPOs

Lessons for the leaders of VNPOs

This research would suggest eight key issues for the managers of VNPOs to consider in the context of the innovative capacity of their organizations. The first, and fundamental one, is to emphasize that it is wrong to perceive innovative capacity as an inherent characteristic of VNPOs. As highlighted above, this has frequently been asserted both by policy makers (Department of Health 1989) and by writers about the sector (Peyton 1989). Yet the research reported above has made it clear that this is not so. VNPOs are not inherently innovative. Only around a third of the organizations identified what could subsequently be classified as genuine innovative activity that they had been involved in, even when invited to do so.

Whilst it is important to dispel the myth of the inherent innovative capacity of VNPOs, there is an important corollary to this: that innovation is not normatively better than any other activity that VNPOs engage in. It is simply one role. Other, potentially equally important, roles that were uncovered by the research included the provision of specialist services, individual advocacy and campaigning for the needs and rights of disadvantaged groups.

In the past, it is true, claims of their innovative capacity have been used by the leaders of VNPOs to assert their equality with, or hegemony over, the statutory services (Carter 1974). This was a useful tactic when VNPOs were marginal to the provision of mainstream public services and were often engaged in a struggle to gain funding. However, the social policy terrain has shifted so that VNPOs are increasingly becoming *the* provider of mainstream public services. To continue with claims of an inherent innovative capability carries real danger for their leaders. They risk not only having their other core organizational capabilities, as above, downgraded and dismissed, but also making themselves hostage to their own rhetoric. They may as a consequence be expected to build innovative capacity into any work that they undertake on behalf of government. There is already evidence that a demonstration of innovative capacity is becoming a precondition of some government funding schemes (such as the Inner City Partnership Scheme of the Department of the Environment). Unless their leaders act to raise the profile of the other potential contributions of VNPOs to public services, these risk being lost.

Finally, in this context, the leaders of VNPOs have to be aware themselves that innovation is not always a normative good or representative of progress. It can be wrong, or can have bad consequences for the beneficiaries of a service. For example, a number of the Intermediate Treatment schemes that many VNPOs set up in the early 1970s, to divert juvenile offenders from custody, had the unintended consequence of increasing the custodial rates for such juveniles (Morris and Giller 1987). In the industrial sphere we are also still coming to terms with the consequences of many technological developments of the twentieth century – such as acid rain and the dispersal of the ozone layer. This is one reason why there have been calls for such innovative activity to be constrained within a wider government policy for sustainable development (Mole and Elliot 1987). Managers of VNPOs need to beware of being seduced by assumptions of the implicit 'goodness' of innovation, when the societal evidence is to the contrary.

The second issue, for those VNPOs which are engaged in innovative activity, is to be clear about the type of innovation that they are pursuing and its managerial implications. This study produced a typology of organizational change which differentiated between innovation and organizational development, as well as classifying three types of innovative activity. The former distinction is especially important. Because of the importance of innovation as a 'talisman' for VNPOs, as outlined above, there has been a tendency for their leaders to call any types of organizational changes 'innovations'. This was apparent here, with even extending the opening hours of a service being called an 'innovation'. However, the dynamics of incremental organizational development, of improving the efficiency and productivity of the existing services of a VNPO to its existing beneficiaries, are quite different from innovation. An especial issue is the *discontinuity* that innovation involves, compared to organizational development (Tushman and Anderson 1985). To take a simple example, an organizational development which modifies the role of play workers in a play scheme is entirely different from an innovation which replaces that scheme with something else entirely – and which may not even require play workers.

As suggested above, this is not to say that innovation is somehow 'better' than gradual development; in the medium term, both could lead to profound improvements in the quality of the services provided. However, in the short term, the managerial issues posed for the organization are quite different and require different strategies with regard to managing their discontinuity with staff and beneficiaries. A useful metaphor has been offered by Herbig (1991) who argues that it is wrong to talk about the 'diffusion' of innovation within organizations. Rather, the process should be modelled around catastrophe theory, which emphasizes precisely this issue of discontinuity.

Further, even within the areas of legitimate innovative activity this research uncovered three different types of innovation – *total* (which changed the service and the beneficiary group of an organization), *evolutionary* (which changed the service to an existing beneficiary group), and *expansionary* innovation (which provided the existing services of an organization to a new beneficiary group). Again it is important for an organization to be clear about the type of innovation that it could or should be adopting, for each will have its own particular challenges. Persuading the existing beneficiaries of an organization to try a new service that it is offering, for example, is different from persuading a new beneficiary group to try services that the organization has previously offered to another group.

The third issue is rather more negative. This is to assume that the structural characteristics or internal environment of a VNPO will automatically give it an innovative capacity. It has often been asserted in the past that the flexibility or autonomy of decision making of VNPOs was a key factor in their innovative capacity (Knapp *et al.* 1990 provide a good summary of this and other arguments). However, *all* the VNPOs in this study exhibited low levels of bureaucracy and formalization and high levels of horizontal and internal communication and autonomy of decision making (at least in a structural sense). Whilst it might be true, therefore, that such characteristics are a necessary precursor to innovative capacity for VNPOs, by themselves they are not sufficient to ensure such a capability.

Further, there was some evidence, suggestive rather than definitive admittedly, that VNPOs with an innovative capacity had a rather *higher* level of centralization than did their developmental and traditional counterparts. It may be that this centralization is important in order to provide sufficient organizational direction and leadership in order to deal with the inertia and resistance that innovation often engenders (Rowe and Boise 1974).

Fourth, and similarly, it is incorrect to put store by the importance of individual action by itself to activate the innovative capacity of a VNPO. Much of the popular management literature of the 1980s put great store by such 'hero innovators' (such as Peters and Waterman 1982; Kamm 1987). Equally, though, others warned that such individuals, by themselves, could not prevail against the mass of organizational inertia (Praill and Baldwin 1988).

This research did indeed find that key individuals, at a range of organizational levels, were influential in stimulating the innovative capacity of VNPOs. Equally, though, it found such strong individuals present in the developmental and traditional organizations, but taking on different roles – such as fundraising or campaigning. Once again, though, the presence of such individuals is a necessary but not a sufficient condition by which to stimulate the innovative capacity of VNPOs. As previously, therefore, this issue poses two challenges for the management of VNPOs. The first is to ensure, if an innovative direction is required, that such individuals of flair and energy are indeed located within the organization. This by itself is not sufficient, however. The second necessary condition is then to ensure that their energies are directed toward innovative activity, rather than other, probably equally important, organizational activity.

It is also important to consider the location of innovation within a VNPO. There is no perfect solution here. One possibility, found frequently in these case studies, was for current managers to take on an innovative role in addition to their existing workload. This ensured that innovation was located in the mainstream of organizational activity. However, it did risk the overload and burnout of these managerial staff members. If such an alternative is pursued, therefore, a realistic review of their workloads needs to be carried out and some time specifically ring-fenced for innovative activity.

The second possibility, found in only a couple of organizations, was to appoint managers whose specific role was the development of innovative work. This meant that such individuals had dedicated time to devote to the complex tasks of innovation and that this did not disrupt the routine work of the organization. However, it had the potential to marginalize innovation from the mainstream of the organization, making it difficult to diffuse across the organization as a whole (because other staff could resent the perceived 'special' status of such individuals or not see the innovative developments as integral to their work). It could also risk the innovating individuals' pursuing initiatives not in tune with the overall tenor of the organization. If such an approach is taken, therefore, one possibility is to second existing staff to these posts, so that they keep an operational focus and a legitimacy with the organization as a whole.

The next two managerial issues relate to the relationships of VNPOs to their external environment. A key finding of the research was that the innovative organizations had an outward orientation to their environment which encouraged their leaders, staff and members both to interact with other actors in this environment (thus gaining information about unmet need and about possible new approaches to providing public services) and to seek opportunities for growth and development. By contrast, the developmental and traditional organizations tended to be far more self-contained and inward-looking, much more aware of potential organizational threats than of opportunities in the environment. In organizational terms, the innovative VNPOs acted more as 'open-systems' organizations, dependent upon interaction with their environment to achieve their mission-critical goals, whilst their non-innovative counterparts were analogous to 'closed-systems' organizations, which were uncoupled from their environments and not dependent upon such interaction to achieve their mission-critical goals (Pfeffer and Salancik 1978; Scott 1992).

The fifth issue, therefore, is for the managers of VNPOs to take a deliberate strategic approach to the relationship of their organization to its environment – in terms of the local community, its key stakeholders and the larger societal environment. In the research, the use of the four strategic gestalts of Miles and Snow (1978) were found to be extremely useful in making extant the strategic directions of the case-study organizations.

Conventional management theory has emphasized for some time the impact of such strategic approaches upon the internal structure and adaptation of an organization to its environment (Zahria and Pearce 1990). However, this present research, confirming that of Beekum and Ginn (1993), has revealed that these strategic approaches could have an equally powerful impact upon the external inter-organizational networks of relationships of a VNPO. These networks of relationships themselves were found to be a powerful activator of the innovative capacity of VNPOs. The innovative organizations invariably had complex and sophisticated inter-organizational networks, whilst the traditional organizations displayed far simpler ones.

Such networks could play a range of functions for the innovative VNPOs. They could provide information about a new approach to service delivery, or an unmet need; they could facilitate the successful implementation of an innovation by locating it within an inter-organizational context or plan; they could be immensely useful in resource-acquisition to find an innovative development; and they could ensure the wider dissemination and/or sustenance of an innovation by providing a supportive environment for its growth.

Yet if such networks were significant for the success of innovative activity, it would be wrong to see 'networking' as an activity in its own right. Previous research by the present author (PSMRC 1991; Osborne and Tricker 1994) has found that such networks gather their import from being a product of other work and so have a demonstrable record of success. Network-building in isolation from such other activity lacks a context and can invariably be a sterile exercise – invariably consuming more resources than it actually creates. The successful management of innovation by managers of VNPOs requires them to be explicit in their strategic direction therefore, rather than falling prey to 'strategic drift', and to use the networks of relationships which have arisen from this mission-critical work to engender and support this innovative activity. A range of possible models for such strategic management of VNPOs exist (such as Lyons 1996) and could be made use of in this context.

The sixth issue concerns the funding pattern of a VNPO and its impact upon its innovative capacity. This research found that the innovative organizations were significantly more likely to receive funding from a governmental source (in most cases from local government, but for a few VNPOs from the Department of Health itself) rather than from voluntary or other income (like donations or fees). This runs counter to much of the conventional wisdom, which has often argued for voluntary income, and the consequent freedom to experiment, as being a key source of the innovative capacity of VNPOs.

In fact, government funding appeared to be important for two reasons. The first was the comparative security that it offered to VNPOs, to allow them room to innovate. Those with a higher degree of reliance upon voluntary sources of income were often more circumspect about experimentation – because of the innate caution and conservatism of their donors. Moreover, those VNPOs in this research that were reliant upon fees for their survival invariably needed to maintain their core services rather than risk experimentation; their market base was usually quite small and provided little margin for error. By contrast, those VNPOs that were funded by government had more comparative stability and 'slack' (Cyert and March 1963) with which to innovate.

A central issue here were the risks (financial and others) that innovation involves. This research found three such risks. These were the risk that an innovation might fail and nobody would want to support it, the risk that an innovation would be successful but not attract sufficient take-up to be viable, and the risk that an innovation might be successful but turn out to be more expensive to provide in the longer term than had been expected or was acceptable.

The leaders of a VNPO must consider, when deciding upon a commitment to innovation, whether it has sufficient resources to bear such risks itself, whether it will need to seek full development funding from an external funder (who would then bear these risks, but who would also be able to dictate the direction of the innovation – and take any resultant credit accruing from it), or whether to share the risk through a joint funding arrangement. The last approach is probably the most sensible. However, it does require a deal of trust between the two parties which the current 'contract culture' for public services in the UK does not always engender. It is, however, a significant component of 'best practice' in contracting in the for-profit sector (Ring and Van de Ven 1992).

The second possible reason for the import of government funding was the impact of the strategic intent of government itself. At both a national and a local governmental level, innovation has become one key policy goal at present. Moreover, it can also be a useful yardstick of managerial success, in the absence of more definitive measures of organizational success (Feller 1981). Funding from such governmental sources has thus frequently had a bias to innovation built into it. Indeed, the problem this posed for many VNPOs has been not so much how to fund innovative activity, but rather how to obtain funding for their non-innovative, but equally important, activity or for the continuance of innovative developments beyond the pump-priming stage. This is not a new observation (Osborn 1985, Smith and Lipsky 1993), but one which remains to be acted upon by both government and VNPOs. Often this process could involve the 'dressing up' of developmental or traditional activity in innovative 'clothing', which approach itself could weaken the direction or effectiveness of this activity (Bernstein 1991).

A key lesson here for the leaders of VNPOs, therefore, is not to seek governmental funding alone. Whilst the present policy goal for government in the UK is indeed innovation, one can predict that this impetus will change in the medium term. If VNPOs want to maintain their independence and ability to choose their own direction then it is essential to maintain a diversity of income sources, even given the potential transaction costs that the multiple accountability requirements of such diversity will impose. Any other strategy, particularly over-dependence upon government funding, leaves a VNPO prey to the whims of government policy rather than being able to follow its own strategic intent (Pifer 1967; Kramer 1989).

The final two issues for the management of the innovative capacity of VNPOs concern the appreciation by their leaders of their institutional context. This can be a diffuse concept for practising managers to grasp. It concerns the way in which organizations are embedded in their social context and the unwritten rules and rituals which enable and constrain their activity (Powell and DiMaggio 1991). In particular it concerns the expectations which exist of VNPOs by their key external stakeholders and how they respond to these in their search for legitimacy and survival (Tucker *et al.* 1992).

The institutional environment of VNPOs is complex and involves appreciation of the factors acting at the societal, industry and local community, and organizational levels. This research uncovered important factors at each of these levels.

The seventh issue for the leaders of VNPOs is therefore to be fully aware of this institutional environment and its impact upon their organization and its innovative capacity. It requires them to be aware of all three levels and their interaction. To take a simplistic example, it is not sufficient to focus solely on the societal level. If such imperatives were paramount then one would expect almost all VNPOs to be engaged in innovative activity. This is not so. One must hence explore, for example, the interaction of the societal framework and the funding policy of the key local stakeholders. Even here, though, these stakeholder expectations are not sufficient. It is quite possible for opportunities for innovative action to be available to a VNPO, but for its leaders to be constrained by its history of traditional, specialist, but non-innovative, activity. Such a scenario could set up both hostility to innovation amongst its staff and a view of it by potential funders as a provider of specialist rather than innovative activity. Managers must thus focus on the interaction between the three levels and how they both constrain and enable the activity of their organization.

The final issue is one which derives directly from the one above. This is that the managers of VNPOs should not see themselves as the passive 'victims' of their institutional contexts. Rather they need to be proactive in shaping it. As Granovetter (1985) has made clear, an institutional approach is not solely a case of simple environmental determinism but of the *interaction* of organizations, their leaders and their environment. Organizations are both enabled/constrained by their environment and act (consciously or otherwise) to shape it. If managers want their organizations to be proactive in innovation, then they need to act to create the perception of their organization as a legitimate vehicle for innovation amongst both its staff and key stakeholders. In such effort the impact of organizational symbols is as powerful as that of explicit messages (Meyer and Rowan 1977). For the staff of an organization, for example, seeing their leaders actually act to foster innovation sends a far more powerful message than any number of policy statements or internal memoranda. Such cultural and symbolic management is certainly not easy (Colville and Packman 1996). It is, however, essential.

In conclusion, this section has drawn out the implications for the managers of VNPOs of the research about the innovative capacity of VNPOs reported previously. It has deliberately avoided a 'cookery book' approach to such capacity; organizational reality and innovation are far more complex than baking a cake (Pelz 1985). Whilst it is possible to highlight key issues and offer guidelines for managers, ultimately the priming of the innovative capacity of an organization is not a mechanistic exercise but rather requires the application of managerial judgement.

It is appropriate to end on the point that was started with, in this context. This is the issue as to whether it is right for the leaders of any particular VNPO to seek to be innovative. There may well be very good reasons for this – to do with the changing needs of its beneficiaries or the need to respond to other changes in the environment. However, there is also the danger at present of innovation's being assumed to be a normative policy good, irrespective of other considerations. Such an assumption should always be challenged. There are many other important roles that VNPOs can perform in providing public services. Innovation may or may not be necessary to this performance, but it may also be counterproductive. The leaders of VNPOs need to be careful to ensure that they do not become forced into a role which is neither inherent to their nature nor conducive to mission-critical goals. Innovation has real costs in terms of financial and human resources, in terms of the risks (for organizations and their beneficiaries) that it requires to be taken, and in terms of the opportunities forgone by a decision to innovate. VNPOs must beware of these costs and be prepared to meet them, or risk organizational demise.

Lessons for local government managers of public services

There are six key issues for local government managers that this research suggests. The first, and overriding, one is for local government to recognize itself as an active factor in shaping the innovative capacity of VNPOs in its locality. Dependent upon the funding strategy that a local authority adopts, it could reinforce the innovative capacity of a small number of VNPOs, could generate opportunities for innovation by a range of VNPOs across the locality, or could indeed 'select out' innovative activity as a desired goal for VNPOs, by de-selecting it as a funding goal or as a performance indicator. Whilst it is true that this would affect only the VNPOs dependent upon local government for their funding, other research (Osborne and Hems 1996) has shown how this is an increasing and significant source of income for many VNPOs.

It is important, therefore, for local government to recognize explicitly its active role. Often such a role is shaped by the unconscious and unplanned fallout of the local policy-making process. Greater efficiency and effectiveness in the meeting of local policy goals will be forthcoming if it becomes instead a conscious and explicit consideration of this process.

Second, it is important equally for local government to be clear about what type of innovation it wants to generate and why. The typology of innovation developed for this study (Osborne 1998) is a useful starting point here. Each type of innovation within this typology both will have its own implications for the development of local public services and will have its own distinctive managerial challenges for VNPOs and for local government. Enabling a VNPO to provide its current services to a new beneficiary group is a task of a different order from enabling it to provide new services to its existing beneficiaries. The focus in the former case would be upon an effective marketing strategy whilst in the latter it would be upon training and staffing needs. It is important, therefore, that local government take strategic decisions about the type of innovation it wants, rather than rely on a general exhortation to innovate, as the current 'flavour of the month' for public services. It then needs to clarify the distinctive managerial tasks that it raises for the authority. Of course, the leaders and staff of VNPOs will themselves have ideas about the types of innovative developments that they would like to instigate. The relative power balance between local government and a VNPO in any particular relationship will determine how influential these ideas are. The important point for those in local government is to take a strategic view of their own position.

Third, it is important for local government to appreciate the opportunity costs of innovation. By adopting innovation as a core goal or performance indicator for VNPOs, local government is forgoing its alternative activities, such as the continuance or expansion of an existing specialist service. The resource realities of the voluntary sector are that a VNPO will not be able to do both – unless, of course, double the funding is available!

Moreover, within the present public-policy framework, with its emphasis on innovation as a normative good, there is a temptation to see innovation as an end in itself. This must be resisted. There may be good reasons to promote innovation in the delivery of local community services, but there may also be equally good, or better, reasons to build upon existing specialist knowledge. Good local management will make positive decisions about such choices, rather than letting them happen by default.

Fourth, local government needs to be careful that 'innovation' does not become one more token in a time- and resource-consuming funding game between VNPOs and itself. Much has been written (such as Bernstein 1991) about the nature of this game, wherein actions and decisions are important as much for their symbolic significance as for their actuality (see also Meyer and Rowan 1977). If it is required to secure funding, a VNPO is quite capable of making a service appear innovative or to have innovative outcomes, irrespective of its actual virtue. Similarly, local government can use innovation as a gatekeeping device, through which to screen 'in' or 'out' VNPOs in the funding strategy.

To an extent, in a time of restricted and other diminishing public resources, such game-playing may be an inevitable part of the local funding process for VNPOs. However, it has its own costs, in terms of both finances and of human resources, and can add a level of cynicism and lack of mutual trust which is counterproductive to efficient local services. There is no easy solution to this problem, but it does require recognition. Once made extant, both parties can then act to engender more trust, both through the contracting process itself (Ring and Van de Ven 1992) and through the management of their joint working relationship (Huxham and Vangen 1996).

Fifth, local authorities need to consider the implications of their approach to co-ordinating the plural provision of local services to their community. Within the PSS, for example, and even assuming a national context of the overall development of the 'mixed economy of care', there are nonetheless different models of implementing and co-ordinating these services at a local level. Dependent upon its approach, a local authority might emphasize the use of the market and price mechanisms to co-ordinate its provision, the use of a hierarchical planning mechanism, or the use of its existing network of relationships with VNPOs, and other organizations, in its area (Osborne 1997). No one approach is right but they do all have discrete managerial implications, and costs. In this context, for example, if the market mechanism was chosen to co-ordinate service provision, there is some evidence that this will make VNPOs cautious, rather than innovative, because of the small size of the market and the high labour costs involved (Smith and Lipsky 1993, Wistow *et al.* 1994).

Finally, as the concept of the mixed economy of care develops, local authorities need to pay close attention to their management of the contractual process with VNPOs. Three issues are relevant here. First, local government needs to consider the actual impact of contracting for mainstream, rather than marginal or 'add-on', public services upon the innovative capacity of VNPOs. Major research in the US (Smith and Lipsky 1993) has suggested that the impact can be deleterious. This is because the move to such mainstream provision of public services means that issues of efficiency take precedence over those of innovation. The worst of all worlds is where local government contracts a service to a VNPO with the expectation both of efficiency *and* of innovation gains. Such expectations invariably set the VNPO up to fail, to the benefit of neither purchaser, provider nor beneficiary of the service.

A second, related, issue is concerned with the costs of the contractual management process, known as transaction costs (Williamson 1986). As the for-profit literature makes clear, the process of innovation is invariably a costly one, because of the risks involved (Best 1990). If further transaction costs are loaded onto a VNPO, through the contractual process, this may make the service financially unviable. Again, no one will benefit in such a situation.

The final issue relating to the management of contractual services and the innovative capacity of VNPOs concerns the evaluation of such capacity by government. On the one hand, there can be an important symbolic content to such evaluation, concerned with organizational legitimacy in the eyes of key internal and external stakeholders. Feller (1981) has suggested that innovation can become a symbol of 'conspicuous production' for organizations where their goals and achievements are diffuse and ambiguous, as is the case with many public services, and especially with the PSS (see also Meyer and Rowan 1977; Bovaird 1993). If this is the case, then local government and VNPOs need to consider together the costs of such an exercise and the extent to which the legitimacy obtained by both parties is worth these costs.

On the other hand, the actual process of evaluating innovation, and identifying the types of performance indicators that might be employed, is fraught. One possible way forward is a multidimensional approach which looks at innovative impact of VNPOs alongside a range of interrelated indicators of organizational performance (Osborne *et al.* 1995). Another alternative, which the Department of Health has recently adopted, is the 'outcome funding' model (Williams and Webb 1992).

Whatever approach is adopted, it is certainly a potentially costly process. If these costs are not to be prohibitive, then the evaluation of innovation by VNPOs requires trust and joint collaboration between local government and VNPOs in both development and management. Nor is such trust antipathetic to either the development of a mixed economy of care or to the management of the contractual process itself. Best practice in the for-profit sector has emphasized how such trust is essential both to the proper working of the contractual process in the market place (Burt 1982, 1992; Ring and Van de Ven 1992) and to the management of the risks of innovation (Best 1990; Alter and Hage 1993).

In conclusion, three points should be emphasized. First, it is essential that local authorities are clear about why they wish to engender innovation in their local services and the type of innovation that they need. The indiscriminate search for service innovation is both inefficient and ineffective, and is in the interests of no one.

Second, the issues of trust and interdependence are important. Unless local authorities are prepared to bear substantial transaction costs in the management of innovation, and to impose similar costs on VNPOs, then trust and collaboration with VNPOs needs to be fostered.

Finally, local government needs to accept and embrace its active role in the release of the innovative capacity of VNPOs. Local government has as much responsibility for the release of the innovative capacity of VNPOs as do the organizations themselves. To act in ignorance of this role will undermine the best use of this capacity in the provision of public services to local communities.

References

1 Voluntary and non-profit organizations and innovation in public services

Anheier, H. and W. Seibel (eds) (1990) *The Third Sector* (de Gruyter, Berlin)

Department of Health (1989) *Caring for People: Community Care in the Next Decade and Beyond* (HMSO, London)

Deutsch, K. (1985) 'On theory and research in innovation' in (eds) R. Merritt and A. Merritt, *Innovation in the Public Sector*, pp. 17–34

Griffiths, R. (1988) *Community Care: Agenda for Action* (HMSO, London)

King's Fund Institute (1987) *Promoting Innovation in Community Care* (King's Fund Institute, London)

Knapp, M., E. Robertson and C. Thomason (1990) 'Public money, voluntary action. Whose welfare?' in (eds) H. Anheier and W. Seibel, *The Third Sector*, pp. 183–218

Knokke, D. and D. Prensky (1984) 'What relevance do organization theories have for voluntary organizations?' in *Social Science Quarterly* (65), pp. 3–20

Merritt, R. and A. Merritt (eds) (1985) *Innovation in the Public Sector* (Sage, Beverly Hills, Calif.)

Paton, R. (1993) 'Organisation and management studies on voluntary and non-profit organisations in the UK: achievements and prospects' (Paper to the Researching Voluntary and Non-profit Organisations in the UK: The State of the Art Symposium, University of the South Bank, London)

Rao, N. (1991) *From Providing to Enabling* (Joseph Rowntree Foundation, York)

Wistow, G., M. Knapp, B. Hardy and C. Allen (1994) *Social Care in a Mixed Economy* (Open University Press, Buckingham)

Wistow, G., M. Knapp, B. Hardy, J. Forder, J. Kendall and R. Manning (1996) *Social Care Markets: Progress and Prospects* (Open University Press, Buckingham)

2 Conceptualizing voluntary activity

Abrams, P., S. Abrams, R. Humphreys and K. Snaith (1989) *Neighbourhood Care and Social Policy* (HMSO, London)

Anheier H. (1995) 'Theories of the nonprofit sector' in *Voluntary and Nonprofit Sector Quarterly* (24, 1), pp.15–24

Anheier, H. and W. Seibel (eds) (1990) *The Third Sector* (de Gruyter, Berlin)

Aves Committee (1969) *Voluntary Work in the Social Services* (George Allen & Unwin, London)

Barker, A. (1982a) 'Quango: a word or a campaign' in (ed.) A. Barker, *Quangos in Britain*, pp. 219–231

Barker, A. (1982b) *Quangos in Britain* (Macmillan, London)

Bennett, J. (1983) 'Classification of charitable purposes' in Charities Aid Foundation, *Charity Statistics 1982/83*, p. 77

Berger, P. and R. Neuhaus (1977) *To Empower People. The Role of Mediating Structures in Public Policy* (American Enterprise Institute for Public Policy Research, Washington)

Billis, D. (1991) 'The roots of voluntary agencies' in *Voluntary and Nonprofit Sector Quarterly* (20, 1), pp. 5–24

Bourdillon, A. (1945a) 'Introduction' in (ed.) A. Bourdillon, *Voluntary Social Services. Their Place in the Modern State*, pp. 1–10

Bourdillon, A. (1945b) *Voluntary Social Services. Their Place in the Modern State* (Methuen, London)

Brenton, M. (1985) *Voluntary Sector in British Social Services* (Longman, London)

Brudney, J. (1990) *Fostering Volunteer Programs in the Public Sector* (Jossey-Bass, San Francisco)

Butler, R. and D. Wilson (1990) *Managing Voluntary and Non-Profit Organizations* (Routledge, London)

Caiden, G. (1982) *Public Administration* (Palisades, Calif.)

Chanan, G. (1991) *Taken for Granted* (Community Development Foundation, London)

Chanan, G. (1996) 'Regeneration. Plugging gaps or pushing frontiers', in *Local Economy* (August), pp. 98–103

Collins, R. and N. Hickman (1991) 'Altruism and culture as social products' in *Voluntas* (2, 2), pp. 1–15

Cornuelle, R. (1983) *Healing America* (Pitman, New York)

Cousins, P. (1982) 'Quasi-official bodies in local government' in (ed.) A. Barker (1982b), pp. 152–163

Darvill, G. and B. Mundy (1984) *Volunteers in the Personal Social Services* (Tavistock, London)

de Oliveira, M. and R. Tandon (1994) *Citizens. Strengthening Global Democracy* (CIVICUS, Washington)

de Tocqueville, A. (1971) *Democracy in America* (Oxford University Press, London)

Etzioni, A. (1961) *A Comparative Analysis of Complex Organizations* (Free Press, New York)

Etzioni, A. (1968) *The Active Society. A Theory of Societal and Political Processes* (Free Press, New York)

Fisher, J. (1993) *The Road from Rio. Sustainable Development and the Nongovernmental Movement in the Third World* (Praeger, Westport, Conn.)

Gamwell, F. (1984) *Beyond Preference. Liberal Theories of Independent Association* (University of Chicago Press, Chicago)

Gladstone, F. (1979) *Voluntary Action in a Changing World* (Bedford Square Press, London)

Gurin, M. and J. Van Til (1990) 'Philanthropy in its historical context' in (ed.) J. Van Til, *Critical Issues in American Philanthropy*, pp. 3–18

Guzzetta, C. (1984) 'Voluntarism and professionalism' in (ed.) F. Schwartz, *Voluntarism and Social Work Practice* (University Press of America, Lanham)

Hague, D., W. Mackenzie and A. Barker (eds) (1975) *Public Policy and Private Interests* (Macmillan, London)

Hatch, S. (1980) *Outside the State* (Croom Helm, London)

Hedley, R. (1992) *Volunteering Today* (Volunteer Centre, Berkhamsted)

Hedley, R. and J. Justin Smith (1992) *Volunteering and Society. Principles and Practice* (NCVO, London)

Home Office (1990) *Efficiency Scrutiny of Government Funding of the Voluntary Sector* (HMSO, London)

Hood, C. (1984) *The Hidden Public Sector. The World of Para-Governmental Organisations* (Centre for the Study of Public Policy, University of Strathclyde)

Horton Smith, D. (1981) 'Altruism, volunteers, and volunteerism' in *Journal of Voluntary Action Research* (10), pp. 21–36

Horton Smith, D. (1991) 'Four sectors or five? Retaining the member benefit sector' in *Nonprofit and Voluntary Sector Quarterly* (20, 2), pp. 137–150

Horton Smith, D. and J. Van Til (eds) (1983) *International Perspectives on Voluntary Action Research* (University Press of America, Washington DC)

James, E. (1990) 'Economic theories of the non-profit sector: a comparative perspective' in (ed.) H. Anheier and W. Seibel – op. cit., pp. 21–29

Knapp, M., E. Robertson and C. Thomason (1990) 'Public money, voluntary action. Whose welfare?' in (ed.) H. Anheier and W. Seibel – op. cit., pp.183–218

Kramer, R. (1990) *Voluntary Organizations in the Welfare State: On the Threshold of the Nineties* (Centre for Voluntary Organization Working Paper, London)

Kramer, R., H. Lorentzen, W. Melief and S. Pasquinelli (1993) *Privatization in Four European Countries* (M. E. Sharpe, New York)

Leat, D. (1995) 'Revising the non-profit/for-profit rhetoric' (Paper to the Researching the UK Voluntary Sector Conference, NCVO, London)

Les, E. (1994) 'The voluntary sector in post-communist East Central Europe: from small circles of freedom to civil society' in (eds) M. de Oliveira and R. Tandon, *Citizens. Strengthening Global Democracy*, pp.195–237

National Center for Charitable Statistics (1986) *National Taxonomy of Exempt Entities* (INDEPENDENT SECTOR, Washington DC)

National Council of Social Service (1970) *Voluntary Social Services* (NCSS, London)

O'Neill, M. (1989) *The Third America* (Jossey-Bass, San Francisco)

Osborne, S. (1993a) *Understanding Voluntary Organizations in Contemporary Western Society* (Public Sector Management Research Centre Working Paper Number 23, Aston University)

Osborne, S. (1993b) *Toward a Theory of the Voluntary Sector?* (Public Sector Management Research Centre Working Paper Number 24, Aston University)

Osborne, S. (1996) *Managing in the Voluntary Sector* (International Thomson Business Press, London)

Osborne, S. and L. Hems (1995) 'The economic structure of the voluntary sector in the UK' in *Nonprofit and Voluntary Sector Quarterly* (24, 4), pp. 321–336

Osborne, S. and L. Hems (1996) 'Estimating the income and expenditure of charitable organizations in the UK' in *Non Profit Studies* (1, 1), pp. 7–18

Osborne, S. and A. Kaposvari (1997) 'Towards a civil society? Exploring its meanings in the context of post-communist Hungary' in *Journal of European Social Policy* (7, 3), pp. 209–222

Palisi, B. (1972) 'A critical analysis of the voluntary association concept' in *Voluntary Action Research 1972*, pp. 39–50

Payne, R., B. Payne and R. Reddy (1972) 'Social background and role determinants of individual participation in organized voluntary action' in *Voluntary Action Research 1972*, pp. 207–250

Pifer, A. (1967) *Quasi Non Governmental Organizations* (Carnegie Corporation, New York)

Pifer, A. (1975) 'The non-governmental organization at bay' in (eds) D. Hague, W. Mackenzie and A. Barker – op. cit., pp. 395–408

Salamon, L. (1987) 'Of market failure, voluntary failure and third party government. Toward a theory of government – nonprofit relations in the modern welfare state' in *Journal of Voluntary Action Research*, pp. 29–49

Salamon, L. and H. Anheier (1994) *The Emerging Sector. An Over-View* (Johns Hopkins University, Baltimore)

Schultz, J. (1972) 'The voluntary sector and its components' in *Voluntary Action Research 1972*, pp. 25–38

Schuppert, G. (1991) 'State, market, third sector: problems of organizational choice in the delivery of public services' in *Nonprofit and Voluntary Sector Quarterly* (20, 2), pp. 123–136

Schwartz, F. (ed.) (1984) *Voluntarism and Social Work Practice* (University Press of America, Washington DC)

Seibel, W. and H. Anheier (1990) 'Sociological and political science approaches to the third sector' in (eds) H. Anheier and W. Seibel – op. cit., pp. 7–20

Shaw, T. (1990) 'Popular participation in non-governmental structures in Africa: implications for democratic development' in *Africa Today* (37, 3), pp. 5–22

Sheard, J. (1992) 'Volunteering and society, 1960 to 1990' in (eds) R. Hedley and J. Justin Smith, *Volunteering and Society. Principles and Practice*, pp. 11–32

Thomas, A. and H. Finch (1990) *On Volunteering* (Volunteer Centre, Berkhamsted)

Titmuss, R. (1970) *The Gift Relationship. From Human Blood to Social Policy* (George Allen & Unwin, London)

United States Department of the Treasury (1977) *Research Papers Sponsored by the Commission on Private Philanthropy and Public Needs* (US Dept. of the Treasury, Washington)

Van Til, J. (1988) *Mapping the Third Sector. Voluntarism in a Changing Social Economy* (Foundation Center, New York)

Van Til, J. (ed.) (1990) *Critical Issues in American Philanthropy* (Jossey-Bass, San Francisco)

Zeldin, D. (1983) 'Mobilization of young volunteers: alternative versions of voluntarism' in (eds) D. Horton Smith and J. Van Til, *International Perspectives on Voluntary Action Research*, pp. 113–122

3   Innovations, innovators and innovating

Abernathy, W. (1978) *The Productivity Dilemma* (Johns Hopkins University Press, Baltimore)

Abernathy, W. and K. Clark (1988) 'Innovation: mapping the winds of creative destruction' in (eds) M. Tushman and W. Moore, *Readings in the Management of Innovation*, pp. 55–78

Abernathy, W. and J. Utterbach (1988) 'Patterns of industrial innovation' in (eds) M. Tushman and W. Moore – op. cit., pp. 25–36

Abernathy, W., K. Clark and A. Kantrow (1983) *Industrial Renaissance* (Basic Books, New York)

Achilladelis, B., P. Jervis and A. Robertson (1972) *Project SAPPHO. A Study of Success and Failure in Innovation* (Science Policy Research Unit, University of Sussex)

Adair, J. (1990) *Challenge of Innovation* (Talbot Adair Press, Guildford)

Ahlbrandt, R. and A. Blair (1986) 'What it takes for large organizations to be innovative' in *Research Management* (29, 2), pp. 34–37

Aiken, M. and J. Hage (1974) 'Organic organizations and innovation' in *Sociology* (5), pp. 63–82

Albrecht, T. and B. Hall (1991) 'Facilitating talk about new ideas: the role of personal relationships in organizational innovation' in *Communication Monographs* (58), pp. 273–287

Aldrich, H. (1976) 'An inter-organization dependency perspective on relations between the Employment Service and its organization set' in (eds) R. Kilmann, L. Pond and D. Slevin, *Management of Organization Design*, pp. 231–266

Alter, C. and J. Hage (1993) *Organizations Working Together* (Sage, Newbury Park, Calif.)

Anheier, H. and W. Seibel (eds) (1990) *The Third Sector* (de Gruyter, Berlin)

Astley, G. and A. Van de Ven (1983) 'Central perspectives and debates in organization theory' in *Administrative Science Quarterly* (28), pp. 245–273

Atuahene-Gima, K. (1996) 'Differential potency of factors affecting innovation performance in manufacturing and service firms in Australia' in *Journal of Product Innovation Management* (13, 1), pp. 35–52

Azzone, G. and P. Maccarrone (1993) 'The energy role of lean infrastructure in technology transfer' in *Technovation* (17, 7), pp. 391–402

Baden-Fuller, C. (1995) 'On strategic innovation, corporate entrepreneurship and matching outside-in and inside-out approaches to strategy research' in *British Journal of Management* (Special edition of volume 6), pp. S3–S16

Baker, M. (ed.) (1979) *Industrial Innovation: Technology Policy and Diffusion* (Macmillan, London)

Baldock, J. (1991) 'Strengthening home based care', in (ed.) R. Kraan *et al.*, *Care for the Elderly. Significant Innovations in Three European Countries*, pp. 141–185

Baldock, J. and A. Evers (1991) 'On social innovation – an introduction' in ibid., pp. 87–92

Barclay, P. (1982) *Social Workers. Their Role and Tasks* (Bedford Square Press, London)

Barley, S. and P. Tolbert (1997) 'Institutionalization and structuration: studying the links between action and institution' in *Organization Studies* (18, 1), pp. 93–117

Barnes, M. and G. Wistow (1992) 'Sustaining innovation in community care' in *Local Government Policy Making* (18, 4), pp. 3–19

Barnett, H. (1953) *Innovation: The Basis of Cultural Change* (McGraw-Hill, New York)

Barras, R. (1989) 'Towards a theory of innovation in services' in *Research Policy* (15, 4), pp. 161–174

Barritt, A. (1990) *Innovations in Community Care* (Family Policy Studies Centre, London)

Baum, J. (1996) 'Organizational ecology' in (eds) S. Clegg, C. Hardy and W. Nord, *Handbook of Organization Studies*, pp. 77–114

Baum, J. and C. Oliver (1992) 'Institutional embeddedness and the dynamics of organizational populations' in *American Sociological Review* (57), pp. 540–559

Beck, S. and T. Whistler (1967) 'Innovative organizations: a selective view of current theory and research' in *Journal of Business* (40), pp. 462–469

Becker, S. and F. Stafford (1967) 'Some determinants of organizational success' in *Journal of Business* (40), pp. 511–518

Beekum, R. and G. Ginn (1993) 'Business strategy and inter-organizational linkages within the acute care hospital industry: an expansion of the Miles and Snow typology' in *Human Relations* (46, 11), pp. 1291–1318

Beer, M. and A. Walton (1987) 'Organizational change and development' in *Annual Review of Psychology* (38), pp. 339–367

Benson, J. (1975) 'Inter-organizational networks as a political economy' in *Administrative Science Quarterly* (20, 3), pp. 229–249

Berry, F. (1994) 'Innovation in public management: the adoption of strategic planning' in *Public Administration Review* (54, 4), pp. 322–330

Bessant, J. and M. Grunt (1985) *Management and Manufacturing Innovation in the United Kingdom and West Germany* (Gower, Aldershot)

Best, M. (1990) *The New Competition* (Polity Press, Cambridge)

Beveridge, W. (1948) *Voluntary Action* (Allen & Unwin, London)

Bhoovaraghaven, S., A. Vasudevan and R. Chaudran (1996) 'Resolving the process vs product innovation dilemma: a consumer choice theoretical approach' in *Management Science* (42, 2), pp. 232–246

Blau, P. and W. Scott (1963) *Formal Organizations* (Routledge and Kegan Paul, London)

Boeker, W. (1997) 'Strategic change: the influence of managerial characteristics and organizational growth' in *Academy of Management Journal* (40, 1)

Burgelman, R. and L. Sayles (1986) *Inside Corporate Innovation* (Free Press, New York)

Burns, T. and G. Stalker (1961) *Management of Innovation* (Tavistock, London)

Burt, R. (1982) 'A note on co-operation and definitions of constraint' in (eds) P. Marsden and N. Lin, *Social Structure and Network Analysis*, pp. 219–233

Burt, R. (1992) 'The social structure of competition' in (eds) N. Nohria and R. Eccles, *Network and Organizations*, pp. 57–91

Butler, A. (ed.) (1985) *Ageing. Recent Advances and Creative Responses* (Croom Helm, London)

Butler, R. and D. Wilson (1990) *Managing Voluntary and Non-profit Organisations* (Routledge, London)

Camagni, R. (1991a) 'From the local "mileau" to innovation through cooperation networks' in (ed.) R. Camagni (1991b), *Innovation Networks, Spatial Perspectives*, pp. 1–9

Camagni, R. (ed.) (1991b) *Innovation Networks, Spatial Perspectives* (Belhaven Press, London)

Carroll, G. (ed.) (1988) *Ecological Models of Organizations* (Ballinger, Cambridge, Mass.)

Carson, J. (1989) *Innovation. A Battle Plan for the 1990s* (Gower, Aldershot)

Carter, N. (1974) *Trends in Voluntary Support for Non Governmental Social Services Agencies* (Canadian Council on Social Welfare, Ottawa)

Child, J. (1972) 'Organizational structure, environmental and performance: the role of strategic choice' in *Sociology* (6), pp. 1–22

Cho, H.-D., J.-K. Lee and K.-K. Ro (1996) 'Environment and technology strategy of firms in government R&D programmes in Korea' in *Technovation* (16, 10), pp. 553–560

Clark, P. (1987) *Anglo-American Innovation* (de Gruyter, Berlin)

Clark, P. and N. Stanton (1989) *Innovation in Technology and Organization* (Routledge, London)

Clegg, S., C. Hardy and W. Nord (eds) (1996) *Handbook of Organization Studies* (Sage, London)

Colville, I. and C. Packman (1996) 'Auditing cultural change' in *Public Money and Management* (July/September), pp. 27–32

Connelly, M. (1994) 'An Act of empowerment: the Children, Young Persons and the Family Act (1989)' in *British Journal of Social Work* (24, 1), pp. 87–100

Connelly, N. (1990) *Raising Voices* (Policy Studies Institute, London)

Connor, A. (1987) *Poachers Turned Gamekeepers* (Scottish Office, Edinburgh)

Connor, A. and D. Wilkinson (1988) *Monitoring Projects Funded by the Unemployment Voluntary Action Fund 1982–87* (Scottish Office, Edinburgh)

Cooper, R. and E. Kleinschmidt (1993) 'Major new products: what distinguishes the winners in the chemical industry?' in *Journal of Product Innovation Management* (10, 2), pp. 90–111

Cornish, D. and R. Clarke (1975) *Residential Treatment and Its Effects on Delinquency* (HMSO, London)

Crompton, J. and C. Lamb (1988) *Marketing Governmental Social Services* (John Wiley, New York)

Cyert, R. and J. March (1963) *Behavioral Theory of the Firm* (Prentice-Hall, Englewood Cliffs, NJ)

Dacin, M. T. (1997) 'Isomorphism in context: the power and prescription of institutional norms' in *Academy of Management Journal* (40, 1), pp. 46–81

Daft, R. and S. Becker (1978) *Innovation in Organizations* (Elsevier, New York)

Damanpour, F. (1996) 'Organizational complexity and innovation' in *Management Science* (42, 5), pp. 693–716

da Rocha, A., C. Christensen and N. Paim (1990) 'Characteristics of innovative firms in the Brazilian computer industry' in *Journal of Product Innovation Management* (7, 2), pp. 123–134

Darvill, G. and G. Smale (1990) *Partners in Empowerment. Networks of Innovation in Social Work* (NISW, London)

Davies, B. and D. Challis (1986) *Matching Resources to Need* (Gower, Aldershot)

Davies, B. and E. Ferlie (1982) 'Efficiency promoting innovations in social care: social services departments and the elderly' in *Policy and Politics* (10, 2), pp. 181–203

Davies, B. and E. Ferlie (1984) 'Patterns of efficiency improving innovations: social care of the elderly' in *Policy and Politics* (12, 3), pp. 281–295

Davies, B., A. Bebbington and H. Charnley (1990) *Resources, Needs and Outcomes in Community Based Care* (Gower, Aldershot)

Delbecq, A. (1978) 'The social political process of introducing innovation in human services' in (eds) R. Sarri and Y. Hasenfeld, *The Management of Human Services*, pp. 309–339

Department of Health (1989) *Caring for People* (HMSO, London)

Despres, C. (1991) 'Information, technology and culture' in *Technovation* (16, 1), pp. 1–20

Deutsch, K. (1966) *The Nerves of Government* (Free Press, New York)

DiMaggio, P. and W. Powell (1988) 'The iron cage revisited' in (ed.) C. Milofsky, *Community Organizations*, pp. 77–99

Doudeyns, M. and E. Hayman (1993) 'Statistical indicators of innovation' in *Economic Trends* (September), pp. 113–123

Douglas, J. (1983) *Why Charity?* (Sage, Beverly Hills, Calif.)

Downs, G. and L. Mohr (1976) 'Conceptual issues in the study of innovation' in *Administrative Science Quarterly* (21), pp. 700–714

Drucker, P. (1985) *Innovation and Entrepreneurship* (Heinemann, London)

Etzioni, A. (1993) 'Normative-affective choices' in *Human Relations* (46, 9), pp. 1053–1069.

Euske, N. and K. Euske (1991) 'Institutional theory: employing the other side of rationality in non-profit organisations' in *British Journal of Management* (2, 2), pp. 81–88

Feller, I. (1981) 'Public sector innovations as "conspicuous consumption"' in *Policy Analysis* (7. 1), pp. 1–20

Ferlie, E. (1983) *Source Book of Innovation in the Community Care of the Elderly* (PSSRU, University of Kent)

Ferlie, E., D. Challis and B. Davies (1984a) 'Models of innovation in the social care of the elderly' in *Local Government Studies* (10, 6), pp. 67–72

Ferlie, E., D. Challis and B. Davies (1984b) *A Guide to Efficiency Improving Innovations in the Care of the Frail Elderly* (PSSRU Discussion Paper 284, University of Kent)

Ferlie, E., D. Challis and B. Davies (1989) *Efficiency Improving Innovation in the Social Care of the Elderly* (Gower, Aldershot)

Fischer, W., W. Hamilton, C. McLaughlin and R. Zmud (1986) 'The elusive product champion' in *Research Management* (29, 3), pp. 13–16

Fisher, M. (1994) 'Man-made carers: community care and older male carers' in *British Journal of Social Work* (24, 6), pp. 659–680

Freeman, C. (1973) 'A study of success and failure in industrial innovation' in (ed.) B. Williams, *Science and Technology in Economic Growth*, pp. 227–255

Freeman, C. (1982) *Economics of Industrial Innovation* (Frances Pinter, London)

Freidland, R. and R. Alford (1991) 'Bringing society back in: symbols, practices, and institution contradictions' in (ed.) W. Powell and P. DiMaggio – op. cit., pp. 232–266.

Frost, P. and C. Egri (1991) 'Political process of innovation' in *Research in Organizational Behavior 1991*, pp. 229–296

Galbraith, J. (1973) *Designing Complex Organizations* (Addison-Wesley, Reading, Mass.)

Gershuny, J. (1983) *Social Innovation and the Division of Labor* (Oxford University Press, Oxford)

Gibbons, J. (1990) *Family Support and Prevention* (HMSO, London)

Giddens, A. (1984) *The Constitution of Society* (University of California Press, Berkeley)

Goldberg, E. (1981) *A New Look at the Social Services* (Policy Studies Institute, London)

Goldberg, E. and R. Warburton (1979) *Ends and Means in Social Work* (George Allen & Unwin, London)

Golden, O. (1990) 'Innovation in public sector human service programs: the implications of innovation by "groping along"' in *Journal of Policy Analysis and Management* (9, 2), pp. 219–248

Gomulka, S. (1990) *The Theory of Technological Change and Economic Growth* (Routledge, London)

Granovetter, M. (1985) 'Economic action and social structure: the problem of embeddedness' in *American Journal of Sociology* (91, 3), pp. 481–510

Grant, G. and M. McGrath (eds) (1987) *Community Mental Handicap Teams* (British Institute for Mental Health, Kidderminster)

Greenwood, R. and C. Hinings (1988) 'Organisation design types tracks and the dynamics of strategic change' in *Organization Studies* (9, 3), pp. 293–316

Gronbjerg, K. (1982) 'Private welfare in the welfare state' in *Social Services Review* (56, 1), pp. 1–26

Hadley, R. (1981) 'Social services departments and the community' in (ed.) E. Goldberg, *A New Look at the Social Services*, pp. 35–45

Hadley, R. and M. McGrath (1980) *Going Local* (Bedford Square Press, London)

Hage, J. (1980) *Theories of Organizations* (John Wiley, New York)

Hage, J. and M. Aiken (1967) 'Program change and organizational properties: a comparative analysis' in *American Journal of Sociology* (72), pp. 503–519

Hage, J. and R. Dewar (1973) 'Elite values versus organizational structure in predicting innovation' in *Administrative Science Quarterly* (18), pp. 279–290

Hammock, D. and D. Young (eds) (1993) *Nonprofit Organizations in a Market Economy* (Jossey-Bass, San Francisco)

Hannan, M. and G. Carroll (1992) *Dynamics of Organizational Populations* (Oxford University Press, Oxford)

Hannan, M. and J. Freeman (1989) *Organizational Ecology* (Harvard University Press, Cambridge, Mass.)

Hardy, B., A. Turrell and G. Wistow (1989) *Innovations in Management Arrangements* (CRSP, Loughborough University)

Hasenfeld, Y. (ed.) (1989) *Administrative Leadership in the Social Services* (Haworth Press, New York)

Hasenfeld, Y. (ed.) (1993) *Human Services as Complex Organizations* (Sage, Newbury Park, Calif.)

Hasenfeld, Y. and H. Schmid (1989) 'The life cycle of human service organizations' in (ed.) Y. Hasenfeld, *Administrative Leadership in the Social Services*

Haveman, H. (1993) 'Organizational size and change: diversification in the savings and loan industry after deregulation' in *Administrative Science Quarterly* (38, 1), pp. 20–50

Healy, P. (ed.) (1989) *Innovatory Management Practice in Social Services Departments* (Local Government Management Board, Luton)

Heap, J. (1989) *The Management of Innovation and Design* (Cassell, London)

Herbig, P. (1991) 'A cusp catastrophe model of the adoption of an industrial innovation' in *Journal of Product Innovation Management* (8, 2), pp. 127–137

Hickson, D., J. Hinings, C. Lee, R. Schneck and J. Denings (1971) 'A strategic contingencies theory of inter-organizational power' in *Administrative Science Quarterly* (16), pp. 216–229

Holloman, J. H. (1980) 'Life cycle, early market conditions and policy implications' in (ed.) B.-A. Vedin, *Current Innovation*, pp. 103–112

Home Office (1990) *Efficiency Scrutiny of Government Funding of the Voluntary Sector* (HMSO, London)

Hughes, B. (1995) 'Openness and contact in adoption: a child-centred perspective' in *British Journal of Social Work* (25), pp. 729–747

Huxham, C. (1993) 'Collaborative capability' in *Public Money and Management* (13, 3), pp. 21–28

Huxham, C. and S. Vangen (1996) 'Managing inter-organizational relationships' in (ed.) S. Osborne, *Managing in the Voluntary Sector*, pp. 202–216

Isaacs, B. and H. Evers (eds) (1984) *Innovations in the Care of the Elderly* (Croom Helm, London)

Iwamura, A. and V. Jog (1991) 'Innovation organization structure and the management of the innovation process in the securities industry' in *Journal of Product Innovation Management* (8, 2), pp. 104–116

Jelinek, M. and C. Schoonhoven (1990) *The Innovation Marathon* (Blackwell, Oxford)

Johnson, N. (1987) *The Welfare State in Transition* (Wheatsheaf, Brighton)

Kahan, B. (ed.) (1989) *Child Care Research Policy and Practice* (Hodder & Stoughton, London)

Kamerman, S. and A. Kahn (1976) *Social Services in the United States* (Temple University Press, Philadelphia)

Kamien, M. and N. Schwartz (1982) *Market Structure and Innovation* (Cambridge University Press, Cambridge)

Kamm, J. (1987) *Integrative Approach to Managing Innovation* (Lexington Books, Lexington, Mass.)

Kanter, R. (1985) *The Change Masters* (Unwin, London)

Kilmann, R., L. Pondy, and D. Slevin (eds) (1976) *Management of Organization Design* (North-Holland, New York)

Kimberly, J. (1981) 'Managerial innovation' in (eds) P. Nystrom and W. Starbuck, *Handbook of Organizational Design*, pp. 84–104

Kimberly, J. (1987) 'Organizational and contextual influences on the diffusion of technological innovation' in (eds) J. Pennings and A. Buitendan, *New Technology as Organization Innovation*, pp. 237–259

King's Fund Institute (1987) *Promoting Innovation in Community Care* (King's Fund Institute, London)

Kingsley, S. (1981) 'Voluntary action: innovation and experiment as criteria for funding' in *Home Office Research Bulletin* (pt. II), pp. 7–10

Knapp, M. (1984) *The Economics of Social Care* (Macmillan, London)

Knapp, M., P. Cambridge, C. Thomason, J. Beecham, C. Allen and R. Darton (1990a) *Care in the Community. Lessons from a Demonstration Project* (PSSRU, University of Kent)

Knapp, M., E. Robertson and C. Thomason (1990b) 'Public money, voluntary action: whose welfare?' in (eds) H. Anheier and W. Seibel (1990), *The Third Sector*, pp. 183–218

Knight, K. (1967) 'A descriptive model in the intra-firm innovation process' in *Journal of Business* (40), pp. 478–496

Knight, R. (1987) 'Corporate innovation and entrepreneurship' in *Journal of Product Innovation Management* (9, 4), pp. 284–297

Knokke, D. and J. Kuklinski (1982) *Network Analysis* (Sage, Beverly Hills, Calif.)

Knokke, D. and D. Prensky (1984) 'What relevance do organization theories have for voluntary organizations?' in *Social Science Quarterly* (63), pp. 3–20

Kondratiev, N. (1978) 'The long wave in economic life' (translated by W. Stolper) in *Lloyds Bank Review* (no. 129), pp. 41–60

Kraan, R., J. Baldock, B. Davies, A. Evers, L. Johansson, M. Knappen, M. Thorsland and C. Tunissen (eds) (1991) *Care for the Elderly. Significant Innovation in Three European Countries* (Campus Verlag, Frankfurt)

Kramer, R. (1981) *Voluntary Agencies in the Welfare State* (University of California Press, Berkeley)

Kreiner, K. and M. Schultz (1993) 'Informed collaboration in research and design. The formation of networks across organizations' in *Organizational Studies* (14, 2), pp. 189–209

Labour Party (1990) *Labour and the Voluntary Sector, A Consultation Document* (Labour Party, London)

Lane, J.-E. (1993) *The Public Sector* (Sage, London)

Langrish, L., M. Gibbons, W. Evans and F. Jervons (1972) *Wealth from Knowledge* (Halsted, New York)

Lawrence, P. and J. Lorsch (1967) *Organizations and Environment: Managing Differentiation and Integration* (Harvard University, Boston)

Le Grand, J. (1991) 'Quasi-markets and social policy' in *The Economic Journal* (101), p. 1256–1267

Lipsky, M. and S. Rathgeb Smith (1989) 'Non-profit organizations, government and the welfare state' in *Political Science Quarterly* (104, 4), pp. 625–648

Loveridge, R. (ed.) (1992) *Continuity and Change in the NHS* (Open University Press, Buckingham)

Loveridge, R. (1993) 'Socio-economics – a bridge too far?' in *Human Relations* (46, 9), pp. 1029–1034

MacPherson, J. M. and L. S. Loven (1988) 'A comparative ecology of five nations: testing a model of competition among voluntary organizations' in (ed.) G. Carroll, *Ecological Models of Organization*, pp. 85–109

Magat, R. (ed.) (1989) *Philanthropic Giving* (Oxford University Press, New York)

Mansfield, E. (1963) 'Size of firm market structure and innovation' in *Journal of Political Economy* (71), pp. 556–576

March, J. and H. Simon (1958) *Organizations* (John Wiley, New York)

Marks, I. and R. Scott (1990) *Mental Health Care Delivery* (Cambridge University Press, Cambridge)

Marsden, P. and N. Lin (eds) (1982) *Social Structure and Network Analysis* (Sage, Beverly Hills, Calif.)

Marshall, A. (1966) *Principles of Economics* (Macmillan, London)

Marshall, M. and A. Sommerville (1983) *New Services for Old People* (Liverpool University Press, Liverpool)

Marx, K. (1974) *Capital* [Vol. 1] (Lawrence & Wishart, London)

Mellor, M. (1985) *Role of Voluntary Organisations in Social Welfare* (Croom Helm, London)

Mensch, G. (1985) 'Trends in perspectives in innovation policies' in (eds) R. Merritt and A. Merritt, *Innovation in the Public Sector*, pp. 253–267

Merritt, R. and A. Merritt (eds) (1985) *Innovation in the Public Sector* (Sage, Beverly Hills, Calif.)

Meyer, M. (ed.) (1978) *Environment and Organizations* (Jossey-Bass, San Francisco)

Meyer, S. and B. Rowan (1977) 'Institutionalized organizations: formal structure as myth and ceremony' in *American Journal of Sociology* (83), pp. 340–363

Miles, R. and C. Snow (1978) *Organization Strategy Structure and Process* (McGraw-Hill, New York)

Milofsky, C. (ed.) (1988) *Community Organizations* (Oxford University Press, New York)

Ministry of Health (1959) *Report of the Working Party on Social Workers in the Local Authority, Health and Welfare Services* (HMSO, London)

Mohr, L. (1969) 'Determinants of innovation' in *American Political Science Review* (63), pp. 111–126

Mohr, L. (1987) 'Innovation theory: an assessment from the vantage point of new electronic technology in organizations' in (eds) J. Pennings and A. Buitendan – op cit., pp. 13–31.

Mole, V. and D. Elliot (1987) *Enterprising Innovation: An Alternative Approach* (Frances Pinter, London)

Moore, J. and J. Green (1985) 'Contribution of voluntary organizations to the support of caring relatives' in *Quarterly Journal of Social Affairs* (1, 2), pp. 93–130

Morris, A. and H. Giller (1987) *Understanding Juvenile Justice* (Croom Helm, London)

Morris, A. and M. McIsaac (1978) *Juvenile Justice?* (Heinemann, London)

Morris, T. and R. Westbrook (1996) 'Technical innovation and competitive advantage in retail financial services' in *British Journal of Management* (7, 1), pp. 45–61

Mort, J. (1991) 'The applicability of percolation theory to innovation' in *Journal of Product Innovation Management* (18, 1), pp. 32–38

Myrtle, R. and K. Willer (1994) 'Designing service delivery systems: lessons from the development of community based systems for care of the elderly' in *Public Administration Review* (54, 3), pp. 245–252

Nadler, D. (1988) 'Concepts for the management of organizational change' in (eds) M. Tushman and N. Moore – op cit., pp. 718–732

National Council for Voluntary Organisations [NCVO] (1991) 'Political supplement' in *NCVO News* (June)

Nelson, R. (1993a) *National Innovation Systems* (Oxford University Press, New York)

Nelson, R. (1993b) 'Technological innovation: the role of non-profit organizations' in (eds) D. Hammock and D. Young, *Nonprofit Organizations in a Market Economy*, pp. 363–377

Nelson, R. and S. Winter (1982) *An Evolutionary Theory of Economic Change* (Belknap Press, Cambridge, Mass.)

Nohria, N. (1992) 'Is a network perspective a useful way of studying organizations?' in (eds) N. Nohria and R. Eccles (1992), pp. 1–22

Nohria, N. and R. Eccles (eds) (1992) *Networks and Organizations* (Harvard Business School Press, Boston)

Normann, R. (1971) 'Organizational innovativeness' in *Administrative Science Quarterly* (16), pp. 203–215

Normann, R. (1991) *Service Management* (John Wiley, Chichester)

North, D. (1990) 'A transaction cost theory of politics' in *Journal of Theoretical Politics* (2, 4), pp. 355–367

Nutley, S. and S. Osborne (1994) *Public Sector Management Handbook* (Longman, London)

Nystom, H. (1979) *Creativity and Innovation* (John Wiley, Chichester)

Nystrom, P. and W. Starbuck (eds) (1981) *Handbook of Organizational Design* (Oxford University Press, Oxford)

Oliver, C. (1996) 'The institutional embeddedness of economic activity' in *Advances in Strategic Management* (13), pp. 163–187

Osborn, A. (1985) 'Short-term funded projects: a creative response to an ageing population?' in (ed.) A. Butler, *Ageing. Recent Advances and Creative Responses*, pp. 125–136

Osborne, S. (1984) 'Social inquiry reports in one juvenile court' in *British Journal of Social Work* (14), pp. 361–378

Osborne, S. (1996) *Managing in the Voluntary Sector* (International Thomson Business Press, London)

Parker, R., H. Ward, S. Jackson, J. Aldgate and P. Wedge (eds) (1991) *Assessing Outcomes in Childcare* (HMSO, London)

Paton, R. (1993) 'Organisation and management studies on voluntary and non-profit organisations in the UK: achievements and prospects' (Paper to the Researching Voluntary and Non-profit Organisations in the UK: the State of the Art Symposium, University of the South Bank, London)

Pavitt, K. (1991) 'Key characteristics of the large innovating firm' in *British Journal of Management* (2, 1), pp. 41–50

Pelz, D. (1985) 'Innovation complexity and the sequence of innovatory stages' in *Knowledge: Creation, Diffusion, Utilization 1985*, pp. 261–291

Pennings, J. and A. Buitendan (1987) *New Technology as Organizational Innovation* (Ballinger, Cambridge, Mass.)

Perri 6 (1993) 'Innovation by non-profit organizations: policy and research issues' in *Nonprofit Management and Leadership* (3, 4), pp. 397–414

Peters, T. (1988) *Thriving on Chaos* (Macmillan, London)

Peters, T. and N. Austin (1985) *A Passion for Excellence* (Fontana, Glasgow)

Peters, T. and R. Waterman (1982) *In Search of Excellence* (Harper & Row, New York)

Pettigrew, A. (1973) *Politics of Organisational Decision Making* (Tavistock, London)

Peyton, R. (1989) 'Philanthropic values' in (ed.) R. Magat, *Philanthropic Giving*, pp. 19–45

Pfeffer, J. (1978) 'The micro-politics of organizations' in (ed.) M. Meyer, *Environment and Organizations*, pp. 29–50

Pfeffer, J. (1981) *Power in Organizations* (Pitman, Boston)

Pfeffer, J. (1982) *Organizations and Organization Theory* (Pitman, Boston)

Pfeffer, J. and A. Salancik (1978) *The External Control of Organizations* (Harper and Row, New York)

Pinchot, G., III (1985) *Intrapreneuring* (Harper & Row, New York)

Poole, M. S. (1981) 'Decision development in small groups I : a comparison of two models' in *Communication Monographs* (48), pp. 1–24

Poole, M. S. (1983a) 'Decision development in small groups II : a study of multiple sequences in decision making' in *Communication Monographs* (50), pp. 206–232

Poole, M. S. (1983b) 'Decision development in small groups III : a multiple decision sequence model of group decision development' in *Communication Monographs* (50), pp. 321–341

Poole, M. S. and J. Roth (1989) 'Decision development in small groups IV: a typology of group decision paths' in *Human Communication Research* (15, 3), pp. 323–356

Porter, M. (1985) *Competitive Advantage* (Free Press, New York)

Poulton, G. (1988) *Managing Voluntary Organisations* (John Wiley, Chichester)

Powell, W. and P. DiMaggio (eds) (1991) *The New Institutionalism in Organizational Analysis* (University of Chicago Press, Chicago)

Powell, W., K. Koput and L. Smith-Doew (1996) 'Inter-organizational collaboration and the locus of innovation: networks of learning in bio-technology' in *Administrative Science Quarterly* (41, 1), pp. 116–145

Prochaska, F. (1988) *The Voluntary Impulse* (Faber & Faber, London)

Ram, S. and H.-S. Jung (1991) 'Forced adoption of innovation in organizations' in *Journal of Product Innovation Management* (8, 2), pp. 117–126

Ramon, S. and M. Giannichedda (eds) (1991) *Psychiatry in Transition* (Pluto Press, London)

Randon, A. (1993) 'Spurs and barriers to innovation by nonprofit organisations. Policy issues and research findings' (Paper to the Annual Conference of ARNOVA, Toronto)

Rickards, T. (1985) *Stimulating Innovation* (Pinter, London)

Robert, M. and A. Weiss (1988) *The Innovation Formula* (Ballinger, Cambridge, Mass.)

Robertson, M., J. Swan and S. Newell (1996) 'The role of networks in the diffusion of technological innovation' in *Journal of Management Studies* (33, 3), pp. 333–359

Rogers, E. and F. Shoemaker (1971) *Communication of Innovation* (Free Press, New York)

Ronen, T. (1994) 'Cognitive-behavioural social work with children' in *British Journal of Social Work* (24, 3), pp. 273–286

Rose, A. (1974) *Theory and Method in the Social Sciences* (Greenwood Press, Westport, Conn.)

Rosner, M. (1967) 'Economic determinants of organizational innovation' in *Administrative Science Quarterly* (12), pp. 614–625

Ross, K. (1995) 'Speaking in tongues: involving users in day care services' in *British Journal of Social Work* (25, 6), pp. 791–804

Rothman, J. (1974) *Planning and Organizing for Social Change* (Columbia University Press, New York)

Rothman, J. (1980) *Social Research and Development: Research and Development in the Human Services* (Prentice-Hall, Englewood Cliffs, NJ)

Rothman, J., J. Erlich and J. Teresa (1976) *Promoting Innovation and Change in Organizations and Communities* (John Wiley, New York)

Rothwell, R. (1975) 'Project SAPPHO – some hypotheses tested' (Paper to the Innovation Symposium, Royal Swedish Academy of Engineering Science, Stockholm)

Rothwell, R. and W. Zegveld (1981) *Industrial Innovation and Public Policy* (Pinter, London)

Rowe, L. and W. Boise (1974) 'Organizational innovation: current research and evolving concepts' in *Public Administration Review* (34), pp. 284–293

Salamon, L. and H. Anheier (1994) *The Emerging Sector* (Johns Hopkins University, Baltimore)

Sapolsky, H. (1967) 'Organizational structure and innovation' in *Journal of Business* (40), pp. 497–510

Sarri, R. and Y. Hasenfeld (eds) (1978) *The Management of Human Services* (Columbia University Press, New York)

Saxon-Harrold, S. (1990) 'Competition resources and strategy in the British non-profit sector' in (eds) H. Anheier and W. Seibel – op. cit., pp. 123–139

Schall, E. (1997) 'Public sector succession: a strategic approach to sustaining innovation' in *Public Administration Review* (57, 1), pp. 4–10

Schon, D. (1963) 'Champions for radical new inventions' in *Harvard Business Review* (March/April), pp. 77–86

Schorr, A. (1970) 'Tasks for voluntarism in the next decade' in *Child Welfare* (49, 8), pp. 425–434

Schumpeter, J. (1939) *Business Cycles* (McGraw-Hill, New York)

Scott, R. (1990) *Organizations. Rational, Natural and Open Systems* (Prentice-Hall, Englewood Cliffs, NJ)

Scott, R. and J. Meyer (1991) 'Organization of social sectors: propositions and early evidence' in (eds) W. Powell and P. DiMaggio – op cit., pp. 108–142

Selznick, P. (1949) *TVA and Grass Roots* (University of California Press, Berkeley)

Sen, A. (1977) 'Rational fools: a critique of the behavioural foundations of economic theory' in *Philosophy and Public Affairs* (6), pp. 317–344

Singh, J. and C. Lumsden (1990) 'Theory and research in organizational ecology' in *Annual Review of Sociology* (16), pp. 161–195

Singh, J., D. Tucker and A. Meinhard (1991) 'Institutional change and ecological dynamics' in (eds) W. Powell and P. DiMaggio – op.cit., pp. 390–422

Smale, G. and G. Tuson (1990) 'Community social work: foundation for the 1990s and beyond' in (eds) G. Darvill and G. Smale, *Partners in Empowerment. Networks of Innovation in Social Work*, pp. 151–163

Smith, A. (1910) *Wealth of Nations* (Dent, London)

Sommerlad, L. and D. Hills (1990) *Managing an Innovative Project* (Tavistock Institute, London)

Starkey, K. and A. McKinlay (1988) *Organizational Innovation* (Avebury, Aldershot)

Stone, M. (1990) *Young People Leaving Care* (Royal Philanthropic Society, Liverpool)

Stroetman, K. (1979) 'Innovation in small and medium sized industrial firms – a German perspective' in (ed.) M. Baker *Industrial Innovation: Technology Policy and Diffusion*, pp. 205–225

Sutton, J., F. Dobbin, J. Meyer and W. Scott (1994) 'The legalization of the workplace' in *American Journal of Sociology* (99), pp. 944–971

Thompson, J. (ed.) (1966) *Approaches to Organizational Design* (Pittsburgh University Press, Pittsburgh)

Thompson, V. (1965) 'Bureaucracy and innovation' in *Administrative Science Quarterly* (10), pp. 1–20

Thorpe, D., D. Smith, C. Green and J. Paley (1980) *Out of Care. The Community Support of Young Offenders* (George Allen & Unwin, London)

Tidd, J. (1995) 'Development of novel products through intraorganizational and interorganizational networks: the case of home automation' in *Journal of Product Innovation Management* (12, 4), pp. 307–322

Tucker, D., J. Baum and J. Singh (1992) 'The institutional ecology of human service organizations' in (ed.) Y. Hasenfeld, *Human Services as Complex Organizations*, pp. 47–72

Tushman, M. and P. Anderson (1985) 'Technological discontinuities and organizational environments' in *Administrative Science Quarterly* (31), pp. 439–465

Tushman, M. and W. Moore (eds) (1988) *Readings in the Management of Innovation* (Ballinger, Cambridge, Mass.)

Twiss, B. (1987) *Managing Technological Innovation* (Pitman, London)

Urabe, K. (1988) 'Innovation and the Japanese management style' in (eds) K. Urabe, J. Child and T. Kagono, *Innovation and Management. International Comparisons*, pp. 3–26

Urabe, K., J. Child and T. Kagono (1988) *Innovation and Management. International Comparisons* (De Gruyter, Berlin)

Utting, W. (1991) *Children in Public Care. A Review of Residential Care* (HMSO, London)

Van de Ven, A. (1988) 'Central problems in the management of innovation' in (eds) M. Tushman and W. Moore – op cit., pp. 103–122.

Van de Ven, A., H. Angle and M. Doole (1989) *Research on the Management of Innovation* (Harper and Row, New York)

Vedin, B.-A. (ed.) (1980) *Current Innovation* (Almqvist & Wiksell, Stockholm)

Von Hippel, E. (1978) 'A customer active paradigm for industrial product idea generation' in *Research Policy* (7), pp. 240–266

Von Hippel, E. (1982) 'Appropriability of innovation benefits as a predictor of the source of innovation' in *Research Policy* (11, 2), pp. 95–116

Wagner, G. (1988) *Residential Care. A Positive Choice* (HMSO, London)

Walsh, K. (1989) *Marketing in Local Government* (Longman, London)

Ware, A. (1989) *Between Profit and State* (Polity Press, Cambridge)

Webb, S. and B. Webb (1911) *Prevention of Destitution* (Longman, London)

Williams, B. (ed.) (1973) *Science and Technology in Economic Growth* (Macmillan, London)

Williams, H. and A. Webb (1992) *Outcome Funding* (Rensselaerville Institute, New York)

Wilson, D. (1992) 'The strategic challenge of cooperation and competition in British voluntary organisations' in *Nonprofit Management and Leadership* (2, 3), pp. 239–252

Wilson, J. (1966) 'Innovation in organization: notes towards a theory' in (ed.) J. Thompson, *Approaches to Organizational Design*, pp. 193–218

Wistow, G., M. Knapp, B. Hardy, J. Forder, J. Kendall and R. Manning (1996) *Social Care Markets: Progress and Prospects* (Open University Press, Buckingham)

Wolfe, R. (1994) 'Organizational innovation: review, critique and suggested research directions' in *Journal of Management Studies* (31, 3), pp. 405–431

Wolfenden Committee (1978) *Future of Voluntary Organisations* (Bedford Square Press, London)

Young, D. (1976) *If Not For Profit, For What?* (Lexington Books, Mass.)

Younghusband, E., D. Birchall, R. Davies and M. Kellner Pringle (eds) (1970) *Living with Handicap* (National Bureau for Co-operation in Child Care, London)

Zahria, S. and J. Pearce (1990) 'Research evidence on the Miles–Snow typology' in *Journal of Management* (16, 4), pp. 751–768

Zaltman, G., R. Duncan and J. Holbek (1973) *Innovation and Organizations* (John Wiley, New York)

4 Research methodology

Abrams, P. (1984) 'Evaluating soft findings' in *Research Policy and Planning* (2, 2), pp. 1–8

Bryman, A. (1988a) *Quantity and Quality in Social Research* (Unwin-Hyman, London)

Bryman, A. (ed.) (1988b) *Doing Research in Organizations* (Routledge, London)

Buchanan, D., D. Boddy and J. McCalman (1988) *Getting In, Getting On, Getting Out and Getting Back* in (ed.) A. Bryman – op cit., pp. 53–67

Cameron, K. and R. Quinn (1988) 'Organizational paradox and transformation' in (eds) R. Quinn and K. Cameron, *Paradox and Transformation*, pp. 1–18

Carmines, E. and R. Zeller (1979) *Reliability and Validity Assessment* (Sage, Beverly Hills, Calif.)

Clare, R. and M. Scott (1994) 'Charities contribution to Gross Domestic Product' in *Economic Trends* (no. 482), pp. 134–141

Cohen, J. (1977) *Statistical Power Analyses for the Behavioral Sciences* (Academic Press, New York)

Denzin, N. (1970) *The Research Act in Sociology* (Butterworth, London)

Department of Health (1989) *Caring for People: Community Care in the Next Decade and Beyond* (HMSO, London)

Deutch, K. (1966) *The Nerves of Government* (Free Press, New York)

de Vaus, D. (1986) *Surveys in Social Research* (George Allen & Unwin, London)

Feeser, H. and G. Willard (1990) 'Founding strategy and performance' in *Strategic Management Journal* (11), pp. 87–98

Ferlie, I. and A. Pettigrew (19, 2) 'Coping with change in the NHS' in *Journal of Social Policy* (19, 2), pp. 191–220

Glaser, B. and A. Strauss (1968) *The Discovery of Grounded Theory* (Weidenfeld & Nicolson, London)

Golden, B. (1992) 'The past is past – or is it? The use of retrospective accounts as indicators of past strategy' in *Academy of Management Journal* (35), pp. 848–860

Griffiths, R. (1988) *Community Care: Agenda for Action* (HMSO, London)

Hall, R. and R. Quinn (eds) (1983) *Organizational Theory and Public Policy* (Sage, Beverly Hills, Calif.)

Handy, C. (1988) *Understanding Voluntary Organisations* (Penguin, London)

Hatch, S. (1980) *Outside the State* (Croom Helm, London)

Huber, G. and W. Glick (1993) *Organizational Change and Redesign* (Oxford University Press, Oxford)

Inkson, K., D. Pugh and D. Hickson (1970) 'Organizational context and structure: an abbreviated replication' in *Administrative Science Quarterly* (15), pp. 318–329

Kanter, R. (1983) *The Change Masters* (Simon & Schuster, New York)

Kim, J.-O. and C. Mueller (1978) *Introduction to Factor Analysis* (Sage, Newbury Park, Calif.)

Kirk, J. and C. Miller (1986) *Reliability and Validity in Qualitative Research* (Sage, Newbury Park, Calif.)

Kirton, M. (1976) 'Adaptors and innovators: a description and measure' in *Journal of Applied Psychology* (61, 5), pp. 622–629

Miles, M. and A. Huberman (1984) *Qualitative Data Analysis. A Source-Book of New Ideas* (Sage, Newbury Park, Calif.)

Miller, C., L. Cardinal and W. Glick (1997) 'Retrospective reports in organizational research: a re-examination of recent evidence' in *Academy of Management Journal* (40, 1), pp. 189–204

Mintzberg, H., D. Raisinghani and A. Thoret (1976) 'The structure of "unstructured" decision processes' in *Administrative Science Quarterly* (21), pp. 256–275

Moser, C. and G. Kalton (1971) *Survey Methods in Social Investigation* (Heinemann, London)

Nystrom, P. and W. Starbuck (eds) (1981) *Handbook of Organizational Design* (Oxford University Press, London)

Office of Population Censuses and Surveys [OPCS] (1992) *County Monitors* (HMSO, London)

Osborne, S. (1997) *Selecting a Methodology for Management Research. Issues and Resolution* (Public Sector Management Research Centre Research Paper RP713, Aston University, Birmingham)

Osborne, S. and L. Hems (1995) 'The economic structure of the charitable sector in the UK' in *Nonprofit and Voluntary Sector Quarterly* (24, 4), pp. 321–336

Osborne, S. and L. Hems (1996) 'Estimating the income and expenditure of charitable organizations in the UK. Methodology and summary of findings' in *Non Profit Studies* (1, 1), pp. 7–18

Pettigrew, A. (1990) 'Longitudinal field research on change: theory and practice' in *Organization Science* (1, 3), pp. 267–292

Powell, W. and P. DiMaggio (1991) *The New Institutionalism in Organizational Analysis* (University of Chicago Press, Chicago)

Scott, W. (1992) *Organizations. Rational, Natural and Open Systems* (Prentice-Hall, Englewood Cliffs, NJ)

Wistow, G., M. Knapp, B. Hardy and C. Allen (1994) *Social Care in a Mixed Economy* (Open University Press, Buckingham)

Wistow, G., M. Knapp, B. Hardy, J. Forder, J. Kendall and R. Manning (1996) *Social Care Markets: Progress and Prospects* (Open University Press, Buckingham)

Wolfe, R. (1994) 'Organizational innovation: review, critique and suggested research directions' in *Journal of Management Studies* (31, 3), pp. 405–431

Wolfenden Committee (1978) *The Future of Voluntary Organisations* (Croom Helm, London)

Yin, R. (1979) *Case Study Research* (Sage, London)

5 Mapping and defining the innovative activity of VNPOs

Chesterman, M. (1979) *Charities, Trusts and Social Welfare* (Weidenfeld & Nicolson, London)

Cyert, R. and J. March (1963) *A Behavioral Theory of the Firm* (Prentice-Hall, Englewood Cliffs, NJ)

DiMaggio, P. and W. Powell (1988) 'The iron cage revisited: institutional isomorphism and collective rationality in organizational fields' in (ed.) C. Milofsky, *Community Organizations*, pp. 77–99

Eisenbis, R. and R. Avery (1972) *Discriminant Analysis and Classification Procedures* (Lexington Books, Lexington, Mass.)

Hedderson, J. and M. Fisher (1993) *SPSS Made Easy* (Wadsworth, Belmont, Calif.)

Kimberly, J. (1981) 'Managerial innovation' in (eds) P. Nystrom and W. Starbuck, *Handbook of Organizational Design*, pp. 84–104

Klecka, W. (1980) *Discriminant Analysis* (Sage, Beverly Hills, Calif.)

Milofsky, C. (ed.) *Community Organizations* (Oxford University Press, New York)

Norusis, M. (1988) *SPSS – Introductory Statistics Guide* (SPSS, Chicago)

Norusis, M. (1990) *SPSS – Advanced Statistics Users Guide* (SPSS, Chicago)

Nystrom, P. and W. Starbuck (eds) (1981) *Handbook of Organizational Design* (Oxford University Press, Oxford)

Osborne, S. and L. Hems (1995) 'The economic structure of the charitable sector in the UK' in *Nonprofit and Voluntary Sector Quarterly* (24, 4), pp. 321–336

Osborne, S. and L. Hems (1996) 'Estimating the income and expenditure of charitable organizations in the UK' in *Non Profit Studies* (1, 1), pp. 7–18

Phillip, A., J. McCulloch and N. Smith (1975) *Social Work Research and the Analysis of Social Data* (Pergamon Press, Oxford)

Porter, M. (1985) *Competitive Advantage* (Free Press, New York)

Smith, S. Rathgeb and M. Lipsky (1993) *Nonprofits for Hire. The Welfare State in the Age of Contracting* (Harvard University Press, Boston)

6   Four causal hypotheses and a process

Abrams, P., S. Abrams, R. Humphreys and R. Snaith (1989) *Neighbourhood Care and Social Policy* (HMSO, London)

Anheier, H. and W. Seibel (eds) (1990) *The Third Sector* (de Gruyter, Berlin)

Ascher, K. (1987) *Politics of Privatisation* (Macmillan, London)

Astley, W. and A. Van de Ven (1983) 'Central perspectives and debates in organization theory' in *Administrative Science Quarterly* (28), pp. 245–273

Beveridge, W. (1948) *Voluntary Action* (George Allen & Unwin, London)

Bryman, A. (1988) *Quantity and Quality in Social Research* (Unwin Hyman, London)

Burridge, D. (1990) *What Local Groups Need* (NCVO, London)

Camagni, R. (1991a) 'From the local "milieu" to innovation through co-operation networks' in (ed) R. Camagni, *Innovation Networks. Spatial Perspectives*, pp. 1–9

Camagni, R. (1991b) *Innovation Networks. Spatial Perspectives* (Belhaven Press, London)

Carson, J. (1989) *Innovation. A Battleplan for the 1990s* (Gower, Aldershot)

Carter, N. (1974) *Trends in Voluntary Support for Non Governmental Social Support Agencies* (Canadian Council on Social Development, Ottawa)

Child, J. (1984) *Organization. A Guide to Problems and Practice* (Harper & Row, London)

Clark, P. (1990) *Describing and Explaining the Structure of Canadian Textile Firms* (Aston Programme Press, Aston University)

Cyert, R. and G. March (1963) *A Behavioral Theory of the Firm* (Prentice-Hall, Englewood Cliffs, NJ)

Darvill, G. and G. Smale (eds) *Partners in Empowerment: Networks of Innovation in Social Work* (NISW, London)

Department of Health (1989) *Caring for People: Community Care in the Next Decade and Beyond* (HMSO, London)

DiMaggio, P. and W. Powell (1988) 'The iron cage revisited: institutional isomorphism and collective rationality in organizational fields' in (ed.) C. Milofsky, *Community Organizations*, pp. 77–99

DiMaggio, P. and W. Powell (1991) 'Introduction' in (eds) W. Powell and P. DiMaggio, *The New Institutionalism in Organizational Analysis*, pp. 1–40

Donaldson, L. and M. Warner (1976) 'Bureaucratic and democratic structures in occupational interest associations' in (ed.) D. Pugh and C. Hinings, *Organizational Structure: Extensions and Replication*, pp. 67–86

Feller, E. (1981) 'Public sector innovation as "conspicuous consumption"' in *Policy Analysis* (7, 1), pp. 1–20

Foxall, G. (1994) 'Consumer innovations. Adaptors and innovators' in *British Journal of Management* (5, special issue), pp. S3–S12

Foxall, G. and P. Hackett (1994) 'Styles of managerial creativity: a comparison of adoption-innovation in the United Kingdom, Australia and the United States' in *British Journal of Management* (5, 2), pp. 85–100

Gladstone, F. (1979) *Voluntary Action in a Changing World* (Bedford Square Press, London)

Granovetter, M. (1985) 'Economic action and social structure: the problem of embeddedness', in *American Journal of Sociology* (91, 3), pp. 481–510

Griffiths, R. (1988) *Community Care: Agenda for Action* (HMSO, London)

Hague, D., W. Mackenzie and A. Barker (eds) (1975) *Public Policy and Private Interests* (Macmillan, London)

Hammack, D. and D. Young (eds) (1993) *Nonprofit Organizations in a Market Economy* (Jossey-Bass, San Francisco)

Hasenfeld, Y. (ed.) (1992) *Human Services as Complex Organizations* (Sage, Newbury Park, Calif.)

Hinings, C., S. Ranson and A. Bryman (1976) 'Churches as organizations: structure and context' in (ed.) D. Pugh and C. Hinings – op.cit., pp. 102–114

Home Office (1990) *Efficiency Scrutiny of Government Funding of the Voluntary Sector* (HMSO, London)

Huxham, C. (1993) 'Collaborative capability' in *Public Money and Management* (13, 3), pp. 21–28

Huxham, C. and S. Vangen (1996) 'Managing inter-organizational relationships' in (ed.) S. Osborne, *Managing in the Voluntary Sector*, pp. 202–217

Inkson, K., D. Pugh and D. Hickson (1970) 'Organizational context and structure: an abbreviated replication' in (ed.) D. Pugh and C. Hinings – op. cit., pp. 12–26

Kamm, J. (1987) *Integrative Approaches to Managing Innovation* (Lexington Books, Lexington, Mass.)

King's Fund Institute (1989) *Promoting Innovation in Community Care* (King's Fund Institute, London)

Kirton, M. (1976) 'Adaptors and innovators: a description and measure' in *Journal of Applied Psychology* (61, 5), pp. 622–629

Knapp, M., E. Robertson and C. Thomason (1990) 'Public money, voluntary action: whose welfare?' in (ed.) H. Anheier and W. Seibel, *The Third Sector*, pp. 183–218

Knokke, D. and D. Prensky (1984) 'What relevance do organization theories have for voluntary organizations?' in *Social Science Quarterly* (65), pp. 3–20

Labour Party (1990) *Labour and the Voluntary Sector, A Consultation Document* (Labour Party, London)

Lane, J.-E. (1993) *The Public Sector* (Sage, London)

Lawrence, P. and J. Lorsch (1967) *Organizations and Environment* (Harvard Business School Press, Boston)

Miles, M. and A. Huberman (1984) *Qualitative Data Analysis* (Sage, Newbury Park, Calif.)

Miles, R. and C. Snow (1978) *Organization Strategy Structure and Process* (McGraw-Hill, New York)

Milofsky, C. (ed.) (1988) *Community Organizations* (Oxford University Press, Oxford)

Ministry of Health (1959) *Report of the Working Party on Social Workers in Local Authority, Health and Welfare Settings* (HMSO, London)

Mischra, R. (1984) *Welfare Work in Crisis* (Wheatsheaf, Brighton)

National Council for Voluntary Organisations [NCVO] (1991) *NCVO News* (June), *Political Supplement*

Nelson, R. (1993) 'Technological innovation: the role of nonprofit organizations' in (eds) D. Hammack and D. Young, *Nonprofit Organizations in a Market Economy*, pp. 363–377

Osborne, D. and T. Gaebler (1993) *Reinventing Government* (Plume, New York)

Osborne, S. (1986) 'It's as easy as A–B–C. Cognitive group therapy with depressed people' in *Behavioural Social Work*

Osborne, S. (1992) 'Lifting the siege? Organizational culture and social services departments' in *Local Government Policy Making* (18, 5), pp. 17–20

Osborne, S. (ed.) (1996) *Managing in the Voluntary Sector* (International Thomson Business Press, London)

Osborne, S. (1997) 'Managing the coordination of social services in the mixed economy of welfare: competition, cooperation or common cause?' in *British Journal of Management* (8), pp. 317–328

Osborne, S. and L. Hems (1995) 'Economic structure of the voluntary sector in the UK' in *Nonprofit and Voluntary Sector Quarterly* (24, 4), pp. 321–336

Osborne, S. and M. Tricker (1994) 'Local development agencies: supporting voluntary action' in *Nonprofit Management and Leadership* (5, 1), pp. 37–52

Paton, R. (1993) 'Organisation and management studies on voluntary and non-profit organisations in the UK: achievements and prospects (Paper to the Researching Voluntary and Non-profit Organisations in the UK: the State of the Art Symposium, University of the South Bank, London)

Pettigrew, A. (1990) 'Longitudinal field research on change: theory and practice' in *Organization Science* (1, 3), pp. 267–292

Pifer, A. (1967) *Quasi Non Governmental Organizations* (Carnegie Corporation, New York)

Pifer, A. (1975) 'The non-governmental organization at bay' in (eds) D. Hague, W. Mackenzie and A. Barker, *Public Policy and Private Interests*, pp. 395–408

Porter, M. (1985) *Competitive Advantage* (Free Press, New York)

Powell, W. and P. DiMaggio (eds) (1991) *New Institutionalism in Organizational Analysis* (University of Chicago Press, Chicago)

Public Sector Management Research Centre (1991) *Managing Social and Community Development Programmes in Rural Areas* (Aston University, Birmingham)

Pugh, D. (1981) 'The Aston programme perspective' in (eds) A. Van de Ven and W. Joyce, *Perspectives on Organization Design and Behaviour*, pp. 135–166

Pugh, D. and D. Hickson (1976) *Organizational Structure in its Context* (Saxon House, Farnborough)

Pugh, D. and C. Hinings (1976) *Organizational Structure: Extensions and Replications* (Saxon House, Farnborough)

Pugh, D. and R. Payne (1977) *Organizational Behaviour in its Context* (Saxon House, Farnborough)

Rao, N. (1991) *From Providing to Enabling* (Joseph Rowntree Foundation, York)

Schein, E. (1985) *Organizational Culture and Leadership* (Jossey-Bass, San Francisco)

Scott, R. (1992) *Organizations. Rational, Natural and Open Systems* (Prentice-Hall, Englewood Cliffs, NJ)

Singh, J., D. Tucker and A. Meinhard (1991) 'Institutional change and ecological dynamics' in (eds) W. Powell and P. DiMaggio – op. cit., pp. 361–389

Smale, G. and G. Tuson (1990) 'Community social work: foundation for the 1990s and beyond' in (ed.) G. Darvill and G. Smale, *Partners in Empowerment: Networks of Innovation in Social Work*, pp. 151–163

Starbuck, W. (1981) 'A trip to view the elephants and rattlesnakes in the garden of Aston' in (eds) A. Van de Ven and W. Joyce – op. cit., pp. 167–198

Thwaites, D. and S. Edgett (1991) 'Aspects of innovation in a turbulent market environment' in *Service Industries Journal* (11, 3), pp. 346–361

Tucker, D., J. Baum and J. Singh (1992) 'The institutional ecology of human service organizations' in (ed.) Y. Hasenfeld, *Human Services as Complex Organizations*, pp. 47–72

Van de Ven, A. and W. Joyce (eds) (1981) *Perspectives on Organization Design and Behavior* (John Wiley, New York)

Van de Ven, A. and M. Poole (1988) 'Methods for studying innovation processes' in (eds) A. Van de Ven, H. Angle and M. S. Poole, *Research in the Management of Innovation*, pp. 31–54

Van de Ven, A., H. Angle and M. S. Poole (1989) *Research in the Management of Innovation* (Harper and Row, New York)

Williams, H. and A. Webb (1992) *Outcome Funding* (Rensselaerville Institute, New York)

Wistow, G., M. Knapp, B. Hardy and C. Allen (1994) *Social Care in a Mixed Economy* (Open University Press, Buckingham)

Wistow, G., M. Knapp, B. Hardy, J. Forder, J. Kendall and R. Manning (1996) *Social Care Markets. Progress and Prospects* (Open University Press, Buckingham)

Wolfenden Committee (1978) *The Future of Voluntary Organisations* (Croom Helm, London)

7   The innovative capacity of VNPOs

Abernathy, W., K. Clark and A. Kantrow (1983) *Industrial Renaissance* (Basic Books, New York)

Alter, C. and J. Hage (1993) *Organizations Working Together* (Sage, Newbury Park, Calif.)

Anheier, H. and W. Seibel (eds) (1990) *The Third Sector* (de Gruyter, Berlin)

Barley, S. and P. Tolbert (1997) 'Institutionalization and structuration: studying the links between action and institution' in *Organization Studies* (18, 1), pp. 93–117

Beekum, R. and G. Ginn (1993) 'Business strategy and inter-organizational linkages within the acute care hospital industry' in *Human Relations* (46, 11), pp. 1291–1312

Bernstein, S. (1991) *Managing Contractual Services in the Non Profit Agency* (Temple University Press, Philadelphia)

Best, M. (1990) *The New Competition* (Polity Press, Cambridge)

Bovaird, A. (1993) 'Current approaches to performance assessment in the public sector: pure symbolism, limited learning systems in the beginnings of TQM?' (Paper to the Public Productivity Working Group, International Institute of Administrative Sciences, Leuven)

Burt, R. (1982) 'A note on cooperation and definitions of constraint' in (eds) P. Marsden and N. Lin, *Social Structure and Network Analysis*, pp. 219–233

Burt, R. (1992) 'The social structure of competition' in (eds) N. Nohria and R. Eccles, *Networks and Organizations*, pp. 57–91

Carter, N. (1974) *Trends in Voluntary Support for Non Governmental Social Service Agencies* (Canadian Council on Social Welfare, Ottawa)

Colville, I. and C. Packman (1996) 'Auditing cultural change' in *Public Money and Management* (July/September), pp. 27–33

Cyert, R. and J. March (1963) *Behavioral Theory of the Firm* (Prentice-Hall, Englewood Cliffs, NJ)

Denzin, N. (1970) *The Research Act in Sociology* (Butterworth, London)

Department of Health (1989) *Caring for People* (HMSO, London)

Deutsch, K. (1966) *Nerves of Government* (Free Press, New York)

DiMaggio, P. and W. Powell (1988) 'The iron cage revisited: institutional isomorphism and collective rationality in organizational fields' in (ed.) C. Milofsky, *Community Organizations*, pp. 77–99

Feller, I. (1981) 'Public sector innovation as "conspicuous consumption"' in *Policy Analysis* (7, 1), pp. 1–20

Granovetter, M. (1985) 'Economic action and social structure: the problem of embeddedness' in *American Journal of Sociology* (91, 3), pp. 481–510

Hasenfeld, Y. (ed.) (1993) *Human Services as Complex Organizations* (Sage, Newbury Park, Calif.)

Herbig, P. (1991) 'A cusp catastrophe model of the adoption of an industrial innovation' in *Journal of Product Management Innovation* (8, 2), pp. 127–137

Huxham, C. (1993) 'Collaborative capability: an intra-organizational perspective on collaborative advantage' in *Public Money and Management* (13, 3), pp. 21–28

Huxham, C. and S. Vangen (1996) 'Managing inter-organizational relationships' in (ed.) S. Osborne, *Managing in the Voluntary Sector* (International Thomson Business Press, London), pp. 202–216

Kamm, J. (1987) *Integrative Approach to Managing Innovation* (Lexington Books, Lexington, Mass.)

Knapp, M., E. Robertson and C. Thomason (1990) 'Public money, voluntary action: whose welfare?' in (eds) H. Anheier and W. Seibel, *The Third Sector*, pp. 183–218

Knokke, D. and J. Kuklinski (1982) *Network Analysis* (Sage, Beverly Hills, Calif.)

Knokke, D. and D. Prensky (1984) 'What relevance do organization theories have for voluntary organizations?' in *Social Science Quarterly* (63), pp. 3–20

Kramer, R. (1989) 'From voluntarism to vendorism: an organizational perspective on contracting' in (eds) H. Demone and M. Gibelman, *Services for Sale* (Rutgers University Press, Brunswick, NJ)

Lawrence, P. and J. Lorsch (1967) *Organization and Environment* (Harvard Business School Press, Boston)

Lyons, M. (1996) '"On a clear day..." Strategic management for VNPOs' in (ed.) S. Osborne, *Managing in the Voluntary Sector*, pp. 87–109

Marsden, P. and N. Lin (eds) (1992) *Social Structure and Network Analysis* (Sage, Beverly Hills, Calif.)

Meyer, S. and B. Rowan (1977) 'Institutionalized organizations: formal structure as myth and ceremony' in *American Journal of Sociology* (83), pp. 340–363

Miles, R. and C. Snow (1978) *Organization Strategy Structure and Process* (McGraw-Hill, New York)

Milofsky, C. (ed.) (1988) *Community Organizations* (Oxford University Press, New York)

Mole, V. and D. Elliot (1987) *Enterprising Innovation: An Alternative Approach* (Frances Pinter, London)

Morris, A. and H. Giller (1987) *Understanding Juvenile Justice* (Croom Helm, London)

Nohria, N. and R. Eccles (eds) (1992) *Networks and Organizations* (Harvard Business School Press, New Haven, Conn.)

Osborn, A. (1985) 'Short term funded projects: a creative response to an ageing population?' in (ed.) A. Butler, *Ageing. Recent Advances and Creative Responses* (Croom Helm, London), pp. 125–136

Osborne, S. (1996) *Managing in the Voluntary Sector* (International Thomson Business Press, London)

Osborne, S. (1997) 'Managing the coordination of social services in the mixed economy of welfare: competition, cooperation or common cause?' in *British Journal of Management* (8), pp. 317–328

Osborne, S. (1998) 'Naming the beast: defining and classifying service innovations in social policy' in *Human Relations* (in press)

Osborne, S. and L. Hems (1996) 'Establishing the income and expenditure of charitable organizations: methodology and summary of findings' in *Non Profit Studies* (1,1), pp. 7–18

Osborne, S. and M. Tricker (1994) 'Local development agencies: supporting voluntary action' in *Nonprofit Management and Leadership* (5, 1), pp. 37–52

Osborne, S., A. Bovaird, S. Martin and M. Tricker (1995) 'Performance management and accountability in complex public programmes' in *Financial Accountability and Management* (11, 1), pp. 19–37

Paton, R. (1993) 'Organisation and management studies on voluntary and non-profit organisations in the UK: achievements and prospects' (paper to the Researching Voluntary and Non-profit Organisations in the UK: the State of the Art Symposium; University of the South Bank, London)

Pelz, D. (1985) 'Innovation complexity and the sequence of innovatory stages' in *Knowledge: Creation, Diffusion, Utilization*, pp. 261–291

Peters, T. and L. Waterman (1982) *In Search of Excellence* (Harper & Row, New York)

Peyton, R. (1989) 'Philanthropic values' in (ed.) R. Magat, *Philanthropic Giving* (Oxford University Press, New York)

Pfeffer, J. (1981) 'Four laws of organizational research' in (eds) A. Van de Ven and W. Joyce, *Perspectives on Organization Design and Behavior*, pp. 409–425

Pfeffer, J. and A. Salancik (1978) *The External Control of Organizations* (Harper & Row, New York)

Pifer, A. (1967) *Quasi Non Governmental Organizations* (Carnegie Corporation, New York)

Poulton, G. (1988) *Managing Voluntary Organisations* (John Wiley, Chichester)

Powell, W. and P. DiMaggio (eds) (1991) *The New Institutionalism in Organizational Analysis* (University of Chicago Press, Chicago)

Praill, T. and S. Baldwin (1988) 'Beyond hero innovation: real change in unreal systems' in *Behavioural Psychotherapy* (16, 1), pp. 1–14

Public Sector Management Research Centre [PSMRC] (1991) *Managing Social and Community Development Programmes in Rural Areas* (Aston University, Birmingham)

Ring, S. and A. Van de Ven (1992) 'Structuring co-operative relations between organizations' in *Strategic Management Journal* (13), pp. 483–498

Rowe, L. and W. Boise (1974) 'Organizational innovation: current research and evolving concepts' in *Public Administration Review* (34), pp. 284–293

Salamon, L. and H. Anheier (1992a) 'In search of the nonprofit sector I: the question of definitions' in *Voluntas* (3, 2), pp.125–151

Salamon, L. and H. Anheier (1992b) 'In search of the nonprofit sector II: the problem of classification' in *Voluntas* (3, 3), pp. 267–309

Salamon, L. and H. Anheier (1994) *The Emerging Sector: An Overview* (Johns Hopkins University, Baltimore)

Salancik, G. and J. Pfeffer (1977) 'An examination of need-satisfaction models of job attitudes' in *Administrative Science Quarterly* (22), pp. 427–456

Scott, R. (1992) *Organizations. Rational, Natural and Open Systems* (Prentice-Hall, Englewood Cliffs, NJ)

Singh, J., D. Tucker and A. Meinhard (1991) 'Institutional change and ecological dynamics' in W. Powell and P. DiMaggio, *The New Institutionalism in Organizational Analysis*, pp. 390–422

Smith, S. Rathgeb and M. Lipsky (1993) *Nonprofits For Hire: The Welfare State in the Age of Contracting* (Harvard University Press, Boston)

Tucker, D., J. Baum and J. Singh (1992) 'Institutional ecology of human service organizations' in (ed.) Y. Hasenfeld, *Human Services as Complex Organizations*, pp. 47–72

Tushman, M. and P. Anderson (1985) 'Technological discontinuities and organizational environments' in *Administrative Science Quarterly* (31), pp. 439–465

Van de Ven, A. and W. Joyce (eds) (1981) *Perspectives on Organization Design and Behavior* (John Wiley, New York)

Williams, H. and A. Webb (1992) *Outcome Funding* (Rensselaerville Institute, New York)

Williamson, O. (1986) *Economic Organization* (Wheatsheaf Books, Brighton)

Wistow, G., M. Knapp, B. Hardy and C. Allen (1994) *Social Care in a Mixed Economy* (Open University Press, Buckingham)

Zahria, S. and J. Pearce (1990) 'Research evidence on the Miles–Snow typology' in *Journal of Management* (16, 4), pp. 751–768

Index